SALT

ARTHUR

ARTHUR
WARRIOR AND KING

Don Carleton

AMBERLEY

For Janice

Jacket illustrations. Two examples of how Arthur becomes all things to all men. *Front, above*: King Arthur fighting the Saxons in the Rochefoucauld Grail manuscript, produced in Flanders or Artois around 1320. Portraying Arthur as a twelfth-century knight is rather like using a picture of of a nuclear submarine to illustrate victory over the Spanish Armada. *Below*: The Avon Gorge at Bristol. Downstream lay Roman Abonae; upstream lies the possible site of the Battle of Badon. *Back of jacket*: This extraordinary early sixteenth-century Netherlands glass roundel from the series of the 'Nine Heroes' depicts Arthur riding on a camel – a crusader perhaps? (Courtesy Metropolitan Museum of Art)

First published 2018

Amberley Publishing
The Hill, Stroud
Gloucestershire, GL5 4EP

www.amberley-books.com

Copyright © Don Carleton, 2018

The right of Don Carleton to be identified as the Author of this work has been asserted in accordance with the Copyrights, Designs and Patents Act 1988.

ISBN 978 1 4456 8257 0 (hardback)
ISBN 978 1 4456 8258 7 (ebook)

British Library Cataloguing in Publication Data. A catalogue record for this book is available from the British Library.

Typesetting and Origination by Amberley Publishing.
Printed in the UK.

CONTENTS

PREFACE

This book began by accident and continued in bloody-mindedness. I had been asked by a publisher to consider writing a history of Bristol and the West Country. There are lots of books published about this part of England, so I said that I would only do it if I felt there was something new to be said. I started reading around the subject to see what areas of novelty or rediscovery might be open. It was then that I came across sixteenth-century references to what purported to be the old Celtic name for the city of Bristol.

That is where the accident came in. At the time, I had recently been reading Anthony Price's excellent thriller *Our Man in Camelot*. The plot of his book turns on a search for the site of the Battle of Badon, said to be the greatest battle of the famous King Arthur. I had, of course, heard of the Battle of Badon and of King Arthur, who apparently played a role in it. Had I not accidentally been reading Anthony Price, it might not have occurred to me that an old place name for Bristol and the battle name might be connected in some way.

That is where the bloody-mindedness came in. I asked a colleague, the distinguished mediaeval historian Professor Paddy McGrath, about a possible link between the two names: had anyone written on the topic? Although he had a vast store of knowledge of local Bristol history, he said he could not recall having read anything on the point. He commended me to other prominent mediaeval historians elsewhere in Britain. I wrote out the substance of my observation – a very short version of the material that appears in Chapters Five and Six of this book – and sent it to them seeking their guidance.

I had a kind and generous reply from Professor Wendy Davies. She said the coincidence of the names was interesting, that she knew of no articles about it, and that the primary sources relating to Badon were very sparse and were all available in good modern editions. I could therefore pursue the point if I wished but she did not see how it could be proved, unless some new documents were discovered, say, hidden in the binding of an old book in some forgotten part of an ancient library. She did not think it would be worthwhile searching the libraries of Europe in the vain hope of such a discovery.

At one level, then, this book is a record of my search for the truth about Badon, King Arthur's other battles, and King Arthur himself. At another, it is the book I wish had existed when I first spoke to Professor McGrath because it brings together in one place some of the evidence and most of the questions that can be asked about the martial career of the warrior Arthur, and his greatest battle, the Battle of Badon. What battles defined him as a warrior? Where were they fought? Where did the Battle of Badon fit in? Where was it fought? When? Why? How? By whom? What connection did it really have with King Arthur? Who was he, anyway? Did he exist? How, why and where did he become a king? What can he, or his legend, tell us about the forces at play in the England of the sixth century – right in the middle of the period we call, with justice, 'the Dark Ages'?

This book is both a record of what I found, and my attempt to make it into a coherent story. I hope readers will find it entertaining and illuminating, but caution should be exercised. Nothing that can be said about Badon and the other battles, or about Arthur, or what we might call 'the Arthurian era', or the 'Age of Arthur', can truly be authentic history, not even perhaps 'Dark Ages History'. Professor Davies is right. The material on which a provable account might be based does not exist for, or in, the sixth century, the Age of Arthur.

My aims in this book therefore became more limited. I wanted to share with others the fun of seeking out neglected sources, of using literature in new ways, and of speculating in a sensible or reasoned way about the legends. The Arthur who emerges is certainly different from the one we all think we know. And that fact may cause us to examine ourselves by asking: what is it about this obscure warrior and implausible king that makes us want him to be true in the way that history is true?

Don Carleton
Piso Livadi, Paros, Greece

I

THE FAMOUS KING ARTHUR

What place is there within the Empire of Christendom to which the winged praise of Arthur the Briton has not extended? Who is there, I ask, who does not speak of Arthur the Briton since he is but little less known to the peoples of Asia than to the Bretons, as we are informed by pilgrims who return from Eastern Lands. The peoples of the East speak of him as do those of the West, though separated by the breadth of the whole earth. Egypt speaks of him, nor is the Bosphorus silent. Rome, queen of cities, sings his deeds, and his wars are known to her former rival, Carthage. Antioch, Armenia and Palestine celebrate his feats.

Alanus de Insulis (Alain de Lille)

This is that Arthur of whom the Britons fondly fable to this present day, a man worthy to be celebrated, not by idle fiction, but by authentic history.

William of Malmesbury, De gesta regum Anglorum

The old quest for King Arthur is fruitless. The documentary evidence cannot respond to those sorts of questions. More seriously, to pretend to have provided answers sought by that romantic quest from the surviving written sources is downright dishonest. ... We can find new questions to ask, ones for which the evidence to hand might be able to provide plausible responses, even if ones always susceptible to refinement and correction.

Guy Halsall, The Worlds of Arthur

Introducing Arthur

Once upon a time there was a man called Arthur who was a
warrior who became a king. About four or five hundred years
after his death, he became so famous that, today, even people
who confess that they know no history say that they know about
King Arthur. They can relate to us their cherished images of him.
He is a tall, handsome man in shining armour who sits with his
beautiful wife, Guinevere, accompanied by his knights – also in
shining armour – in a glorious sunlit court called Camelot. Some
people can also name his bravest knights – Galahad, Lancelot and
Bedivere – and know stories about them and how they interacted
with Arthur. They know that the famous knights sat with the
famous king and their fellows at the Round Table, and from
time to time they went on 'quests': missions to rescue maidens in
distress, to fight in single combat with other mysterious or sinister
knights, or to slay dragons, and to seek the Holy Grail. Of course,
none of that is true, and merely gets in the way if we want to find
out more about this warlike monarch and his battles.

The biggest obstacle is King Arthur himself. He is perhaps the
most famous warrior of the last 1,500 years, but we know almost
nothing of him that can be described as 'historical'. He is not
named in any contemporary document, nor does any gravestone
from the time remain to serve as his monument. His fame derives
almost entirely from an explosion of literature in the twelfth
century when he emerges as a 'culture hero', a dominant figure to
whom all manner of good things was attributed. His reputation
was so pervasive that men hoped, and possibly believed, that he
would come again to save them from their foes and to end all the
troubles that afflicted them. Arthur, for them, was 'the once and
future king'. Even if that was always a vain hope, it indicates his
status in the minds of men. We can ask: what is it about this sixth-
century warrior that made him, in the twelfth century, the most
famous king of the Britons, and, in our own times, a man whose
name who is known to millions, even to people around the world
who otherwise know little of Britain, and even less of its history.
Why is he famous?

The person most responsible for this fame is Geoffrey of
Monmouth (*c.* 1095–*c.* 1155), an ambitious *magister* (teacher)
at Oxford who wanted to be Bishop of St Asaph in the north-
eastern corner of Wales. He had no spiritual ambitions and he

did not want to lead a flock to salvation or to astound men by his saintly life. He simply wanted a good, well-paid job with very few formal duties. In his day, being an absentee bishop meant a man appointed to such a post could enjoy the income without ever feeling the need to visit his diocese. Geoffrey set out to write a book that would bring him to the notice of important men who could award him the post he desired.

Geoffrey's Arthur

Geoffrey tells us he was given an old book by his friend and colleague Walter, Archdeacon of Oxford, and based his book about Arthur on what he read there. Medieval writers often claimed sources of this kind to give a spurious authority to their own original work, and most scholars writing about Geoffrey have doubted its existence. More recent research, however, indicates a stratum of material in Geoffrey that appears to date from a possible, although otherwise unknown, collection of historical material. His other sources include king lists and charters, and some Welsh saints' biographies ('lives' – *vitae*). He may also have had some Breton material from his own birth family, or from Walter.

Geoffrey skilfully blended all this into a roaring yarn – *Historia regum Britanniae (The History of the Kings of Britain)*. He started with one Brutus, a descendant of Aeneas of Troy, who founded Britain. He wound up with the Norman kings of his own day. The bulk of the material was devoted to the magically-born Arthur and the wizard Merlin, who assisted in his conception and directed his early career.

Geoffrey's Arthur is an all-conquering military superhero. In his battles, Geoffrey's Arthur ranged the length and breadth of Britain, invaded Norway and Iceland, and concluded his campaign by marching across France to the Alps, finally defeating there the Procurator, or Ruler, of Rome. Returning to Britain, he was betrayed and attacked by his own nephew Modred. That led to a great civil war, culminating in the Battle of Camlan from which Arthur retired, mortally wounded, to the Isle of Avalon where he was tended by his sister, Morgan Le Fay, and her holy women.

Right from the start, people knew that the story was not true. Gerald of Wales tells a catty story about Geoffrey's work. When a copy was placed on the body of a sick man, the lies in the text attracted devils and demons to the patient; when Geoffrey's book was removed and a copy of the Gospel replaced it, the true word of the Lord expelled the demons, who immediately took flight. The sick man arose cured of his illness. William of Newburgh was more direct in his criticism. He said: 'Only a person ignorant of ancient history would have any doubt about how shamelessly he [Geoffrey] lies in almost everything ... It is quite clear that everything this man wrote about Arthur and his successors, or indeed about his predecessors from Vortigern onwards, was made up partly by himself and partly by others.' From the outset, Geoffrey's book was known to be a work of fiction and yet the picture of Arthur he painted, and the sites of the battles he determined, have passed into history. They taint almost every account written thereafter.

That is because, despite Newburgh's strictures (which modern scholarship confirms), Geoffrey's work became the medieval equivalent of a bestseller. Although all books then had to be copied by hand, the book's appeal was such that even today more than two hundred copies survive. The *scriptoria* (writing rooms) of monasteries, wherever in Europe they were located, were kept busy making or translating copies. The French theologian and mystic Alanus de Insulis reported that the work was known throughout Europe, the Middle East, and the nearer parts of Asia. In the generation after Geoffrey, two other writers, Wace and Layamon, elaborated on his fiction. Geoffrey's tale also inspired Chrétien de Troyes, and other French poets and troubadours took it up and created a body of work that collectively became known as the *Matter of Britain*. This body of work consisted of imaginative stories usually called *romans* (romances) that told of an Arthur who was wise and sagacious, and the love of his wife Guinevere; they told of Lancelot, the Holy Grail, and other loves and romantic adventures designed to meet the tastes of Queen Eleanor of Aquitaine, her daughters and the ladies of the court. This is really where Arthur first acquired his shining armour, and where the Arthur known today made his first appearance.

Geoffrey's Arthur was always a warrior rather than a wooer of ladies. Geoffrey created him to meet the tastes and interests of his carefully chosen prospective male patrons. They were the Bishop of Lincoln, who could obtain advancement for him in the Church, and Robert, Earl of Gloucester, the uncle and mentor of the young King Henry II, who might bring power and influence in the State.

Geoffrey intended his work to be both flattering and useful. He set out to create an Arthur whose Christianity was inspirational and whose military objectives were much the same as those of the ruling family. The battles his Arthur fought in Britain followed very closely, in overall strategy and locations, the pattern of the campaign fought by William the Conqueror to subdue England in the years after 1066. Geoffrey updated his scheme to include the issues of his own day. His Arthur fights to bring Norway and Iceland under his rule before departing to France where he mounts a vigorous campaign that takes him to the Alps. His political and military aims are not very far distant from the objectives of Henry II, Henry's mother the Empress Matilda, and Henry's uncle, Robert of Gloucester. Geoffrey was in the business of creating precedents for his royal patrons to justify and give legal colour to actions they were planning.

His book proved to be popular in Europe too; not just because it was a rattling good yarn, but also because it was pertinent for many peoples at a time when what we may call 'nation-building' was in process. The King of France, for example, had an uncertain grasp on his notional dominions, and the area he actually ruled directly was scarcely more than a dukedom. His control over the provinces of France was exerted through obligations on the part of dukes and counts to do homage to him for their lands. Henry II, who was ruler of Anjou through his mother's marriage to his father, of Aquitaine through his wife, and of Normandy by descent, owed such a duty and was not always ready to discharge it. Other French princes and provincial lords shared his view. A story about a warlike king who had unified territories, creating precedents that cast doubt on traditional duties of homage, was very much to their taste. They could see parallels between this old king of the Britons and their own ambitions. Geoffrey's account of the warlike Arthur was thus popular because it spoke to the age in which it was created. The fact that it had little to do with an Arthur who had lived in the sixth century and fought battles then did not matter to those who read it.

Mallory's Arthur
The next major version of Arthur shared some of the same characteristics of Geoffrey's work; it also spoke to its age and it

was also a bestseller. The buoyant sales were perhaps due more to its publisher and printer, William Caxton (1422–91), than to the efforts of its author. Caxton seems to have done some judicious editing and shaping of the text, and it was he who hit on the name *Morte d'Arthur*.

The new book was about far more than Arthur's death. We know from a preface (likely also to have been composed by Caxton) that it was written by a knight who was a prisoner. This man is now thought to be Sir Thomas Malory (*c.* 1415–71) of Newbold Revel in Warwickshire. Malory was imprisoned as a thief, extortionist, rapist, ordinary lawbreaker and political terrorist charged with plotting an attack on the life of, and a coup against, King Edward IV. He nevertheless seems to have retained the good opinion of many of his peers. He was at least twice elected a Member of Parliament (more by patronage than democracy), and fought as a soldier in the Wars of the Roses, initially on the Yorkist side but, in the end, for the Lancastrians. His book, while it is a vivid retelling of the Arthur story, has underlying themes – chivalry, loyalty, and the proper conduct of knights facing various physical and moral dangers. It is, in a sense, a moral debate cast in the form of attractive stories. It asks, in several guises, the fundamental question for knights and local power holders: what is loyalty, and how and why should it be given to a liege lord? In the context of the Wars of the Roses – a civil war – these were lively themes, and the fact that they were in a fictional setting permitted discussion, and even emulation.

These topics alone might have made the book popular, but the fact that it was a printed text meant many copies were readily available. *Morte d'Arthur* became a medieval bestseller, and its fame may have achieved one of Malory's objectives: he wanted people to understand and sympathise with the dilemmas he had faced, and why he had made the decisions he had made, and most of all he wanted his freedom. Arthur, for him, was the key that might unlock his prison cell by engaging the good opinions of influential readers. It worked; not long before his death, he was released from prison. It worked at another level, too; after Malory, Arthur and the knights of his court set the standard for chivalry and good behaviour in the face of dilemmas and misfortunes. Malory's Arthur created the example of the '*verray parfit gentle knight*'.

Malory's Arthur was very clearly a work of fiction rather than history, and Malory did nothing to disturb the romantic and inaccurate picture created of Arthur's wars and conflicts by Geoffrey of Monmouth and his successors. Two centuries later, the poet John Milton considered an epic on King Arthur – possibly because he too was involved in a civil war – but, in the end, he decided on a grander conflict in the divine civil wars of *Paradise Lost*. It was left to John Dryden, a generation or two later than Milton, to take up the warrior king again in his opera *King Arthur*.

Dryden's Arthur

Dryden had first thought of the idea of an Arthurian work to mark the twenty-fifth anniversary of the accession of King Charles II after the Cromwellian Protectorate. At that time, it probably would have simply celebrated the return of the monarchy and depicted the cheery halls of old Camelot. Unfortunately, Charles died before the idea could reach fruition and Dryden put it aside. When he took it up again, England was a nation sharply divided, and Dryden found himself in considerable personal difficulties. In making his opera libretto, he accidentally discovered something new: Arthur as a symbol of the British nation.

In the 'Glorious Revolution' of 1688, the Catholic King James II (whom Dryden, as a Catholic, favoured) had been replaced by the Protestant joint monarchy of the Dutch Prince William and his Stuart wife, Mary. There was therefore not just a religious tension in Britain; there was also, perhaps for the first time since the Norman Conquest, a lively sense of foreign invasion and threatened national integrity. Dryden did not lack moral courage in confronting his dilemmas. His King Arthur is a 'British Worthy', the hero who opposes in arms the Pagan king of Kent, Oswald, in rivalry for the rule of Britain. The contending forces are also fairly transparently Tories (James II's supporters) and Whigs (William's men), and it is possible to identify real individual people in the characters portrayed. That identification was not without political risk.

Dryden was already on the wrong side. Under the Williamite regime, he had lost the salaried post of Poet Laureate he had held under James II because he refused to give up his faith. He was now forced to earn a living as a man of the theatre. His personal feelings had to be subordinated to both the box office and political reality. He therefore tempered his treatment of Oswald so that both Arthur and his rival emerged as decent but different people. As Dryden said, 'But not to offend the present Times, nor a Government that has hitherto protected me, I have been obliged so much to alter the first design, and take away so many beauties from the Writing ... it is now no more what it was formerly.' He also had to adapt his lines to the musical settings of Henry Purcell.

In his libretto, Dryden showed no interest in the chivalrous knight Malory had created, nor in the wise king the French minstrels and troubadours had written about in the *Matter of Britain*. His Arthur is a patriotic warrior, a man determined to oppose the Saxon foreigners, and to recover his lost love – the blind Cornish Princess Emmeline (who represented the British people). Actors spoke the roles of the main characters – Arthur, Oswald and Arthur's beloved Emmeline – but the piece progressed by a musical narrative or commentary featuring Valkyries, nymphs, sirens, Venus, Pan and other deities including the Cold Genius – a sort of personification of the cold weather of the 1680s that permitted 'frost fairs' on the frozen Thames. Henry Purcell produced a splendid, frothy, dramatic and entertaining score including a hymn to Britain, 'Fairest Isle, All Isles Excelling', which became very popular. The tune and the words were so effective that they were shamelessly plundered, adapted, and given a sort of permanence by Charles Wesley in the hymn – still widely sung today, especially at weddings – 'Love Divine, All Loves Excelling'. Thomas Betterton, the producer/director, threw considerable resources at the piece – the sets were outstanding, characters were wafted in on high on wires, and he played Arthur himself, and the leading actress of the day, Mrs Anne Bracegirdle, played Emmeline. The soprano Charlotte Butler made a great hit as Phillidel (a sort of politically moderate, airy spirit) despite covering her face with a veil because she didn't want her fans to see her contort it to reach the notes demanded by Purcell.

Quite obviously, there was much to admire in the cast, the spectacle and the attractive production values, but the real reason for its success was the ability of the character of Arthur to express the spirit of the age. His contest with the foreigners was patriotic, but there was also a sense that maybe the new foreign ruler was the way forward to achieve national unity. The closest Dryden got to a political statement was the fact that Emmeline recovered her sight; the British people, he seemed to be saying, might eventually see clearly again and know that the Revolution was mistaken. Dryden's decent patriotic Arthur, more than the insipid Emmeline, was in many ways the real embodiment of the nation. Thereafter, King Arthur became symbolic of the best qualities of the British nation.

Tennyson's Arthur

That same quality is manifest, but in a more restricted, private way, in the next great literary Arthur – the Arthur who appears in Alfred, Lord Tennyson's *Idylls of the King*. The twelve *Idylls* of Tennyson were published between 1859 and 1885, and Tennyson was probably aiming initially at just a collection of poems linked by the personality of Arthur and designed to offer compliment to Prince Albert, the husband of Queen Victoria. With the sudden and unexpected death of Prince Albert in 1861, however, they acquired a more sombre, elegiac tone. The royal link has coloured how the *Idylls* have been received ever since. Tennyson's generalised regret for an old and passing world, which was already in the text, turned into a personal mourning of a lost ruler and a forgotten golden time. Arthur became the dead Prince Albert, and the whole Arthurian world became imbued with a sense of nostalgia.

Tennyson was not much interested in Arthur the warrior. In the first story – *The Coming of Arthur* – he dismisses the battles of Arthur the warrior in a few lines:

> And Arthur and his knighthood for a space
> Were all of one will, and thro' that strength the King
> Drew in the petty princedoms under him,
> Fought, and in twelve great battles overcame
> The heathen hordes, and made a realm and reign'd.

There is much to admire in the *Idylls*, not least Tennyson's feel for landscape and the music of his verse which, taken together, can acquire an operatic grandeur. This is his picture of Camlan.

> So all day long the noise of battle roll'd
> Among the mountains by the winter sea
> Until King Arthur's Table, man by man,
> Had fallen in Lyonesse about their Lord,

King Arthur. Then, because his wound was deep,
The bold Sir Bedivere uplifted him,
And bore him to a chapel nigh the field,
A broken chancel with a broken cross,
That stood on a dark strait of barren land:
On one side lay the Ocean, and on one
Lay a great water, and the moon was full.

As the dying Arthur is conveyed away to the Isle of Avalon, his
last surviving brother-in-arms, Sir Bedivere, returns to the theme
announced in the first Idyll. He says:

'Ah! Lord Arthur, whither shall I go?
Where shall I hide my forehead and my eyes?
For now I see the true old times are dead,
Where every morning brought a noble chance,
And every chance brought out a noble knight.
…
But now the whole Round Table is dissolved
Which was an image of the mighty world,
And I, the last, go forth companionless,
And the days darken round me, and the years,
Among new men, strange faces, other minds.'

And slowly answer'd Arthur from the barge:
The old order changeth, yielding place to new.

The death of a popular prince, the mourning of a respected
queen, the sonorous and at times almost Shakespearean verses,
all combined to make the *Idylls* a great publishing success.
Tennyson's audience, however, also saw the regret for the old,
the excitement of the new, and the fundamental shifting in society
that characterised the mid-Victorian period, with the old rural
order ceding ground to the new industrial nation. The *Idylls* also
spoke to those new dilemmas. King Arthur had once again found
a literary expression that enabled him, as the old prophecies
maintained, to return and comfort his people. The abiding
impression, however, was one of profound nostalgia, and the
sense that Arthur's time had been glorious and that we would not

see his like again. Tennyson had also placed a distance between Arthur and his battles. The sixth-century king and warrior had faded into almost total obscurity.

Arthur the Musical

This new nostalgia, and power to personify in a generalised way the feelings of a nation, was not confined to Victorian times, or indeed to Britain. Only four days after President John F. Kennedy was murdered in Dallas in 1963, his widow, Jackie Bouvier Kennedy, agreed to an interview with *Life* magazine. She told the interviewer, Theodore H. White, that the President's favourite music, which he often played before going to bed at night, was the musical *Camelot*.

Lerner and Loew, who had composed the work after the success of *My Fair Lady*, turned for their plot to another T. H. White – Tim White, who had written a series of 'Arthurian' novels. Lerner and Loew, for their own reasons, rejected Arthur the warrior, and the magic of Merlin which feature in White's books. They concocted a musical play about Arthur and the unfortunate love his wife Guinevere had for his friend, Lancelot. It is a tale about unfaithfulness and betrayal of friendship and so on. Their King Arthur was not a soldier; he was more Arthur the worrier, a man concerned about an affair between his wife and his best friend.

An American Camelot

One might think therefore it was an odd choice for Mrs Kennedy to make – not least because her husband was notoriously and repeatedly unfaithful to her – but, possibly advised by Pierre Salinger, Jackie Kennedy quoted one song which comes right at the end of the musical. King Arthur is knighting a young boy and he sings (somewhat ungrammatically):

> Don't let it be forgot
> That there was once a spot
> For one brief shining moment
> That was known as Camelot.

'There will other great presidents,' she told Theodore White, 'but there will never be another Camelot.'

At a stroke, by her reference to Camelot and Arthur, she had redefined her husband's period in office and determined the reaction of the American people. The Kennedy White House could have been justly remembered as ineffective, bombastic and corrupt. Jackie Kennedy turned her husband's short thousand days in office into 'one brief shining moment' that Americans would recall with love and affection, another example of the nostalgic vision established by Tennyson.

Resounding Silences

It is important, however, not to get too carried away as we review the way King Arthur emerged as the most significant king in two millennia through literature and the imagination of poets. There are two resounding silences we should note. First, we should note that, while Arthur features in some of the greatest achievements of the literature of France, Brittany, Spain, Germany, and Italy as well as England, Scotland and Wales, Ireland is silent. Ireland has her own epics like the *Tain bo Cuailnge* (*the Cattle-Raid of Cooley*), and has not lacked poets, historians and men of words and imagination, but, alone among the nations of western Europe, Ireland has no literature of Arthur. His name doesn't attach to prominent features of its landscape, and in times of trouble and anguish its people have never reached out for the consolations of Arthur. Irish nostalgia for the 'old days', which is very potent, doesn't involve him.

The second great silence is William Shakespeare. Shakespeare understood his country's history and seized upon narratives from the 'Arthurian period', or pre-medieval Britain, for his dramas. He found Lear and Cymbeline, and perhaps Macbeth, in the national story of that time and made them his own. He was not, however, attracted by the rich Arthurian narratives, and he only mentions King Arthur once. In *Henry V* (Act ii, iii), Mistress Quickly, describing the death of John Falstaff, says, 'He is in Arthur's bosom.' It seems that Arthur, for Shakespeare, was some sort of saint or religious figure – perhaps even a 'Jesus double'. The rich tapestry of the *Matter of Britain*, the battles of the warrior and the troubled loyalties of the king, didn't excite Shakespeare's imagination at all. Shakespeare found nothing in Arthur's story that related to his own experience, or to the common experience of men in Elizabethan England. Arthur did not speak to him as he had done to other writers.

This odd fact might repay further study, because the secret of Arthur, the appeal of the king and warrior as he has descended to us in literature, is that people find something in him to which they can respond at a personal level. Geoffrey of Monmouth found a man set on creating a nation at a time when Robert, Earl of Gloucester, was advising his nephew, the young Henry II, on just that task. Geoffrey's account of Arthur's wars matches closely the campaigns of William the Conqueror in England and the ambitions of Henry II in France. Thomas Malory, imprisoned and perhaps wrongly accused for political reasons of various misdeeds (he never faced trial for most of them), found an Arthur who could serve as a focus for a meditation on war, chivalry and loyalty, the perfect type of knighthood. John Dryden found an Arthur who could reflect the struggle of James II to establish his rule in the face of a strong foreign rival, and in Emmeline a paradigm of the British people, who in the end might lose their blindness. Tennyson, in his time, found an Arthur who behaved like a Victorian gentleman with moral challenges about the nature and role of women, love and loyalty between friends, and who was worried about the future while regretting the passing of a much-loved prince.

After Tennyson, Arthur is always nostalgic. Alan Lerner, struggling to make a workable show about Arthur, found himself in the middle of a divorce, and therefore wrote an Arthur who was like a mid-twentieth-century chief executive wondering if he should dump his wife. The dreadful coincidence of a presidential assassination gave the whole world created by Lerner a wider and more lasting relevance – defining a failing administration as a high point in American political life, a golden age to which we cannot return.

In all these ages, the image of Arthur created was wildly popular because the writers touched upon the spirit of the times. Arthur, in any reality a sixth-century warrior and king, became a mirror in which men could see themselves, not perhaps as they really were, but as they might wish to be. That fact alone made him a very attractive figure. It is also why people who know no history think they know King Arthur. We all can think we know Arthur, because we know ourselves, and we know our dreams.

A Quest Begins

It is hard to get past the potency of that golden, nostalgic image to reveal, if we can, the historical Arthur, the man who lived in the sixth century. To begin that task, we have to accept that almost everything we know, or think we know, about King Arthur is wrong and has to be rejected from our study. It is merely an accumulation of a thousand years of dreaming from Geoffrey of Monmouth to Jackie of Hyannis Port. However dear that Arthur in shining armour may be to us, however great the appeal of golden Camelot, it has to be set aside. We have to forget everything we thought we knew and start afresh with a study of the evidence and the legends. That is what this book is about.

We must turn to whatever the sparse contemporary records, stone monuments, archaeological digs, ancient forgotten literature and pious saints' lives can tell us, and recognise that it may not be much, and that some of it may be uncongenial and challenging. We will have to rely at times on guesswork, and our conclusions may not commend themselves to everyone. We have always to be careful and watchful that the potent dream figure created by Geoffrey of Monmouth and others is not influencing what we are seeing.

If we set all that nostalgic and golden tradition aside, and strip back our viewpoint to the bare wall, as it were, we are left with the statement with which we began and not much else: 'Once upon a time there was a warrior called Arthur who became a king.' That at least may be true. If we are to know more, we must go only where the evidence and legends lead us, and, however surprising the results, see if we can make sense of them. That is our task – or, since this is about Arthur the king, let us call it 'our quest'.

As we set out on our quest, we can find comfort in that there is an immediate signpost in our bald blank wall of a statement. Warriors fight wars, are brave or cowardly, achieve victory or endure defeat. That leaves a trace. Kings always have subjects, and sometimes palaces, queens and courtiers. Their rule often has political and social effects and we may be able to discern them. By looking at what we can find of the battles, and the actions of rulers of the time, we may recover the real sixth-century man who stands behind the legends, Arthur the king and warrior, who was obscured by the vivid and enduring imagination of Geoffrey of Monmouth and those who followed him.

CONCLUSIONS

1. The 'Arthur of literature' is a potent figure who excites national and personal loyalties and affection, but he is misleading.
2. To find the 'real Arthur of the sixth century' we have to look at his battles for the warrior and at political and social events to reveal his kingship.

2

WAR IN THE SIXTH CENTURY

The Background

Finding the real King Arthur and his battles in the history of the sixth century is not an easy task. For a start, there is nothing very much that we can call history, or use to make historically accurate accounts of events in that time. We have only two authentic documents, and both are religious writings. The first is a proclamation of faith (*Confessio*) by Saint Patrick of Ireland, and the other is a sermon by the British monk (and later saint) Gildas. Neither mentions Arthur, and, while Gildas mentions a battle – the Battle of Badon Hill – later associated with Arthur, neither saint gives us hard, accurate information about the military or political contentions of the time. We know nothing of Arthur the warrior, or of Arthur the king, from any documentary source of the time.

Archaeology is not much help for this period either. There is no grave, monument or settlement definitely associated with Arthur, where the objects found can offer us a way forward. If we are to forget and eschew the wild military imaginings and the lovely sunlit romances of Geoffrey of Monmouth, Thomas Malory and those who followed them, and to pursue the arid course of truth urged upon us by William of Newburgh, we have to approach this part of our quest by indirect methods.

The Technology of War

We can, for example, make an assertion that appears to be true and see where that leads us. We can reasonably suggest that the technology of war did not change materially in the thousand years between the arrival of the Romans and the invasion of the Normans. Archaeology tells us that swords similar to the Roman infantry sword (*gladius*) or the longer cavalry or gladiator sword (*spatha)* went on being used by warriors.[1] Spears of varying weights and sizes were still employed for throwing or stabbing. There were some changes. The chariot warfare of the Britons disappeared, and, at some point, stirrups for horsemen came into use. Roman cavalry, as we can see on various monuments and triumphal arches, did not have stirrups. Norman knights did, and the more secure seat on the horse that allowed enabled them to deploy in their fighting longer lances, longer swords and heavier battleaxes. Long-range stone-throwing artillery devices went on being used. Perhaps the most significant advance was the introduction of the longbow. Most fighting, however, continued to be of the hand-to-hand variety.

The strategic and military objectives of those who ruled in England varied in the thousand years between the Romans and the Normans. We may be able to deduce significant information by looking at that more closely. We can do that because, up to about AD 400, there is a comparative wealth of material, both archaeological and documentary, about the Roman conquest and occupation. We can use that evidence, and know that what we have found is securely based. Starting around AD 700, and ranging up to around AD 900, there is an accumulation of Saxon charters, plus the *Anglo-Saxon Chronicle* initiated by King Alfred, the *Ecclesiastical History of the English People* written by Bede, and archaeology from many Saxon cemeteries that again offer us a gradually increasing quantity of the raw material of authentic history. By the time we reach *Domesday Book* (1086) and other Norman written records, a clear 'historical' picture is again visible. The dark time, the time where we really have to guess, lies between AD 400 and AD 700, and that is the Age of Arthur. With Arthur, we can only attempt informed speculation. In the centuries that preceded him and the long years that followed him we can see more clearly, so we must now turn to the Romans and the Normans to discover what we can find that is useful.

The Coming of the Romans: Creating Britannia
When Julius Caesar invaded Britain, first in 55 BC and then the next year, he did not enter a place called Britain (*Britannia*) in any

political sense. The native peoples called it *Pretania* (Early British; in Middle Welsh it became *Prydein*, in Irish *Cruithne*)[2]. Caesar had not invaded a unified country or a single state. He arrived in an island that was inhabited by tribes who sometimes worked in alliance with one another, but often, at other times, were bitterly opposed. Political differences of this kind offer great opportunities to the invader bent on conquest, but Julius Caesar did not try to seize them. His aim was not conquest, but a demonstration to people in Rome that he had carried Roman power to the farthest corners of the Earth. His desire was, in modern terms, to achieve better public relations and to build his image in Rome, not power in Britain.

Caesar's two British campaigns were in any case surprisingly poorly planned. On the first occasion he landed late in the summer, almost outside even the Roman campaigning season, on an open beach where his fleet was exposed to storm damage. Returning a year later with five legions, he again landed on an open beach rather than seizing a harbour, and drove north, facing a sort of guerrilla campaign by his main opponents, the Catuvellauni tribe. He succeeded in making his way over a defended ford on the Thames (probably at Wallingford or Brentford). Having seized a stronghold of the enemy – possibly around modern St Albans – he forced his opponents to submit to new rulers and a new political system that he dictated to them. However, he then departed for Gaul, leaving not a single legionary in Britain to enforce the settlement he had made. He left Britain essentially politically unchanged.

Aulus Plautius, almost a hundred years later, had a clearer sense of purpose. Landing on the south coast, he seized several crossing points on the Thames and waited for the Emperor Claudius to arrive in person with war elephants and heavy artillery. He also secured alliances with the tribal enemies of the Catuvellauni, the Atrebates (mid-Thames) and the Dobunni (upper Thames). Then he moved Eastwards against the Catuvellauni and the Iceni. It was not just a frontal assault. Aulus outflanked his British opponents by landing troops (from the mouth of the Rhine) in Kent at Ebbsfleet. These troops then attacked across the estuary, moving westwards to take the British forces in the rear, having made a concerted landing in what is now Essex.

The Romans soon revealed their new strategic objective: not to subdue the Catuvellauni and reimpose a local settlement, but to occupy the whole island of Britain. They were engaged in a war of conquest. Not long after the victory of Claudius and Aulus, another commander, the future emperor Vespasian, moved along the south coast by sea and by land. This 'combined operations' approach may have been novel to the Britons at the time. It was certainly notably effective, and the Romans continued to use it in later British campaigns. Agricola, for example, used it with great success in the conquest of the north and what is now Scotland.

Vespasian at first met considerable resistance, but he pushed up the river valleys (of modern Dorset), taking hill fort after hill fort (the Romans called them *oppida* and claimed to have seized more than thirty) until he reached the area around modern Ilchester. The local tribes, the Durotriges and Dumnonii, could not resist the Romans, and their failure on the battlefield was mirrored elsewhere in Britain. By the end of AD 47, the Romans controlled everything south and east of the Exeter–Lincoln route of the Fosse Way ridge path. They later pressed into south Wales, subduing the Silures, and, in North Wales, conducted a punitive raid as far as *Mon* (modern Anglesey), a centre of the Druid religion. Then they pressed further north into modern Scotland, right up the east coast of Britain as far as Aberdeen.

The Romans had come to stay. This was not warfare as the tribes of Britain had known it. It was not at all like an inter-tribal seasonal raid, designed to exact tribute and hostages and establish a sort of temporary local superiority. It was sustained and had determined, well-planned, and clear objectives. It was, and was intended to be, permanent and transforming. Above all, the political unity it sought encompassed most of the island of Britain. This new region of Britannia was to be governed and administered nationally.

The Romans were aware of external threats to good order and government. They maintained two fleets – one on the west coast to control or mitigate attacks by the Irish and the Picts, and the other on the eastern or 'Saxon Shore' to control the North Sea. In general, they planned their military disposition on the basis of suppressing internal insurrection, and the ease of the collection of the *Annona* – the military tax that supported the legions. As soon as they had established military superiority over Britain's tribes, the Romans set about imposing upon the landscape and the peoples of Britain a pattern of social, administrative, political and military organisation which reflected their concerns. Any revolt by the tribes would in future be suppressed quickly and efficiently by armies that would not be held back by concerns about the landscape, which had dominated men's thoughts for generations.

Before the Romans, the raiding parties (or war bands) and the armies of the British tribes that had moved around in Britain had used the natural landscape. They moved up or down navigable rivers, or along the great ridge paths. Some of these paths, such as the Icknield Way and the Fosse Way, provided invaders from the sea with a high road that led them straight to the interior. Only when raiders had to descend to ford a river were defenders placed at an advantage. At fords and other places where the ridge paths met water obstacles, there was often a great hill fort that dominated the crossing point, and which would have to be overcome before further progress could be made.

The Romans did not attempt to destroy these paths; they were too extensive. Instead they replaced them. Their built their own roads; straight, fast, all-weather surfaces which showed little regard for the curves of hills and had scant need for the traditional fords. Bridges – in stone or timber – carried roads across rivers where necessary. Where junctions or crossing points needed protection, new legionary towns were created. Some former tribal centres became *civitates* (cities). Britain acquired a new urban dimension.

The spine of this new unified country, 'Roman Britain', was defined and controlled by roads. The route called Stane Street ran from the south coast to London, and continued as Ermine Street north from London via Lincoln to York. The Roman Fosse Way ran from Exeter via *Corinium* (Cirencester) and *Ratae* (Leicester) to Lincoln. West of the Fosse Way, another road ran from Caerleon-on-Usk via *Bravonium* to Chester (*Deva Victrix*), providing a road that effectively sealed off Wales from Romanised Britain. Other, less important roads guarded the south coast of Wales (to Carmarthen) and the north coast (to Anglesey). Scotland was controlled by two walls – the Antonine Wall and the more southerly Hadrian's Wall. The Romans showed little interest in Scotland north of the walls, Wales beyond the roads, East Anglia generally, and the western peninsula beyond Exeter and Ilchester. They had no interest in Ireland at all.³ What mattered most to them was the area of England south of the York–Manchester (*Mamucium*) line and east of the Welsh borders.

The economy of Britain changed. The old function of the hill forts as occasional economic gathering places became redundant. The new towns offered market places and centres of craftsmanship. The new *civitates* and the legionary towns were organised into provinces. Agriculture was enhanced by new methods and became focussed on new villa estates whose surplus was sold in the new markets in the cities, mainly to the army. Britain had been given an economy that depended on the army and the tax that supported it. Transactions were carried out using coinage developed for the purpose. By the time the Romans left at the beginning of the fifth century, they had provided Britain with a legacy of roads, bridges, strong points, cities and provincial organisation. They had created the idea of Britain as a unified country.

The Norman Conquest: Reviving 'Britannia'
The strategic vision of the Normans was very similar to that of the Romans. The Normans saw all of Britain, or certainly all of England, the former Roman 'Britannia', as one entity to be ordered, administered and taxed on a 'national' basis. Orderic Vitalis (1075–1142), who offered both his own account and a summary of the contemporary work of William of Poitiers and William of Jumieges, said of King William: 'The king rode to all the remote parts of his kingdom and fortified strategic sites against enemy attacks. For the fortifications called castles by the Norman were scarcely known in the English provinces and so the English – in spite of their love of fighting – could only put up a weak resistance to their enemies.'

These novel structures were not initially the stone-built castles we think of as Norman today. Many were, and some remained, earth mounds thrown up behind wooden palisades. All were located in or very close to settlements, markets or existing towns. Although the Normans were less worried about Irish incursions or Nordic or Germanic intruders, some castles were located along the coasts to deter raiders. The purpose of the castles was not just a defence against an external enemy; they served to dominate and intimidate the local population, and ensured the accurate and prompt payment of taxes.

Armed elites (the Norman knights) were established in castles and given surrounding lands. Ownership was often asserted by renaming the area, and these names lasted; we still have places in England like Ashby de la Zouch (Saxon and Norman), Herstmontceux (Saxon and Norman), and Frome St Quintin (Brythonic/Early Welsh and Norman). Local powers ensured local collection of national taxes, and these taxes, plus a duty of service to a local lord for all men, could be quickly built into a well-equipped and supported national army when required.

Efficient national tax collection was a Norman characteristic. When he came to rule in Britain, after a vigorous military campaign right up to the northern borderlands, King William was quick to organise what came to be known as *Domesday Book* – a very detailed account of who held what land and what his tax liability might be. The aim of this efficient tax collection system was the same as that in Roman times – it was to pay for the defence of the realm and the maintenance in power of the ruler. Nationally used coinage became important again as a means of exchange, and markets began to thrive in the castle-dominated towns and cities. In King William's time, England began to function again as it had under the Romans – as a single administrative unit, organised in local areas (counties now rather than Roman provinces), capable of sustaining a professional warrior class (the knights) and waging war on a nationwide basis, sometimes with international objectives.

When Norman writers like Geoffrey of Monmouth created their King Arthur, they assumed he must have been like King William or his immediate successors, and they believed that his wars and strategic concerns would have been like William's – national in Britain, with some desire and capacity to become involved in wars on the Continent. That was not so. Arthur's battles were carried out in a different context – the almost total collapse of Romanised Britain.

The Romano-Britons: Losing Britannia

The involvement of the Romanised Britons in warfare in the first four centuries of the Christian era appears to have been largely financial. The Romanised Britons were quite prosperous around the beginning of the fourth century, but, in AD 350, they supported a usurper called Magnentius, who ultimately failed in his attempt to gain the Imperial throne. The Imperial authorities sent Paul the Notary, a senior civil servant with wide powers, to make sure that the Britons could never again finance an army that could seek to intervene on the Continent.

Paul – sometimes called Paulus Catena (Paul the Chain) – was a notoriously cruel man. The historian Ammianus, who had met him, thought him the cruellest man in the whole Empire, but he was also extraordinarily efficient. He reduced the otiose wealthy British villa-owning class to penury. Where he did not ruin them with his tax demands and fees to avoid torture and imprisonment, he forcibly seized their estates and sold them to speculators in Rome. By the time the last legions left half a century later in AD 410, the Britons could no longer afford to finance usurpers. The towns and cities of Roman Britian had become decayed and unoccupied, partly perhaps because the tax and political burdens had fallen mainly on town councillors. Men found that it was better to live obscurely in the country. Soon there were no cities and no town councillors. Coins had ceased to circulate, and the craftsmen who made luxury goods had gone out of business or had migrated. There was no tax income to support any kind of army.

That was unfortunate, because the raiders from across the North Sea and the Irish Sea who had troubled Roman Britain, even in the time of the legions, had not gone away. The Britons could no longer pay for fighting men who might resist border infringements from these raiders. All coherent national social organisation disappeared. No authentic names of powerful rulers have come down to us. It appears that, in eastern England at least, the despairing Britons turned to the Saxons, initially to some of the auxiliaries or retired soldiers left behind by the Roman armies, but eventually to new military elites who migrated from their German homelands. By the mid-century, it was clear to observers in Gaul that Britain had passed into the power of the Saxons.[4]

Successful Raiders: The Saxons

For many years even professional historians spoke of a 'Saxon Invasion' of England in the fifth century, but that invasion, we now know, did not happen – at least not in the way it has been portrayed. Historians were misled by Bede's talk of the *'Adventus Saxonum'*. *Adventus* (arrival) was interpreted as a military invasion designed to seize and hold land, and to expel, or to enslave, the original population. It was thought that the Saxons came in numbers and in arms, and by force drove the Britons before them to the west into the fastnesses of Wales, Cornwall and Devon. Archaeology in recent years has demonstrated that, while substantial numbers of Anglo-Saxons arrived and lived in eastern England, that population replacement simply didn't happen. Britons and Saxons went on living side by side, and post-Roman British society, as evidenced by grave goods and building remains, only slowly took on a demonstrably Saxon flavour.

The possibly legendary story of how King Ida came to rule around AD 547 in Bernicia may illustrate the mechanism of the Saxon arrival. He appears to have been invited from his Germanic homeland by resident Angles who were the dominant – perhaps the only – military force in north-eastern England and south-eastern Scotland at the time. They may have been Anglo-Saxons who were, or were descended from, auxiliaries who had served in Britain alongside the Roman legions. The Romans often settled retired soldiers and redundant auxiliaries in small towns and farming settlements known as *colonia*. What a Saxon *colonia* may have looked like is unrecorded, and quite how Ida was selected and invited is not known. Having arrived, he set about creating one of the most powerful of the post-Roman kingdoms of Britain, extending his power south to the Humber Estuary, ruling territory comprising most of the eastern coast of Britain, northwards to modern Edinburgh. His lands seem broadly to correspond to the territory occupied by the Brigantes at the time of the coming of the Romans, and descendants of the 'British' people who were there then – especially in Cumbrian-speaking Elmet, near present-day Leeds – were still there under Ida.

We can see in more detail how it may have happened through an example drawn from a better-documented age: the careers of two Norman knights in the time of Henry II. The first, Richard de Clare, of *Striguli* (Chepstow), found himself disinherited by King Henry II, and denied the Earldom of Pembroke and other lands which were rightfully his. The de Clares had come over with William the Conqueror and were therefore one of the prominent Norman families, but Richard found himself, in his late thirties, unable to marry because of the king's distrust. He was effectively a landless knight with many debts, some of them owed to Robert FitzHarding of Bristol. FitzHarding introduced him to Dermot MacMurchada, king of Leinster, in Ireland. Dermot offered Richard the hand of Aoife (Eva), his daughter, and the right to succeed him as Lord of Leinster in return for military assistance in his Irish wars.

It was too good a chance to turn down. With the permission of King Henry II, Richard accepted and arrived in Ireland with two hundred men-at-arms and around a thousand archers. He quickly took Waterford in late August 1170, and marched on Dublin (taking time off after the first victory to marry Aoife MacMurchada). By the end of September, much of south-eastern Ireland was in his hands. Having demonstrated his loyalty to the king by sending troops from Ireland to support Henry in France, he was later confirmed as Governor (or *Comes*) of Ireland, and Aoife was able to sign a charter as Countess of Ireland (*comtissa de Hibernia*). By then, although the Irish had a 'High-King' in place,[5] Richard and Aoife were effectively king and queen of Ireland.

The second man we should look at is Gerald Fitzwalter of Windsor (1075–c. 1135). Gerald held a castle in Wales and married Nest, the daughter of Rhys ap Tewdwr, the last king of *Deheubarth* (southern or south-western Wales). Gerald's sons (especially Maurice) and grandsons, the Fitzgeralds (descendants of Gerald), carved out considerable territories for themselves in Ireland, one branch becoming Earls of Kildare and later Dukes of Leinster. Another branch became Earls of Desmond. They and their descendants all found Irish wives, adopted the Irish language, and became leading political figures in Ireland. In the middle of the fourteenth century, the 3rd Earl of Desmond wrote some of the finest poems in Irish, and the 8th and 9th Earls of Kildare each became Deputy Lieutenant of Ireland. Later Fitzgeralds became heroes of Irish nationalism. The Irish Parliament is now housed in their ducal palace, Leinster House, and the Union Flag of the United Kingdom features the red saltire (St Patrick's Cross)[6] of their family heraldry. Warrior elites can have long-lasting effects.

The careers of these two men and their descendants show that a small but elite group of warriors, determined and properly led, could establish a kingdom, or at the least an earldom. They could, by invitation as in the case of Richard de Clare, or aggression as in the case of the Fitzgeralds, win the right to rule on the battlefield and then find acceptance of their status by a strategic or dynastic marriage. They only needed a weak and divided host population to create the opportunity. Post-Roman Britain appears to have been such an opportunity for warriors without other prospects. Ida, the Anglo-Saxon from Germany, found his kingdom in the north and east of England. We can see his advent there as a triumph by the peoples who had frequently raided eastern England, the Saxon Shore, from the North Sea in Roman times.

The Irish and Pictish raiders of Roman Britain from the west – called by the Welsh the Goidels (Welsh *gwydol*, a raider) – had also not gone away. It is reasonable to assume that the Goidels too were aware of England as a land of opportunity, but what happened in the west has been little studied and remains rather hidden from view. We should expect, however, that there would have been invading war bands, and perhaps some indigenous opportunists, ready to exploit any perceived weaknesses in what had been Rome's southern and western British provinces. Successful Western war bands may have established rule over some regions of the country. Like the Saxons in the east, they too may have generated fights and feuds among themselves as they sought for regional superiority.

In the east, we can see signs of that kind of struggle in the evidence that grows increasingly available in the seventh century. By about AD 600, England comprised seven smaller kingdoms, called by most historians 'the Anglo-Saxon Heptarchy' – East Anglia, Mercia, Northumbria (split into Bernicia and Deira), Essex, Kent and Sussex – plus a large number of smaller entities, such as the Hwicce (on the Severn) and the Haestingas (on the Sussex coast). Their kings, like the old British tribal rulers before the Romans came, conducted campaigns against their neighbours, striving to establish some form of local hegemony.

We can see that the wars of the Heptarchy were all provincial wars. Although some kings claimed the title *Bretwalda* (wide ruler – not ruler of Britain),[7] no one was seriously trying to become the ruler of a united England. The Pagan Penda of Mercia, for example, contended with the Christian forces of Northumbria to the north and east of his borders. Northumbria harboured ambitions to the north and north-west. East Anglia and Kent managed to stay out of most of the wars, but faced pressure from Mercia as the power of Penda grew. The Saxons of the Middle Thames also faced some pressure from Mercia, with whom they shared a Christian bishop. In AD 660, they decided to move their capital, and the bishop, from Dorchester-on-Thames to Winchester. The move allowed them to develop westwards, and then to the north, to form the region that became the Kingdom of Wessex in the time of King Alfred.

New Model Armies

The agent of change that led to the formation of Wessex (and perhaps many of the other Saxon kingdoms) was the Saxon equivalent of the 'mobile land army' devised in the last years of Roman Britain. This force, called the *comitatenses* or 'companions', was based on the elite Imperial bodyguard of the Eastern Roman Empire, the *hetairoi*. It had never achieved much in Britain because Roman commanders, even those in Gaul apparently facing invasion by Barbarian hordes from Germany, concentrated their efforts on overcoming other Romans. In Britain, there was no Roman dimension, although there may have been some attachment to the name of the *comitatus,* or the idea of it, as a kind of nostalgic recollection of Roman security. Whatever its name, the mobile land army was really a warrior elite, a war band.

Local names developed for these forces. The Saxons in the south called their elite troops the Gewisse, and for a time that term was used interchangeably with 'the West Saxons' or 'Wessex' as the name of their kingdom. A similar body on the Severn was called the Hwicce, and in Wales and north-west England these military adventurers gave their name to the country (the Cymry and Cumbria). In England, whatever the local names may have been, they were all war bands.

Mobile armies proved to be very effective organisations in the conditions of the sixth century. Even in Ireland, which was never occupied by the Romans, a similar force – the *fianna* – had emerged, possibly as early as the third century, led by the legendary giant warrior Fionn MacCumhaill (Finn McCool).[8] This field army usually numbered between 200 and 400 soldiers who formed the core of the war band (Welsh *teulu*). The *teulu* was supported by a wider group called the 'hosting'. The wider 'hosting' included men who were really farmers, shepherds or fishermen who briefly joined the guard for either defensive or aggressive expeditions, usually in the early summer between the planting and the harvest.

We do not know if farmers, fishermen and the like were compelled to serve, or served happily. It may have offered them a chance of betterment, to share in plunder and to acquire new livestock or better boats. For the elite troops and their leaders, it may have offered something more. It has been suggested that successful war bands were 'tribes in the making'. In fact, they were something more than that in sixth-century Britain. Successful war bands, as they did for the de Clares and Geraldines five or six centuries later, offered the chance to acquire land and position. They were the means by which new 'kingdoms' were formed.

The Western Warlords

In the obscure Age of Arthur, we have no good records of where the war bands fought or exactly how they imposed themselves on a host population.[9] We can see plainly from about AD 600 how and where the Saxon war bands situated themselves in eastern England, but we currently know little about incursions by Irish, Pictish or other western war bands. We do, however, possess some compelling and trustworthy details about their commanders, the western warlords who led them into battle. The monk Gildas attacked five of them by name in a sermon, which is one of the few documents of the early sixth century to survive. Only two of these leaders can be identified with certainty. However, it is not their names but their characters that matter. The character of the warlords tells us something both revealing and reliable about the battles of Arthur and about Arthur himself.

Gildas begins (c.28)[10] with Constantine, 'the tyrant whelp of the filthy lioness of Dumnonia' (possibly modern Devon, but also possibly the lost land of Lyonesse, inundated by the sea and lying now off the Cornish coast). Gildas says this man, despite having sworn peace, dressed himself in the habit of an abbot or falsely accepted appointment as an abbot. Thus disguised, using both sword and spear, Constantine slew two royal princes in the arms of their mother before the altar of a church. Furthermore, 'overcome by the stench of frequent and successive adulteries', he put away his lawful wife, and turned to the 'bitter vine of the men of Sodom',[11] which he watered 'with public and domestic wickedness'.

Gildas then turns to Aurelius Caninus (c.30). He says that Aurelius is engulfed in the same slime as Constantine – 'parricide (killing of near relatives such as parents, offspring, nephews or cousins), fornication, and adulteries' which 'rush upon him like sea waves'. Aurelius is also addicted to civil war and the search for plunder.

The next leader he attacks is Votepor, leader of the Demetae, a tribe who lived in modern Pembrokeshire. He is a possibly historical character known from other sources: a grave stone found in Carmarthenshire records in Latin '*Memoria Voteporigis Protictoris*' ('the memorial of King Votepor the Protector'). There is also an Irish ogham inscription on the stone which repeats, in Irish apparently, the same message; the name form, as read by the distinguished Welsh scholar Sir John Rhys, is an Irish genitive, *Voteporigis*.

Rhys was in no doubt that they were the same man, but more recently linguists[12] have argued that the King Votepor of Gildas and the person memorialised in Carmarthen are two distinct individuals. The argument turns on whether or not a letter 'r' was removed or inserted into either name (Vortepor or Votepor), and whether the dating of the grave stone is correct. While we may find ourselves inclined to side with Rhys, the important thing in the quest for Arthur is not the stone but the description in Gildas. Gildas says King Votepor sits on a throne 'full of guile (cunning) and is stained by diverse murders and adulteries' where he sucks down 'violent surges of sin as if it were vintage wine'. These sins include the 'rape of a shameless daughter' who may or may not be his own child.

Gildas then turns to Cuneglas (c.32). He hails him as '*Urse, multorum sessor aurique currus receptaculi ursi dei contemptor sortisque eius depressor*'. We need to take this phrase by phrase to untangle it. '*Multorum sessor*' means 'the pilot of many'. It may perhaps offer a dual meaning – the 'exemplar or guide to whom many look', but also, in a nautical sense, 'fleet commander'. The next phase can be 'the driver of the chariot of the bear's stronghold', but again a nautical meaning may be preferred: 'helmsman of the ship of Dinerth' (Dinerth translates *receptaculi ursi* in Welsh and Cornish and is a known place name, probably Bryn Euryn in Conwy, Wales). *Receptaculi* can also have shameful connotations so we might suggest 'brothel' here as an alternative to 'stronghold'.

It may have been possible for the readers of Gildas to be aware of both meanings simultaneously. This process of deliberate and resonant ambiguity is not unknown in early religious writing. In full, the salutation then reads, 'You bear, Cynglas, fleet commander and helmsman of Dinerth's ship, belittler of God and sinker of his message.' We can express that more loosely and more offensively – 'Cynglas, you bear, admiral and pimp of the ursine brothel, who mocks God and tries to scuttle his Gospel.' Gildas goes on to denounce him as an out-of-control war-dog. He also accuses of him of leaving his lawful wife for her villainous sister who seems to have been a nun, a widow who had dedicated herself to God after the death of her husband.

The last evildoer is Maglocunus, known in later texts as the Welsh king of Gwynedd, Maelgwn. Gildas says that, when Maelgwn was a young man, he seized his throne by force and used spear, sword and flame to destroy his uncle and his soldiers. Then, repenting somewhat, he became a monk, but broke his chaste vows to marry. Gildas says he is like 'a lively foal to whom everything unknown is attractive'. Having married illegally, after a while he left his unlawful wife for the wife of his nephew, murdering both his wife and his brother's son so that he was free to marry the widow.

Gildas, of course, may be too sweeping in his condemnations. Maelgwn is a historical character known from other sources. Welsh tradition remembers Maelgwn as a founder of churches, and he may also have been a monk, bishop or abbot. If he was, he is by no means the only ruler in these early times to have wielded both civil and religious power. Although Gildas condemns the practice, it may have been a shrewd way to obtain, or to wield, power in the circumstances of the Age of Arthur.

We do not have to accept every accusation that Gildas makes as true. A priest reproving sin is under no obligation to be precise, or even entirely accurate, in his diatribes. We can, however, believe the generality of what he says about the characters of the rulers he describes. The details of their offences are likely to be accurate, at least in a general sense. Men who led armies in the sixth century were usually not kings. Sometimes they were landless young men, like the later Norman warriors Richard de Clare and the sons of Gerald, seeking a reputation, a territory and a wife. As Gildas says, they were 'tyrants' – that is, rulers who owed their status to their strong sword arm rather than to any concept of descent or legitimacy. Murder for them may have been simply a means to an end, or the way to a throne. The business they were all in was ravaging and the search for plunder. We should no more disapprove of their search for booty than we might regret the firm, and sometimes brutal, tax collections of the Romans or the Normans. The plunder the tyrants looked for was sought for the same reason as the Roman and Norman taxes: the support of a military effort. A successful chieftain could reward his soldiers with a share of the spoils, and he could rearm them or provide them with new boats with the profits he generated in the disposal of loot. Tyranny was an economic system as much as a military enterprise.

A New Colonisation

There is another economic point we should consider: the necessity to generate income to sustain the war bands inevitably led to a species of colonisation. Archaeology tells us that, after the Romans left, within a generation or so, coins ceased to circulate and market exchanges had to be conducted by barter. Plate and other valuable objects or treasures ceased to be made. Neither readily portable coins, nor treasure in gold or silver objects, was available to be carried off. The raiding war bands had to make do with what was available, and very often that was simply people or livestock.

That caused a transportation problem: how were the spoils of victory to be transported and kept in good condition? The solution became obvious. The raiders decided to stay, and keep the animals and people where they were. That, in turn, generated a strategic need to defend what they had won against other raiders, or mercenaries employed by the original inhabitants, their relatives, or those who feared they might share the fate of their neighbours. That situation determined that there would be no grand national campaigns to subject all of England. Fighting would be for local reasons, and battles would be perhaps annual events at times when farming, fishing and looking after animals could take a backseat. Most fighting men in the sixth century did not want, or have, to travel far to find opponents.

The weapons the troops used – sword, shield, spear and fire – plus the qualities exhibited by their warlord leaders – the amoral cunning, determination and ruthlessness mentioned by Gildas – are what we might reasonably expect in a sixth-century context. These fighting men were most emphatically not knights in shining armour[13] set on rescuing maidens in distress or seeking elusive Holy

Grails. They were professional 'companions', the 'full-time war band', allied sometimes with the part-time warriors of the hosting who were taking time out from their farming or fishing activities. Their leaders did not search for a kingdom that might encompass the whole island of Britain. The military and logistical capability of the war bands, to travel, sustain themselves with food, water and shelter, and be in a fit state to fight, was constrained by what and where they were. Because the capability of their troops was restricted, the ambition of their leaders too was limited, to local or, at best, regional warfare.

Arthur the Warlord

If Arthur was of their number, and we must think on this evidence he may have been, he was likely to have been the violent and cunning leader of a ruthless and bloodthirsty group of 'companions', armed with swords and spears, backed by more ordinary men called to their hosting, all of them hell-bent on invading and burning out their neighbours while seeking whatever treasure or plunder in goods, chattels and possibly slaves they could find to carry off. In the first half and in the middle of the sixth century, that is what war was like in Britain.

If, by our indirect approach, we now understand a little more about war in the sixth century, what have we found out about Arthur? We can say, with a great deal of certainty, that Arthur himself was not the knight in shining armour beloved in literature. It is very probable that neither Arthur nor his soldiers behaved well. War in the sixth century was short-lived but it was very nasty. It did not allow chivalry, nor the pious search for objects of religious interest. No maidens were rescued. Women, on the whole, were poorly treated, raped or killed, not saved from dragons. There was no respect for rights or for law. Murder, plundering and land seizure was a way of life. As we shall see, perhaps much more clearly as our quest develops and progresses, Arthur was a man of his age, conducting wars as they had to be conducted in his time, with whatever troops and hopes of strategic benefit that the age allowed. As his campaigns developed, he may have seen an opportunity to become a king – whatever being a king meant then. He may have seen too a local or regional territory that he thought he might be able to seize, hold and rule.

That is about as much as this line of enquiry can tell us. To know more, to find the real Arthur – warrior and king – we now have to turn to what is known of the twelve battles associated with his name in traditions developed perhaps as long as three hundred years after his death. Warriors and kings define themselves by their victories or defeats; we need now to look at his battles.

CONCLUSIONS

1. The Romans and the Normans had a concept of Britain as a territory that could function as a united entity for military and tax purposes.
2. When Romanised Britain became impoverished and unable to defend itself, there was no longer any sense or concept of a unified realm.
3. There was an opportunity for warlords to carve out kingdoms in both eastern and western England.
4. Eastern Britain fell to the Saxon warlords and western Britain fell to the Goidels (raiders) or to indigenous British leaders.
5. If Arthur was a successful warrior at this time, he must have been a warlord.

3

THE ENGLISH CAMPAIGN: TWELVE BATTLES OF KING ARTHUR

The Authentic Background of the Battle Texts

In 1753, under a new Act of Parliament setting up the British Museum, Henrietta Cavendish Holles, the widow of Edward Harley, 2nd Earl of Oxford and Mortimer (1689–1741), and her daughter, Margaret Cavendish Bentinck, Duchess of Portland, sold Edward Harley's collection of books and manuscripts to the British public. The collection had been started in 1704 when Robert Harley, 1st Earl of Oxford and Mortimer (created 1711), bought the collection of Sir Simonds D'Ewes (d. 1650). The Harleys added to the library by a programme of vigorous collection right across Europe, partly directed by Humfrey Wanley (1672–1726), a palaeographer and a founder of the Society of Antiquaries. The Harleys and Wanley were among the best and most honest book collectors of their day. They were alert to fraud and misrepresentation among the agents they employed, in Britain and in Europe, to acquire material for them. The provenance of much that they brought together is known, and the material in the 'Harley Library' is as authentic as any early set of documents can be.

The Harleian Collection today, administered by the British Library, comprises more than 7,000 manuscripts, nearly 15,000 charters, and 500 rolls (the old format for books). Among them is a group of documents called Harley 3859. Because of the way it was collected, maintained, and acquired, we can assume that Harley 3859 is not a recent forgery made to serve some interest. It is a miscellany of genuine documents of various dates. If appropriately used it can be a good source for our quest, but it is a late source. The part that deals with Arthur has been dated to around the first few decades of the ninth century. Put simply, it was written three hundred years after the events it purports to describe. It is, nevertheless, the only real record we have of the battles of the warlike Arthur, and we must see what we can make of it.

Nennius

Harley 3859 includes, among other matters, a Kentish chronicle, the *Historia Britonum* (HB – 'the History of the Britons'), the *Annales Cambriae* (AC – 'the Annals of Wales'), some genealogical lists, and short notes of curiosities, mainly associated with Wales. This part of the Harleian Collection used to be associated with a monk called Nennius and bore his name, but scholars now refute that attribution, and poor Nennius, if he ever existed, is fading from history. That is a pity because Nennius offered one of the most endearing prefaces to be found in any historical document. He says:

> I, Nennius, a student of the Holy Elvodug, have undertaken to write down some extracts that the stupidity of the British threw out; for the scholars of the Island of Britain had no skill, and set down no record in books. I have therefore made a heap of all that I found, both from the Annals of the Romans, and from the Chronicles of the Holy Fathers, and from the writings of the Irish and the English, and out of the traditions of our elders.
>
> Many learned scholars and copyists have tried to write [about this] but somehow, whether through repeated plague and pestilence, or from frequent military disasters, they have left the subject more obscure. I ask every reader who reads this book to pardon me for daring, like a chattering bird or an incompetent judge, to write so much here after so many. I yield to whoever may be better acquainted with this skill than I am.

Limitations of 'Arthurian Knowledge'

All who aspire to write about King Arthur, or who pursue quests to know more about him, should keep the wise words of Nennius always before them. There is always a danger of making a somewhat misty subject even more obscure, and there are those who believe that no further attempts should be made. In 1977, Dr (as he then was) David Dumville, of Cambridge University, published a devastating article which more or less brought to an end the serious academic study of King Arthur as a potentially historical figure.[1] Dumville pointed out, in a way that it was difficult not to agree with, that the raw materials for authentic history – history as we might write it of, say, the Second World War, where many documents and multiple witness testimonies are available – are not available in the Age of Arthur, the Dark Ages. Dumville concluded, 'We must reject him from our histories and, above all, from the titles of our books.'

While Dumville's first principle has been widely adopted in universities, his second remark has been more honoured in the breach than in the observance. Authors, and their publishers, still find themselves compelled to invoke the magic of Arthur's name to sell books, even dry-as-dust volumes intended only for the small professional market. Serious academic work is no longer focussed on the historicity of the warrior and king; it is now really the study of the literature compiled since Geoffrey of Monmouth's version of King Arthur, and how the figure of Arthur has changed through the ages, what we may call 'the Reception of Arthur'. Some very fine books have been written about that Arthur, the 'Arthur of literature'. The pursuit of the 'historical Arthur' has followed more what we may call the 'tradition of William of Newburgh' – a profound scepticism resulting from the silence of the record. In the end, that, for the 'historical Arthur', has led to an investigative silence in serious academic circles that has lasted now for over fifty years.

Finding Arthur

In our search for Arthur the warrior and king, we will never satisfy the 'Dumvillians' or the 'Newburghers' or, for that matter, probably no one currently active in serious academic circles, but we can adopt a standard that may give some merit to our labours. We can follow, for example, an idea suggested by Kathleen Hughes, historian of early Christian Ireland.[2] She suggests that incidental information in the *vita* of St Columba can be trusted; we can in general trust incidental information even in the most fantastic accounts. Put simply, if we read that a saint gets up in the morning, eats some porridge and then drives demons from the sick, turns his staff into a snake, reproves a sea monster and raises the dead, we can disregard the miracles and believe in the porridge. If we can aggregate sufficient plausible details, a trustworthy picture may emerge.

We may also be able to use incidental information to find Arthur as men find comets – by detecting their influence. Scientists do not know what the dark matter is that holds such importance in our universe, but they infer its reality through the effect that it has. In looking for Arthur, we are searching for what we may call the 'dark matter of Britain', something that is there, can be inferred, but at the current level of techniques and research data cannot be proved, or even seen clearly. We may always hope too that the 'historical Arthur' turns out to be a bit like the Higgs boson, the existence of which was inferred and announced as a theory by Peter Higgs in the 1960s, but only appeared experimentally very recently, decades later. Until that happens with Arthur the warrior and king – if it ever happens – our conclusions and our methods will always be controversial.

We cannot hope that anyone will find the case we make proved, and therefore, even at the outset, we must accept that we may be able to do no more than what dear old Nennius said he did – 'make a great heap' of what we have found. We can also avoid, like the foolish judge in Nennius, making up in length what we lack in sense as we write about Arthur. In all humility, we too, like Nennius, may find that we should yield to anyone who can show that he/she can do it better. Perhaps, in honour of that spirit, as we pursue our quest for Arthur, we can allow ourselves from time to time to refer to 'Nennius' when we really mean the *Historia Britonum* (HB) and the *Annales Cambriae* (AC), and *The Wonders of Britain* held in the documents described in that arid British Library reference number, Harley 3859.

The Battles of the 'Warlike Arthur'

In any case, the really important thing for our quest is not the possible reality or unreality of Nennius, a Welsh monk who may or may not have flourished about AD 820, but the fact that Harley 3859 contains in the *Historia Britonum* (HB) a short passage in Latin entitled *de Arturo rege belligero* ('about the warlike King

Arthur'). It is worthwhile giving the full Latin text because we will have to refer to it as the quest for the 'true Arthur' continues.

It is presented in two passages. The first occurs in a sort of table of contents. It is the headline to gain the reader's attention: *De Arturo rege belligero et duodecim bellis quae adversus Saxones habuit, et de imagine sanctae Mariae in qua triumphaverit, et quot adversariorum uno impetu prostraverit.* (About the warlike King Arthur and the twelve battles he fought against the Saxons, and about the image of Saint Mary in which he gained victory, and how many of the enemy he killed in a single charge.)

The full text of the passage begins with a reference to the Saxon kings of Kent and ends with some information about the Anglian kingdom of Bernicia, and, while that may have some relevance, it is the core of the passage that is important; it gives us a list of battles, and assures us that Arthur won all of them:

Tunc Arthur pugnabit contra illos in illis diebus cum regibus brittonum, sed ipse dux erat bellorum. Primum bellum fuit in ostium fluminis quod dicitur Glein. Secundum, et tertium, et quartum et quintum super aliud flumen quod dicitur Dubglas et est in regione linnuis. Sextum bellum super flumen quod vocatur Bassas. Septimum fuit bellum in silva Celidonis, id est Cat Coit Celidon. Octavum fuet bellum in castello Guinnion, in quo Arthur portavit imaginem sanctae Mariae perpetuae virginis super humeros suos et Pagani versi sunt in fugam in illo die, et caedes magna fuit super illos per virtutem Domini nostri Jesu Christi et per virtutem sanctae Mariae virginis genitrices ejus. Nonum bellum gestum est in urbe legionis. Decimum gessit bellum in litore fluminis quod vocatur Tribruit. Undecim est factum bellum in monte qui dicitur Agned. Duodecim fuit bellum in monte Badonis, in quo corruerunt in uno die nongenti sexaginta viri de uno impetu Arthur, et nemo prostraverit eos nisi ipse solus et in omnibus bellis victor extitit.

(Then Arthur fought with the kings of Britain against them [the Saxons?] at that time [a time when the numbers of Angles and Saxons in Britain were increasing] but he himself was the leader of the wars. The first battle was at the mouth of the river called Glein. The second, third, fourth and fifth battles were on another river which is called the Dubglas, which is in the territory of Linnuis. The sixth battle was on the river called Bassas. The seventh battle was in the woods of Celidon and is [therefore] called 'the battle of Celidon Wood'. The eighth battle was in the fort [or possibly shelter/refuge] of Guinnion, in which battle Arthur carried the image of the Eternally Virgin Saint Mary on his shield [or possibly shoulders] and the Pagans were put to flight that day and there was great slaughter through the power of our Lord Jesus Christ and the power of the Holy Virgin Mary, his mother. The ninth battle was fought in the City of the Legion. The tenth battle was fought on the bank of the river called Tribruit. The eleventh battle was on the hill called Agned. The twelfth battle was on Badon Hill in which in one day 960 men fell to the ground from one charge by Arthur, and no one laid them low but him alone, and he emerged victorious in all the battles.)

We should note that the Vatican Library version of Nennius gives us more information about the eleventh battle. It says, *'in monte qui nominatur breguion, ubi illos in fugam, quem nos cat bregion appellamus'* (on the hill we call Breguion, where they were put to flight, and which we call the Battle of Bregion).

We should also note that some scholars have detected some rather odd numerology going on. Including the Saxon references at the end and the beginning, the passage comprises 240 words in Latin (twenty times twelve) and the number of men killed in one charge is 960 (eighty times twelve). Guy Halsall, who has commented on this, believes that the twelve battles are an invention.[3] Without the additional battles on the River Dubglas, we would have a pattern of four battles, then Guinnion, and then another four battles. Halsall concludes that this means, before the additional Dubglas battles appeared, Guinnion was intended to be the most important encounter. Guinnion is therefore given the greatest number of words.

That may well be the case, and we should bear it in mind, but the relative importance of battles is not the object of our study.[4] We want to use the battles to see if they shed any light on the reality and character of Arthur. Our immediate task is to try to find out when and where these battles were fought, who was involved, and whether Arthur was indeed the supreme commander, leading reigning kings into battle.

We might also wish to test whether or not he really did win all the battles. Geoffrey of Monmouth, who had access to the Harley 3859 HB material, or something very like it, had no doubts. His Arthur, as we have seen, ranged over all Britain putting down insurgent Saxons in a widely scattered range of locations. For Geoffrey, and for many who followed him, the twelve battles of King Arthur were a national campaign. That may not be the case. We should be guarded too about claims made by, or on behalf of, some specific locations. It is easy to find some evidence that appears to support a location for some of the battle sites. Superficially attractive evidence of this kind has been favoured by enthusiastic local investigators, or even, on occasion, by reputable historians, following the misleading star of some pre-existing notion of who Arthur must have been and what his objectives may have been. The fact is that finding convincing, or even persuasive, battle sites is a very difficult task.

The Battle Sites
The battle sites could be almost anywhere in Britain. Most of the battle names involve river names, and similar, or identical, river names are widespread throughout Britain. Names like *Glein*, *Avon* and *Dubglas*, in its various forms, are to be found in most regions of Britain. There is, however, some mild hope of identifying battle sites through river names. Studies have revealed that Celtic (Brittonic, Early Welsh or Irish) river names survived mainly in the west. There is a sort of gradient from east to west in England. Eastern England has few Celtic river names, but gradually they increase in number as we move westwards. By the time we reach Hampshire, they begin to predominate. In our Nennius battle lists, all the rivers named are Celtic. Without being conclusive in any way, that suggests western locations for the battles.

We have nonetheless to fit them into a credible strategic scheme. As we have seen, the circumstances in which war had to be waged and sustained in the first half of the sixth century did not really allow for national campaigns. The twelve battles must have been in one region.

There are two possible regions: Scotland and western England. Pressure from an emerging Anglian kingdom of Northumbria in the Edinburgh area may have established one line of contention between the Anglo-Saxons and forces led by Arthur. We may note that Welsh historians are prepared to admit that Arthur, and other major figures of his time, may be part of the *gwyr y gogledd* – the men of the North – whose tales were later relocated to Wales. The 'Welsh Arthur', they concede, may be a literary artefact, a mere fabrication like 'Geoffrey's Arthur'. The 'true Arthur' may have been located in modern Scotland. If we rely on northern British river names, and on various topographical features of the landscape that later tradition associated with Arthur's name – such as 'Arthur's Seat' at Edinburgh – there may not be a difficulty in regarding Arthurian battles as a feature of northern British history. The west of England and the Welsh Marches, however, offer more compelling evidence that the line of contention between Arthur and his Saxon foes is to be found there. In the spirit of Nennius, we can leave the question of a 'Scottish Arthur' to those who are more skilled than perhaps we may claim to be.

Battle One
(For all the battles see Fig. 2 in plates)
The account of King Arthur's twelve battles begins with a battle on a river, the River Glein. *Glein* is quite common as a river name because the word itself describes an aspect of the water: clearness or brightness. In some parts of England, it may have been conflated with similar names of a different origin. The rivers Glen in Northumberland and Lincolnshire, for example, both take their name from Celtic *glen*, meaning a valley. Attributing a battle with a river name to a specific location is always going to be necessarily speculative.

In searching for the River Glein, the site of Arthur's first battle, we are fortunate that Asser, the biographer of King Alfred, has given us a name, *Guilou*, for the modern River Wylye. This is the Welsh word *gloyw*, which means bright or clear, the same qualities described by *glein*. The Wylye is a typically clear chalk stream that rises in Wiltshire (to which county it gives its name) and flows south toward the southern edge of Salisbury Plain – an area currently used by the British Army for military training purposes. There it joins the River

Nadder, which, in turn, joins the River Avon to flow eventually into the sea at modern Christchurch in Hampshire. The fact that it gives its name to the county of Wiltshire and to several villages along its course suggests that, at one time, it may have been regarded as the primary named river in what we tend to regard now as 'the Avon River system'.

If that were the case, the 'mouth of the Wylye' in Harley 3859 HB may be the junction with the Nadder, but it could also be the mouth of the present River Avon. That places it precisely in the area of England, southern Hampshire, through which, in Roman times, Vespasian made his western march towards the territory of the Durotriges.

Christchurch is also a credible battle site. The first battle was possibly a fight by sea raiders, following the same campaign course as Vespasian and trying to establish a bridgehead, a foothold in England. A hostile force landing successfully in this area in Arthur's time, moving northwards, would be well placed to follow the Roman roads, encountering defenders close to the great earthworks of Bokerly Dyke and the Iron Age fort at Old Sarum near Salisbury. Alternatively, it may be the case that an army, seeking plunder, might emerge from Dorset or Somerset, and encounter defenders on the banks of the Southward-flowing Hampshire rivers. Any of the fords or crossing places on the present River Avon system may have been the site of the battle, but modern Christchurch (where the graves of some Saxon warriors were found) at the sea mouth of the present River Avon, or around modern Salisbury near the confluence of the River Wylye and the River Nadder, must be the prime possibilities. With no other documents or archaeology to guide us, there is no way to take it further.

Battles Two to Five

Nennius says the sites of the second, third, fourth and fifth battles were on the river which is called *Dubglas* and which is in the region of Linnius (*flumen quod dicitur Dubglas et est in regione Linnius*). *Dubglas* means 'blackwater' and is also widespread as a British river name. It occurs as Douglas, Dulais, Dawlish, Divelish and Devil's Brook, and in many locations as 'Blackwater'. Two rivers of this name form a north/south axis across the North Dorset Downs. To the north, the Divelish rises near the impressive earthworks of Rawlsbury Camp and Bulbarrow Hill, and, near Sturminster Newton, flows into the River Stour. The Stour (another common river name) flows to the south-east, and, like the Wylye, also joins the River Avon, reaching the sea at Christchurch. To the south, the Devil's Brook rises in an area full of ancient barrows, tumuli and hill forts, and flows past a small village called Dewlish, a few miles east of Roman Dorchester, into the Piddle or Trent. This river flows to the east and south, parallel to the larger River Frome (another very common river name) reaching the sea at Wareham and Poole Harbour.

Wareham was a significant place from early times. It appears to be have been a settlement as long ago as the fifteenth century BCE. There was a small Roman camp, and inscriptions thought to be 'Brittonic' or 'Brythonic' (that is pre-Saxon British) have been found there. Wareham was named by the Saxons (it means 'fish-weir village'), and King Alfred designated it as a *burh* (fortified town) of 1,600 hides – by this measurement the third-largest in his kingdom. At one point it was occupied by the Danes, and King Alfred thought it worthwhile to pay considerable sums to get rid of them. Two kings of England (or Wessex) may be buried there – Beorhtric (d. 802) and Edward the Martyr (d. 978). Edward is regarded as a saint by Catholics, Orthodox and Anglican communions, and that makes Wareham not only important in the military sense but also significant as a holy site.

Wareham went on being militarily important. Apart from the invasion by the Danes, and its destruction by Canute, Wareham was the scene of violent clashes in medieval times in King Stephen's wars, and in the English Civil War when it was besieged by over two thousand Cromwellian soldiers. In military as much as in religious terms it has been much prized through the centuries, and that makes it a plausible battle site in the Age of Arthur.

In considering the Devil's Brook (Dewlish) and the Divelish, we are clearly looking at an area which has been significant for a very long time. Apart from the important hill forts, and other strong points, such as the vast harbour at Poole and Wareham, the Frome, the Stour and the Trent have always been useful pathways for invaders from the south and east, or raiders from the west with their eyes on the rich villa estates of the south coast.

Both rivers are in a region called by names that may be a version of *Linnius*. Harley 3859 HB gives *Linnius*, but other manuscripts of Nennius give *linuis* or *inniis*. The archaeologist Leslie Alcock, and others who have written about this word, suggest that the word intended was *lininuis*, a word that could be formed from the Roman name of the people of this region, the Lindinienses, the people of *Lindinis*. This tribe was part of the Durotriges who inhabited Dorset, and major parts of Hampshire, Somerset and Wiltshire. Their tribal centre was Ilchester. Their power may well have extended to the line of the Divelish and the Devil's Brook. We may note that the Piddle bears a name that is of Germanic origin and therefore must be a replacement Saxon name for a river previously called Divelish, Devil's Brook, Dewlish or *Dubglas*. Before the Saxons came to that area in numbers, a name like Divelish or Dewlish may well have applied to the whole present River Piddle/Trent system all the way down to the sea at Wareham.

The two Dorset river systems offer many possible sites which armies intent on plunder, or determined to defend home and hearth, may have chosen for an encounter. Although we can bear in mind that multiple battles on the Dubglas may have been made up, as Halsall suggested, it is also the case that several encounters may have taken place along the river system as one army or another strove for supremacy (which is what, *contra* Nennius, Gildas tells us happened). It may be, for example, that one of the battles on the Dubglas was fought on the shore at Wareham as a sea-raiding group tried to establish a bridgehead. Others may have been contested in, or near, the many hill forts on the rivers, as that same group attempted to extend its power beyond the bridgehead into the interior.

The likely strategy for such invaders in the region is clear. When the Romans attacked this area, they advanced up the line of the Stour, past major hill forts like Badbury Rings and Hod Hill to the hill fort that overlooks Ilchester. Their commander, Vespasian, also saw the importance of the approach along the Trent. The Romans created a road to Dorchester and Maiden Castle (hill fort) to facilitate trade and future military actions against any insurgency by the Durotriges. The Romans used an offshore fleet to assist their advance and may have placed forts at bridgeheads as they did on their initial beaches further east. They certainly fortified both Christchurch[5] and Wareham. Wareham, and the two interior rivers of its hinterland, were always worth contesting. South Hampshire and south Dorset were important places around this time in

British history. Whoever controlled the Stour, the Trent (aka the Piddle) and Ilchester controlled a port, two major routes and a vital watershed. There is nothing inherently unlikely in several persisting struggles for control in the region.

Battle Six

The sixth battle, Nennius tells us, took place on the River *Bassas*. The name means a 'shallow or muddy stream' and probably derives from Old Welsh *bas*, a pool or shallow place. Around the sixth century, Welsh, then an inflected language like Latin, changed and became the clear uninflected ancestor of modern Welsh and behaved more or less like modern English to indicate meaning. The pronunciation of Welsh changed too. The sound indicated by the letter 'b' became more like 'v' or 'f', then 'w'.[6]

That change is recorded in how the language was written and can be used to date documents. *Bas* is an early form, and still exists in a later form in the name of the Britain's largest inlet of the sea, the Wash. Around the same time as the sound change from 'b' to 'w' took place, *bassas* would have become *wase* or *wasa*. A tenth-century glossary confirms the word existed: '*wase vel faen, caenum vel lutum sub acqua fetideum*' (*wase* is like a fen, mud, or dirty and stinking under the water). It persisted as a place name in Gloucestershire. Walter de Grey Birch found it as *wasa* in so many Saxon charters and parish boundaries that he was inclined to regard it as a generic term for the River Thames.[7] The nature of the water implied by the term *wase* is slow moving or meandering. We are looking for shallow water, muddy, and perhaps stagnant water meadows, and a ford on the mid-Thames where the river flow slows and its course meanders.

There are of course many fords of that kind on the Thames where a battle may have been fought, but one prime candidate must be Wallingford, close to a major earthwork, the Grimsdyke, which dominates the Icknield Way as it descends from the Chiltern Hills. King Alfred believed that Caesar's expedition into Britain used this crossing point, and Caesar may have fought a short battle there. Alternatively, we might look at another Grimsdyke which flanks the Roman road, Akemannes Street, leading to Bath and which is close to the Fosse Way. Here, at the junction of the Evenlode River and the Thames, Eynsham became another later battle site – a conflict in 571 between Saxons and a foe who may have been Britons or western-based raiders. The strategic aim was probably control of the important Swinford crossing.

In language terms, *bassas* is an early, possibly sixth-century term, and may therefore be an indication that the Nennius narrative is based on a record made at, or close to, the time of the battle. In Arthurian terms, the truth is that this battle could have been fought anywhere on the Thames from eastern Gloucestershire to London. A 'battle on the Thames' is about as close as we can get. Swinford, on conjectural strategic grounds, may be the best choice among many options.

Battle Seven

The seventh battle was fought '*in silva Caledonis*' (in the Caledonian woods), and is almost universally agreed to have taken place in Scotland. The evidence for a Scottish site is in fact slight, and rests almost entirely on the ancient Alexandrian geographer Ptolemy's placing of a tribe called the Caledonii north of the Forth/Clyde line. Ptolemy produced his geography about AD 150. Later Welsh tradition moves the scene somewhat to the south. It suggests that forest of Celidon (*Coit Celidon*) was to be found just north of modern Carlisle.

Against that, we have the evidence of Julius Caesar's expeditions to Britain, which are securely dated to 55 and 54 BCE. We know that Caesar scarcely penetrated further than the boundaries of the modern counties of Kent and Surrey. He did cross the Thames, but went no further than the area around modern St Albans. He certainly didn't reach Scotland or visit Carlisle. The Roman writers Lucan (AD 39–65) and Florus (AD 74–130), speaking of Caesar's Second Expedition to Britain, also refer to *unde Caledonis fallit turbate Britannos* ('from where he deceived the confused Britons of Caledon') and *rursus Britannos, Caledonis sequatus in silvas* ('on the contrary he pursued the Britons towards the woods of Caledon'). Pliny (d. AD 79) noted in his history (*Book IV*, c.30) that, after Caesar returned to Gaul, the Romans didn't go back to Britain for nearly a hundred years, and that in any case they had scarcely penetrated 'beyond the vicinity of the forest of Celidon'. Pliny thought that they had gone less than a hundred miles inland from their coastal landing places. For Lucan, Florus, Pliny and Caesar the 'forest of Celidon' can only be the great forest (*Coit Mawr*) which ran, virtually unbroken, all the way from Kent to Somerset. The

Roman armies that invaded Kent around 55 BCE never went north to Scotland or Carlisle. They knew a different Celidon, and they knew it a hundred years before Ptolemy made his map, when he placed 'Celidon', or a version of it, in modern Scotland.

Celidon may not be a native name used by the Britons. It is possible that Caesar and the Romans derived the name from the ancient city of Calydon in Aetolia which was famous for a boar sent by the goddess Diana. This fabulous boar was destroying all the vines, and it was killed by Meleager and his girlfriend, the huntress Atalanta. If it was not a jokey reference by Caesar to the boar-hunt style of the guerrilla battles with the Catuvellauni,[8] we are forced to conclude that it was a generic name for a forest like *afon* or *abon* is for a river, and therefore is difficult to assign to a particular locality.

Celidon may have been used as a personal name. In the Welsh story of *Culhwch ac Olwen* the grandfather of the hero Culhwch is called *Kyleddon Wledig*, which roughly translates as 'Lord of the Forest'. *Culhwch ac Olwen* is located in south Wales, so it may not be unreasonable to assume that the forest in question may be in that area, perhaps the Forest of Dean.

While we cannot locate Kyleddon or *Silva Celidonis* securely, other known battles may offer further clues. Saxon records say they met the Britons in battle at *Peonnum* (modern Penselwood), just west of the River Wylye, where a Roman road runs north-west from Salisbury to join the old line of the Fosse Way. This gap in the great forest dates back to the time when the Romans built their road, and it may still have been there before the Saxons came in numbers. It was clearly a strategically important area because the Romans felt it necessary to build a road to control it. Its importance seems to have lasted, and we can see why by looking at the Saxon victory at Penselwood. That victory enabled the Saxons to drive the Britons all the way back to the River Parret, opening up the Somerset coast before them. We can reasonably assume that the strategic and military objectives of the sixth century may have been the same as, or similar to, those of the Romans in the first century and the Saxons nearly six hundred years later. Persisting military strategy suggests that Penselwood is a persuasive site for an Arthurian battle in, or near, a forest. Unless some new archaeological or documentary evidence comes to light, there is no way to be sure.

Battle Eight

If Arthur failed to impose his will completely at Celidon, the eighth battle may have resulted. It was fought at Castle, or Fort, Guinnion, and the location we are to propose may suggest that the two battles are closely linked strategically. Before we get to that it should be noted that, unusually for Nennius, we are given quite a lot of additional information – he attributes Arthur's victory of this occasion to the Virgin Mary – and that may lead us to suspect another later editorial hand has been at work.

We may doubt that anyone in sixth-century England was much interested in the Virgin Mary. Although Saint Mary is apparently depicted[9] in the Roman catacombs which date from the early days of Christianity, her cult as 'the Virgin Mother' doesn't begin until after the Council of Ephesus in AD 431. Although the Church recognised her as *theotokos* (the Mother of God) at Ephesus in the 'Church of Mary', other churches dedicated to her were relatively slow to develop. The first Marian churches in Rome itself, for example, date only from the late fifth and sixth centuries. Devotion to the Virgin Mary in England in the early sixth century, the time of the Arthurian battle, is very doubtful.

Two or three hundred years later, in the ninth century, when the Nennius text may have been created in its present form,[10] churchmen in Ireland, Wales and significant parts of England were well along the path to the 'Romanisation' of what may have been previously an independent, or perhaps even a Pelagian, Christianity in the British Isles. In Wales, Bishop Elvodug (*fl.* AD 768) was said to be among the leaders of this movement, and Elvodug of course is the man claimed by Nennius, in the preface to our list of battles, as his mentor. Devotion to the Virgin Mother increased and became widespread as the process of 'Romanisation' continued. William of Malmesbury, in the twelfth century, had a particular devotion to her. The attribution of victory to her may therefore date from the time of Elvodug and Nennius rather than the Age of Arthur, and we will return to this point shortly. For the moment, we can say that it is extremely unlikely that Arthur, or anyone else in Britain, had a particular devotion to Saint Mary the Virgin Mother as early as the first half of the sixth century.[11]

It is nonetheless a potentially informative detail, and perhaps should not be entirely discounted. We are told by Nennius that, in this battle, Arthur carried the image of the Virgin Mary on his shoulders (or on his shield if there was a mistranslation). It was through her virtue, and that of her son Jesus Christ, that victory was obtained. With this divine help, the Pagans were put to flight and there was great slaughter. Even if we rule out the direct intervention and inspiration of the Virgin Mary, the battle at Fort Guinnion may very well have been recorded at the time as a 'Christian victory', or was claimed as such in subsequent years.

A supposed 'Christian victory' should, of itself, remind us to be cautious and sceptical. It may simply be a copy of Constantine's victory at the Milvian Bridge in 312, after he had been told that he would win *in hoc signo* (in this sign, the chi-rho, the first two letters of Christ's name). While Constantine certainly attributed his victory to 'divine aid', the Arch of Victory he erected to mark his success had no Christian symbolism at all. Constantine seems to have remained partly faithful to his original belief in the 'Unconquered Sun' as a battle symbol, and his Arch of Victory only claims unspecified divine help. The chi-rho story may be just a story, a useful fable for an emerging faith. The 'Christian victory' of Guinnion may be a narrative of similar inspiration.

For the purposes of our search, the key element in Arthur's eighth battle remains not the alleged 'Christian victory' but the fort name, *Guinnion*. Sir John Rhys noted that 'n' and 'r' were sometimes scribally confused in Welsh and Latin because of the way the letters were formed. That may lead us to wonder if Guinnion is actually *gwen* (Welsh, white or holy) plus *rian* (Welsh, maiden, girl or young woman), so the fort becomes the 'castle of the holy woman or women' – *Caer Gwen Rian*. We may also note that *castellum* can be translated as 'refuge', so the apparently military 'Fort Guinnion', which may require us to find a Roman camp or a hill fort, may have been no more than a wicker-delineated compound that was regarded at the time as a sanctuary.[12] We simply don't know what word may have been used to denote a house of religious women in the sixth century; 'convent' – from Late Latin *convenire*, 'to come together, an assembly' – was not then in use, nor was 'nunnery', which comes into our present version of English via Saxon *nunne* from Latin *nonna*, a 'religious woman, a female monk'.[13]

Those who prefer a Scottish or northern English Arthur may note with pleasure *Cairn Ryan* near modern Stranraer, but there is no tradition of a battle or religious women there. Geoffrey of Monmouth and the French romances note a 'castle of girls' (*castellum puellarum*) and a *chateau de pucelles* (castle of the virgins) which has usually been regarded as Edinburgh, mainly – and solely – because that is where Geoffrey of Monmouth placed it. We may note that there is an association of healing women at Glastonbury which is independent of Geoffrey. The romances, for example, insist it was to Morgan Le Fay at Avalon that the dying Arthur was borne after the disastrous Battle of Camlan. Yder, wounded in another Arthurian fight, was also taken to Glastonbury where he was tended by Guinevere.

There is no local tradition of a battle at Glastonbury, but many years ago the great Welsh scholar Sir John Rhys (1840–1915) pointed out a very obscure note in Harley 3859, which refers to the origin of the name 'Glastonbury'. The passage reads *unu'st glastenic qui vener q:vocat' loyt coyt*. This is obviously some form of scribal shorthand, and needs to be unpicked to be understood. Rhys's near contemporary, the antiquarian and historian of ancient Britain and Wales E. G. B. Phillimore (1856–1937), expanded the text to read *unum sunt glastenic qui venerunt que vocatur loyt coyt*. His solution read, 'The Glastenic are one people who venerate what they call the grey trees.' Rhys himself suggested *unde sunt glastenic qui venerabiliterque voca(n)tur loyt coyt* which he translated as 'from whence (i.e. Glast) are the Glastenic which are reverently called the grey trees'.

This is still obscure and not quite convincing. Rhys took it that Glastonbury was derived from a conjectural Late British word meaning 'oaks', similar to *glasten* (Breton, oaks) or *glastanen* (Cornish, oaks).[14] Without disagreeing with him on that point, we might hazard an expansion of the Harley 3859 text to read, '*unde sanctus Glastenic qui veneritur quod cat loyt coyt*', which finds the Welsh word for battle (*cat*) in the Latin text while conflating *unum* to *unde*, *st* to *sanctus*, and joining the isolated q to the *vo* or *uo* which precedes *cat*. The text would then read, 'Glastonbury's name comes from the holy (*sanctus*) people of Glasten (*Glastenic*) who are to be honoured because of the battle of the grey trees.' Put more colloquially, Glastonbury gets its name from 'the holy people of the oaks who are honoured because of the battle of the oak grove'. We may even take this further to speculate that the meaning is the 'battle of, or in, the holy grove'.

Was there such a grove at Glastonbury which might also have served as a hospital or sanctuary? Had that 'holy grove' (which sounds a bit pagan) been Christianised? Was it in effect a monastery for women, or a joint monastery with women alongside men? If there was a monastery of holy women, or a joint monastery, in the sixth century at Glastonbury, there is only one likely founder, and that is Saint Bridget of Ireland, or one of her immediate successors. Bridget was known in Ireland as Bridget of Kildare (*kildare* means 'church of the oak' or the 'oak grove'). Irish churches were often associated with oak groves – Saint Columba, for example, was very protective of the one at Derry.

The question then becomes: can we connect Bridget independently with the region? The Bristol county librarian Ernest Sibree, over a hundred years ago, speculated that the name of the City of Bristol (originally *Bricg-stow*) derived not from the bridge (built 1272, and the city name existed before that) but from *bricg* – a form of Bridget plus the word *stow* (a place where people gather for religious purposes). Other place names in the region indicate that there may have been a widespread devotion to Bridget, and to oaks as symbols. Della Hooke, in her study of the Hwicce (who lived north of Bristol in an area roughly equivalent to the old diocese of Worcester, which included Bristol), noted that they marked their borders with crosses affixed to oak trees. Saint Augustine of Canterbury famously met the Christians of Britain somewhere near Bristol 'on the borders of the Hwicce and the West Saxons' (Bede says) at a holy oak which was appropriated by Bede and Catholic historians as 'Augustine's Oak'.

Oaks in Arthur's time, it appears, were very much linked with Christianity. There is nothing inherently improbable about a monastery of holy women and an oak grove at Glastonbury. Place names offer a local tradition associating Bridget with Glastonbury which goes back before AD 1100, and Glastonbury Abbey appears to have been an Irish foundation. It is a plausible site for a monastery of holy women offering curative services headed by a woman of some importance, perhaps by Bridget herself.

Was there a battle there? Glastonbury is a likely place for a battle in the sixth century because the area has a long history that illustrates its strategic importance. It occupied a site that is close to the Roman roads and gaps in the great forest, and offers connections to the sea. Sea levels have changed, and Glastonbury may have been more directly linked with the sea then. It is, in any case, still accessible up the River Brue. As we know from the Saxon invasion of the region, a force successful at Penselwood could drive forward easily to Wedmore, Cheddar, Axbridge and Congresbury, as well as to Glastonbury itself.

The broader Glastonbury area had strong defensive possibilities for the beleaguered. It was at nearby Athelney that Alfred hid from the Danes, and began to assemble his forces for his successful counter-attack against them. The ninth-century *Cormac's Glossary* says Glastonbury was 'fortified by the Irish in the time Crimthann Mor' (around the time of Arthur) when it was known as 'Glastonbury of the Gael' or 'Irish Glastonbury'. There are several prominent Iron Age hill forts and other features, such Glastonbury Tor, that may have been reoccupied in the sixth century, and which could have served as contested strong points. Without substantial archaeological evidence – and that is currently lacking – there is no way of proving the point, but it is at least feasible that Glastonbury was Fort Guinnion.

There is one further point. The oldest church at Glastonbury was the very old church of Saint Mary whose foundation date is unknown. We may enter some doubt about its antiquity, which enthusiasts insist goes back to very early Christian times, around AD 63. It is more plausibly seen as a religious site founded, like so many West Country churches, in the sixth century. We may also enter a doubt about which Mary it was dedicated to. If there was any link with Saint Bridget, who had a caring and medical mission, there may be an association, real or imagined, with the caring ministry of Mary Magdalene at Bethany. If Bridget did indeed have a monastery for women, defended by Arthur and his men, the sign of Saint Mary they fought under may not have been that of Saint Mary the Virgin but that of Saint Mary, the companion of Jesus.[15] Fort Guinnion may have had both religious and military significance, but that lies beyond proof.

Battle Nine
Arthur's ninth battle is somewhat simpler as a conundrum. Nennius says it took place 'in the city of the legion which is called in the British language Cair Lion'. Chester and Caerleon-on-Usk

were both so named, and both may be possible. Welsh tradition, as we shall see later, places Arthur himself in south Wales rather than at Chester, where Bede later, joyfully, reports a battle in which many Welsh monks were slaughtered. There may of course have been other Roman centres that were for a time locally known by this name. Wareham, if we judge by the Burghal Hideage numbers, may have required a legion as a garrison, but we do not know what the Roman camp there was called. In view of the broader picture of a continuing conflict in the south-west of England, we may prefer Caerleon-on-Usk to the other candidate sites. There is nothing inherently difficult in believing that a military base might be the subject of an attack by insurgents, but we know nothing of what was at stake at Caer Leon.

Battle Ten

The tenth battle is more puzzling. Nennius tells us that it took 'place on the bank of the river we call trat treuroit' (*in litore fluminis quod nos vocamus trat treuroit*). Another version of the text gives the river name as Tribruit (*quod vocatur Tribruit*). Some later translations into English give a reconstructed Welsh name, *Tryfrwyd*. References in later Welsh poetry confirm a river with that name, but whether it is the right river for the battle remains problematical. If this form is correct (it also appears as *Trywruid*), it means 'variegated in colour'.

The Latin form *Tribruit* offers the best way forward. *Cormac's Glossary* in the ninth century refers to an Irish occupation of Glastonbury and remarks that 'the Irish dwelt on the East side of the Irish Sea and built habitations and royal forts there'. Among these forts was one called '*Din Tradui*, the triple-fossed fort of Crimthann Mor'.

If we accept a possible Irish connection, we can substitute the Irish word for a fort instead of the usual *din* or *dun*: *rath*. If we postulate that the Welsh word for a battle, *cat*, at one time stood in front of this word and transferred a 't' to it, we can get to the odd form in the text of Nennius, *trath*. *Tribui* (three ditches) would in pronunciation exchange 'b' for 'v' or 'f' so we find *trivui* as a possible form. If we assume that a later scribe didn't understand Trath, but knew there had been a fort involved and re-attached the Welsh *caer* or *dun*, we reach a conjectural form *Caer Trattrivui*.

This is close to a known name, *Caer Draitou* (an exchange of Welsh 'd' for Irish 't'), and to a *Caer Traitou* which was number twenty-four in a list of cities or forts of Britain offered in another part of the Harley 3859 collection.

This name also turns up in a twelfth-century *vita* of Saint Carantoc which records a meeting between the saint and a man called Cato at *Din Drathou*. *Din Drathou* in the saint's biography is thought to be Carhampton on the shores of the Severn Estuary, about 4 miles east of modern Minehead. Carhampton (*Carumtune*) was a royal fortress in Saxon times, and King Egbert fought a large force of Scandinavians there in AD 836. It has an impressive hill fort (Bat's Castle), was an early Christian centre, and was a strategically important place over several centuries. It may well have been the site of Arthur's battle. Precise and conclusive evidence, however, is lacking.

Battle Eleven

The eleventh battle fought by Arthur, according to Harley 3859, was 'on the mountain which is called Agned' (*in monte qui dicitur Agned*). The Vatican MS of Nennius provides a different name and some additional information. It says the battle was fought 'on the mountain that is called Breguion, where they were put to flight, and which we call the Battle of Bregion' (*in monte nominatur breguion ubi illos in fugam vertit, quem nos cat bregion appellamus*).

In the twelfth century, Geoffrey of Monmouth confidently identified *Breguion* as Edinburgh, but there seems little reason on linguistic or other grounds to support his view. Later writers associated *Breguion* with a battle site known to be associated with the famous warrior Urien of Rheged. He fought *kat gellawr brewyn* (the battle in the cells of Brewyn), which has been identified as the Roman fort of High Rochester below Cheviot. That may fit well with the idea of an Arthur whose area of operation lay in modern Scotland and the north of England. There is, however, good reason to prefer another Roman fort. If *Breguion* is assumed to be a scribal error for *Breguien*, the battle site can more confidently identified as the Roman fort and supply depot of *Bravonium*, modern Leintwardine in Herefordshire.

Leintwardine is situated at the junction of the rivers Clune and Teme. The name is partly Celtic and partly Norman. *Leint* is a torrential stream and *wardine* is a protective enclosure. It was a major centre in Roman times, and seems to have been some sort of military headquarters and logistics centre. The Roman army base (*Branogenium*) was located less than half a mile from the town (*Bravonium*), which is located on the Roman road Watling Street. *Bravonium* boasted a bathhouse and a *mansio* (a superior sort of villa estate).

It still has the appearance of a significant military position. The crossing place on the rivers is dominated by the surrounding high ground, which features a number of ancient hill forts. One of them, Brandon Hill, is still particularly impressive, and the whole location is one of the key routes into, or out of, central Wales. Whoever held Leintwardine was in a position to protect, or to threaten, the middle reaches of the River Severn. In military terms, it is an entirely plausible place for a battle, and, as at Caer Leon, its use as a military base may have invited the interest of dissident forces. Archaeology carried out locally reveals that Bravonium and other neighbouring Roman towns were probably destroyed by fire, which suggests some sort of violent military campaign in the area. The remains of the fire, however, are undated, and form the only real evidence that a major battle ever took place there. There are no local traditions linking Arthur with the site.

Battle Twelve

The sequence of battles in Nennius is completed by the Battle of Badon. Nennius insists that in all twelve battles Arthur was the victor (*in omnibus bellis victor extitit*), and that may well have been the case, but we should not too readily accept it as truth. Gildas, the better witness, who was there at the time, says first one side and then the other won in a sequence of battles leading up to battle twelve, the siege, or battle, of Mount Badon (*obsessionis Mons Badonis*).

Badon was said by tradition to be 'King Arthur's greatest battle', and that reputation demands that we study it in more detail. We shall do that in the next chapter. For the moment, we should try to take a view of what the twelve battles may tell us about wars and warriors in the sixth century, and specifically what the battle narratives can reveal about 'Arthur the warrior'.

A Regional War

What was going on? If we are right about the battle locations – and that will be at best contentious, and at worst simply rejected by some – we can see that they fall into three groups. Battles 1, 6 and 7 appear to be a contest for the mid-Thames and Wylye River areas. Battles 2, 3, 4 and 5 follow the route taken by Vespasian, and must have been designed to take and hold the valleys of the Trent, Piddle and Divelish, and perhaps also the watershed to Ilchester – the region of the Lindinienses. Battles 9 and 11 seem directed to the control of Wales, or at any rate the Welsh borders. Battle 10 and, possibly, Battle 12 are linked to the control of the Severn and its estuary.

The aim of the whole campaign can be seen as seizing land and peoples from princes and potentates too weak to hold them. Some encounters may have seen Arthur combat other claimants. In his campaign aims, Arthur was what our earlier study of war in post-Roman Britain would have led us to suspect; he was a warlord working in a defined region towards a crown and a kingdom.

The Enemy

The battle list does not name the enemy faced by Arthur. The 'warlike Arthur' section in Nennius begins with a brief Kentish history; we may choose to accept an implication that his opponents came from Kent. Nennius simply says that they (*ipsi*) were defeated by Arthur and sought help from Germany. They were thus able vastly to increase their numbers, and later brought over kings from Germany to rule them.

We should note that Nennius here may be importing into the 'Arthurian story' a quite different and later contest from north-eastern England. At the end of the 'warlike Arthur' section, Nennius names King Ida of Bernicia as the first king of this 'new German' kind. While Ida was roughly contemporary with Arthur, and seems to have begun his reign in 'Arthurian times', about AD 547, he and his sons fought mainly with peoples to the north and west of their Northumbrian Anglian kingdom, such as those led by Urien Rheged. If Arthur was involved in that conflict, he was a Scottish figure, and all our conjectures about a southern English campaign are misplaced.

The *Dux Bellorum*

There are two pieces of information in the narrative of the Nennius battle list that stand out. First, we are told that Arthur fought alongside the 'kings of Britain' but he was the *'dux bellorum'* – the leader of the wars, the battle commander. That suggests that, at the time of this campaign in southern England, he was not, or not at that time, a king, but that he had been accepted by 'kings' as their leader in the search for country, settlement and plunder – 'England, home and booty', as it were.

It is difficult to see how he may have managed that appointment by his own strength without a civil war of some kind. That war does not feature in either Gildas or Nennius, but Arthur's commanding role could have arisen in two other ways. It is a choice that involves either a very weak ruler or a very powerful monarch. First, Arthur may have been appointed by a ruler as a mercenary to lead local levies, and then betrayed and turned on his master. In that connection we may note the place name *Liss* (Welsh, a palace) in Hampshire, but we have no idea what prince or king may have ruled there. Alternatively, and perhaps more probably, we may think that Arthur was appointed by a more powerful 'over-king', or 'High King', who could order his subservient rulers to accept Arthur as their 'leader-in-war'. The English campaign of the twelve battles tells us that Arthur was either a double-crossing mercenary, not unlike the unscrupulous tyrants denounced by Gildas, or he was the appointed general of a 'sea-king' with a fleet powerful enough to seize and hold Wareham, and command kings to his hostings.

Secondly, the Nennius narrative reveals Arthur, as battle leader and field commander, to have exhibited a remarkable military quality much prized in soldiers even today. It is the ability to maintain focus on a strategic objective despite the distractions of plans going wrong, the enemy being found in greater strength than suspected, and the lie of the land or even the weather not being as predicted. It appears that Arthur pursued an overall scheme for a period of ten or more years (if we measure the time required for twelve battles as ten to twelve successive 'fighting seasons'). Maintaining the objective in those circumstances shows determination, tenacity and perseverance, coupled with an unusual ability to lead men and sustain over time their enthusiasm, direction and belief. Only the great commanders in history have shown these qualities. Arthur, on this evidence, was a considerable warrior.

There are two further points to be made about the campaigns of Arthur as set out by Nennius. The twelves battles fall squarely into the 'wars against external enemies' described by the monk Gildas, and do not involve the later 'civil wars' that he regretted. Arthur's opponents were different from whatever ethnic or political group he, and the kings who fought alongside him, belonged to. That group also included Gildas himself.

Although Gildas, in his accounts of Arthur's wars, speaks from a religious viewpoint, religion doesn't appear to have been a factor. The battle list of the warlike Arthur does not describe a simple 'Christians *versus* pagans' series of conflicts. Arthur may have been a pagan, or a Christian of a type different from the Catholic orthodoxy preferred in the ninth century. The account of Arthur's wars in Harley 3859 can be read as an attempt to suppress or distort the real achievement of Arthur. There seems to be an attempt to co-opt him into the cult of Saint Mary the Virgin Mother. We should not lose sight of the fact that the battle list, as we have it in Nennius, was written three hundred years after the events it purports to describe, and that it reflects the political and religious imperatives of its own day. In the account of the wars we have, the religious orthodoxy of the ninth century may have overcome the real military truth of the sixth. Nennius is not a clear window on the sixth century; he may be a distorting mirror.

Battle Lessons

What are we left with? Well, not very much. We have somewhat tainted reports of battles fought in dubious locations, and we really can't establish any history to modern standards from any of them. We can see some indications that Arthur, although he was in many ways the sort of amoral tyrant we should expect to see in the sixth century, was probably a remarkable leader. He may too have been the surrogate or agent of a powerful king in the shadows.

On the other hand, if we are sceptical about the narrative of the twelve battles of the 'warlike Arthur', we may see the Nennius narrative as no more than a charming set of traditions, edited to fit in with the prejudices and priorities of the time when that part of Harley 3859 was written, in the first two decades of the ninth century. To know more about the life, times and battles of Arthur, only Battle 12, the siege of Mount Badon, is important, and it is to that battle that we now turn.

CONCLUSIONS

1. The pattern made by the battle sites proposed reveals a regional conflict.
2. Arthur either betrayed a British leader or was appointed *dux bellorum* by a shadowy 'over-king' who could command other subservient kings to serve under Arthur's direction in repeated battles.
3. Arthur was a remarkable leader, able to keep the support and backing of his war bands for a period of ten to twelve years and to maintain his focus on strategic objectives over that time.
4. Arthur is unlikely to have fought under the sign of Saint Mary in battle.

4

WHEN WAS BADON?

The Traditional View

The traditional view of the Battle of Badon is that it was one of the most important battles fought between the Britons (the Welsh or native Celtic peoples of the British Isles) and the Anglo-Saxons (the Angles, Saxons, Jutes and other invading Germanic peoples). The battle resulted in a victory for the Britons, and it was widely believed to have set a limit for two or three generations on Saxon expansion in England. It may even have led to some of them returning to their Germanic homelands. It may also have been an opportunity to reverse the Barbarian tide from Germany then engulfing Gaul and other parts of the Roman Empire.

If all of that were true, it would be sufficient to make it perhaps the most significant battle fought in England between the departure of the Romans and the arrival of the Normans. If its wider European significance had been pursued, and the Barbarian tide had been reversed, it would have made Badon a turning point in world history, but the Britons did not follow up their advantage, and the chance of reversing the Barbarian tide, if it ever existed, was lost. Badon may therefore have a legitimate claim on our attention as a turning point in world history where the world resolutely failed to turn. There is, however, one aspect of the battle which transforms its interest into fascination: it is said to have been the greatest victory of the man we know as King Arthur.

Sources of Information

What do we know of this battle? There are only two authentic contemporary documentary sources of information. The first is Saint Patrick of Ireland, who left us his *Confessio* or 'Proclamation of Faith' and a letter to a chieftain called Coroticus. The other source is an *admontiuncula* or a 'Little Admonishment' or 'Little Warning', a sermon called the *De Excidio Britonum* ('The Ruin of Britain') by a monk called Gildas. Saint Patrick has nothing to say of military matters. While Gildas mentions the Battle of Badon, he has nothing to say of King Arthur.

Gildas

Gildas therefore is our sole unchallenged contemporary witness. According to his *vita*, he was the son of a leading ruler in the north of Britain. Welsh tradition says his brothers were great warriors. He studied with Saint Illtud, one of the most famous of the Welsh saints, and was the teacher of Saint Finnian, one of the most important of Irish saints (in Ireland he was called Giltas – the Irish spelt things differently ['t' for 'd']). He wrote a *penitential* – a code of practice for monks – which was widely followed by monasteries in Scotland, Ireland, Wales and England. Saint David of Wales later adapted and refined it into a more ascetic fashion which was also widely followed by the Celtic churches.

In short, Gildas knew, or was known by, everyone who was anyone in the religious life of the British Isles in the sixth century. Since leading monks and abbots were usually members of the ruling tribe in any given area, and indeed often wielded a great deal of temporal power, he also knew most of the political and military leaders of the places that he visited or where he was honoured. He probably heard directly, or was otherwise aware of, the stories told in the courts of the kings and tyrants by the bards who recorded, in the prevailing oral tradition, the deeds of the chieftains in battle. He also knew and was respected by the men who decided what should be written down in the monasteries – the great abbots, the publishers of the day. The abbots liked him and his work. His own written works – his penitential and his little sermon – were 'bestsellers', copied and available in many monasteries. He knew many of the fighting men too, and may himself have been present at, or taken part in, battles. His main activity, however, was spiritual. After an honoured life of great sanctity and learning in England and then Ireland, he retired to Brittany where he founded a monastery which to this day bears his name – Saint Gildas de Rhuys. Through his family connections and his religious links, Gildas was very well placed to know what had happened, and to see that it was written down correctly. That makes him a witness of great potential authority.

The Ruin of Britain

The Ruin of Britain is a work of the earlier part of his life, written before his reputation for spiritual merit was fully established. Gildas intended it to have an immediate, and entirely spiritual and theological, effect. He wasn't interested in telling yarns about King Arthur or anyone else. His aim was to eradicate sinful behaviour among the clergy, leading citizens and rulers of his time. His method was to relate the history of Britain and to use it to show that, in the past, sinful ways of life were always punished by God. He concluded that the errors he could see around him, if they were to persist, would lead to similar exhibitions and examples of divine wrath.

As we have already seen (in chapter 2), he particularly attacked five ruling kings of his day for their loose behaviour and called upon them to reform their lives. In so far as we can identify their kingdoms, all the condemned monarchs ruled in Wales, Cornwall or Devon. Three cannot be identified with certainty with any real rulers known from other sources, and only two can be dated. Votepor is thought to be a king whose memorial stone was said to be of the mid-sixth century (the date has been questioned more recently). The other king is Maelgwn Gwynedd, who, despite Gildas's strictures upon him, is remembered in Welsh Christianity as the founder or supporter of churches and monasteries, some of them run by his relatives. His death was likely to have been accurately recorded by the monks of the monasteries he had helped to found, and the Welsh Annals (*Annales Cambriae*) say he died in AD 545 or 549. We can say, on the basis of the now controversial date of the memorial of Votepor and the obit date of Maelgwn, that the Battle of Badon was fought before AD 545.

Gildas himself is not much help on the date. His mention of Badon is almost incidental to his main purpose, and he uses the battle only a sort of marker in time that his audience might know. He says, 'From that time onwards, first our countrymen, then the enemy, were victorious. This lasted right up to the year of the siege of Badon Hill (*obsessionis Badonici montis*) which was more or less the latest (*novissimaeque*) though not the least defeat of the villains. Since then, as I know, one month of the forty-fourth year has already passed because that was the year of my birth.' A little later he continues, 'Wars against the external enemy ceased, but not the battles among our own people.' Badon, for Gildas in *the Ruin of Britain*, was a watershed in time, a moment when a long sequence of wars against foreigners turned into a period of civil war.

Dating

The Latin style of Gildas makes accurate translation difficult and several alternative versions of what his Latin text says are possible. Bede, for example, writing about two hundred years after Badon, uses his passage about the battle almost unchanged, but believed, based on whatever text was before him, that it meant Badon was fought forty-four years after the arrival of the Saxons in Britain, which he placed about AD 450. Bede implies Badon was fought about AD 500.

That same date has appealed to some modern translators who think the text means that the Battle of Badon was fought in the year of Gildas's birth, which they calculate may have been around AD 500. *Novissimae*, however, means 'very recently or 'a short time ago', and would be a very odd word to employ about an event that took place forty or more years earlier. Gildas may mean that sequence of alternating victories lasted for forty-four years, which he knows personally and particularly because that sequence began in the year of his birth, and that the Battle of Mount Badon, fought very recently at a time that his readers or listeners could be expected to know, was the last battle in that sequence.

The latest scholarship on his sermon suggests that it was written around AD 530. Gildas says he delayed for ten years before publishing his thesis, which would seem to confirm a date about AD 520 for the battle, but, depending on how we read Gildas, it could be AD 530. It may even have been as late as AD 540.

The Birthdate of Arthur

We are not likely to get closer than that for the time of the battle and we can turn now to the consideration of its location. Before we leave Gildas, however, we may note that there is other information to be deduced from this date for the Battle of Badon. If, as we have supposed, Arthur commanded the armies that fought the twelve battles of Nennius and that they may have taken as long as ten or twelve years to accomplish, we may be able to say something about Arthur. We may be able to make a guess at his birthdate.

It is unlikely that any warrior would have found himself placed in charge of an army that included kings before demonstrating his own military competence. If Badon was fought in AD 530, and came at the end of the sequence of battles we have been looking at, Arthur must have assumed field command at least ten years earlier. While he may have shown precocious ability as a warrior, he can hardly have emerged as an overall commander without having three to five years' previous experience. If he was about eighteen or twenty when he began his career, he must have been born about AD 495, plus or minus five years. He was around thirty-five years old when he fought Badon. The archaeology of contemporary graves suggests that, at that age, he was on the outer edge of average life expectancy for men.[1] He was a veteran warrior when he fought at Badon.

CONCLUSIONS

1. The best guess we can make is that the Battle of Badon took place in AD 530.
2. If Arthur was a commander who led men in a series of battles over a ten-year period culminating at Badon, he must have been born in the last decade of the fifth century.
3. He was at the upper end of male life expectancy when he fought Badon.

5

WHERE WAS BADON?

The Background

The search for the site of the Battle of Badon is essentially an exploration of place names and how over the centuries they have remained, or have been altered, forgotten or misunderstood through translation, false etymologies, the fortunes of war, and ethnic and linguistic changes among the peoples who inhabited the land. Language change is a major and sometimes unseen difficulty. People and places we actually know, and can see now, appeared at that time under different names, and in languages that are no longer spoken. We may not recognise even familiar places under old names.

To progress we will sometimes have to make guesses about such places, and we have to use documents whose authors a thousand years ago also made guesses about words, people and places. Their guesses, like ours, could be wrong, but they sometimes deliberately changed texts about events to bring them into line with their own thoughts. Like us, they sometimes reflected in their guesses, amendments and commentaries their own time rather than that of the 'real King Arthur'. Then there is the potent personality King Arthur himself has acquired in the tradition that has come down to us. We may be reflecting not what the evidence tells us but what we hope it may tell us, or confirm about a much-loved figure. King Arthur himself is, and always has been, a particular source of error and confusion.

A Combination Name

Researchers in the last hundred years or so interested in Badon, or in King Arthur, have achieved one element of common ground. They have agreed that Badon as a name is composed of two elements: *Badde* (a personal name) and *dun* (a Celtic word meaning 'fortification'). Researchers have been aware of language changes, so they have also considered that *dun* might be recorded as *down* – a Anglo-Saxon upland, or, translated to another commonly found Celtic word – Welsh *caer* (fort) or Cornish *dinas* (fort) – or to its Anglo-Saxon equivalent – *burh* (fort) or *bury* (fortified town). If it was located near the sea, two other words may come into play. They are *pen* (Welsh) and *ken* (Irish) and both mean 'head' but are commonly used to describe promontory hill forts by the sea. In that sense *ken* and *pen* mean 'headland fort' or just 'headland'.[1]

A Fort and a Ford

In considering all these words, we should remind ourselves again that what we are really looking for, in the context of the sixth century, when we seek a battle site where a siege took place, is not something like a Norman castle, but is more probably an old Iron Age hill fort, with a wall, or walls, of stone or earth, built on the summit of a prominent hill. The Romans called them *oppida* (singular *oppidum*). We are not just looking for the name. We are seeking an Iron Age hill fort that shows archaeological evidence of having been reused in the sixth century, probably one close to, or astride, a major travel route such as an ancient ridge path, a Roman road or a river. We might also hope to find a local tradition of a battle, or even some archaeology that points in that direction.

Sources

Researchers have used four main documents as evidence. They are the *Anglo-Saxon Chronicle*, Bede's *Ecclesiastical History of the English Nation*, the *Historia Britonum* in Harley 3859 (Nennius) and the Welsh Annals (*Annales Cambriae*), also part of Harley 3859. All, in the versions we have now, date from the ninth century, and most of the earliest copies still extant were made about two or three hundred years later than that. Careful examination of them, however, has revealed that they all derive from religious annals, long lists of significant religious and political events written, kept and copied in monasteries. Some of the ancestor annals, especially those of Irish origin, may go back close to the date of the battle – the Irish started keeping annals at Bangor in Northern Ireland in or around AD 550.

Annals, or materials based on them, are not entirely reliable about dates or indeed events.[2] There were genuine problems through disagreements about when the year began – November, December or March were used in different systems, and that meant dates for the same event in different sources could vary by up to five years. Copying errors in assigning an entry to one column rather than another in an annal could introduce an error of up to a hundred years. Scribes making copies often altered texts to enhance the reputation of a lay leader, or the prestige of their religious foundation. Errors and amendments of this kind mean annals are not to be trusted as impartial and accurate records. For deeds and dates, annals should be treated with suspicion, but on place names they are reliable. If a place is mentioned, it means that it existed. In some cases, the place mentioned may even have been a familiar location to the scribe who wrote it down – monks sometimes added a helpful note about location in the margins of whatever they were copying.

The Candidate Sites for Badon

Four major 'Badon' candidates have emerged from the scrutiny of the annalistic place names and modern and recent maps. They range geographically from Penrhyn Badon in the far north of Scotland to Bedon on the coasts of Brittany. They include the present city of Bath because of its Late Welsh name *Caer Vaddon*.[3] The most favoured is Bayden, north of Ramsbury in Wiltshire. *Badde + Dun* candidates include Badbury Rings, a very impressive Dorset hill fort; Badbury Hill near Faringdon in Oxfordshire; and Liddington Castle, a hill fort above a village called Barbury in Wiltshire.

All have their supporters and detractors. Few people have maintained support for Scotland and Brittany. Badbury Hill and Liddington Castle are clearly strategic and close to old trackways and Roman roads. Bath has Roman roads, but was never a fort or military base. The nearest hill fort to Bath is Solsbury Hill, but there appears to be no archaeological evidence of sixth-century reoccupation there.

There is, however, another candidate that has been missed. E. K. Chambers, examining a text of Gildas, saw a helpful note by a scribe about Badon: *qui prope sabrinum hostium habetur* (which is close to the mouth of the Severn). Chambers looked at the handwriting and concluded that the note had been written in the thirteenth century. This is late evidence and might be discounted as likely to be wrong were it not for another remark by an even later writer, John Leland.

Leland and Camden

John Leland (1503–52) is an impressive witness. He was an antiquarian, one of the founding fathers of English topography, bibliography and local history. Beginning in 1533, he undertook a ten-year journey round the kingdom recording the country as he saw it then. He noted hill forts and recorded finds of Roman coins, and provided descriptions of major buildings, speculating on their origins and antiquity. He, and one of his distinguished successors in his tasks, the finest of England's topographers and antiquarians, the great William Camden (1551–1623), noted something that they thought might be an old British or Welsh name for Bristol: *Caer Odor in nante Badon.*

Leland knew right away that something was not quite right. The modern city of Bristol grew originally from a 30-acre mound fortified by the Normans near the River Avon. The Normans later built a bridge to serve the castle and the emerging port, but that bridge, which is thought to provide the name of the city of Bristol (*Bridge + stow*), was not built until 1272. It was, however, enough to focus development around it. Previous inhabitants of the area, including the Romans, didn't see the mound as a suitable place to fortify. Some villa estates in the locality aside, the main Roman centre was their military port at *Abonae* (modern Sea Mills). Bristol, as a name and a place, didn't really exist before about AD 900 in any form. If Bristol didn't exist when the name *Caer Odor* arose and was current as a place name, to what did it refer?

Downriver from the centre of modern Bristol at Clifton, three Iron Age hill forts face one another across the Avon Gorge, the two on the western bank being separated from one another by a narrow defile. The location is now the site of a famous suspension bridge built by the great Victorian engineer Isambard Kingdom Brunel. It is an impressive site and, before the bridge was built, would have been a positively Wagnerian setting for a battle. It was also likely to have been economically and militarily important. In the gorge directly below the forts, there was a ford which permitted travellers to descend from the ridge paths, cross the river and ascend again to continue their progress. Before the development of Bristol, the three forts were the local focus of power, a stronghold of both economic and military significance.

Leland puzzled about the language of the name. He was inclined to see the name Badon as referring to the city of Bath (following the Late Welsh name *Vaddon*) but he could not see that *nante* could refer to the broad open valley in which that city sits. *Nante*, he knew, meant a gorge and the gorge which separated the three Clifton forts was one of the most spectacular in all Britain.[4] Leland concluded that *Badon* was an error and the name should be *Caer Odor in nante Avon*. Although he believed firmly in King Arthur and wrote about him in other places, he didn't consider the possibility of the text he had before him being a scribal mistake for *in monte Badon*. Nor did he explore the meaning and significance of *Caer Odor*.

Caer Odor

Caer is clearly a fort and *Odor* may be a personal name. There are many warriors and kings called *Odor* in Irish records at this time and some of them, in the form *Yder*, turn up in French romances about King Arthur. *Odor* may also be a mutated form of the Welsh word for a river. A tributary of the River Teme which flows from mid-Wales to join the Severn near Worcester is called the *Codre* and its name is derived from two words: *cou* (a basin in Old Welsh) and *dwr* (water in Welsh). Old Welsh words sometime lose their initial letter for grammatical reasons – *Codre* could be an old general name for any river and over time possibly became *Odre*. Thus the name that Leland found might mean 'the river fort at the Badon Gorge'.

There is, however, a more persuasive solution. There are two place names in Cornwall that interest us: Hudder Cave and Hudderdown. The Cornwall authorities Morton Nance and Charles Thomas say the 'h' is intruded. The real name is *udder*, and it is derived from two words, *or* and *tyr*, which combine to mean 'borderland'. That is interesting because Bede says that

Saint Augustine of Canterbury met the British bishops in 603 on the borders of the West Saxons and the Hwicce (*in confinio Hwiccorum et occidentalum Saxonum appelatur*). Not much is known about the Hwicce except that their territory corresponded broadly to the diocese of Worcester, and Worcester's ecclesiastical power in early times reached to Westbury-on-Trym, hardly more than a mile from the Clifton forts.

Bede also only used the term *confinio* to refer to one other place, and that is the border formed by the Humber Estuary between the Anglian kingdom of Deira (modern Yorkshire) and Lindsey (modern Lincolnshire). On the Lincolnshire side, there is a very small village whose Celtic name stands out like a beacon among the Saxon and Scandinavian names that now surround it. It is the hamlet of Odder and its name is a direct translation of the Latin term *confinio*.

Bede was writing in AD 731, when the Anglo-Saxon occupation of his part of England was almost 150 years old. As a surviving Celtic place name, *Odder*, or *Odor*, clearly predates the coming of the Anglo-Saxons. That makes it pre-AD 600 and the Bristol/Clifton name should therefore be considered as being of the same date. *Caer Odor in nante Badon* – 'the border fort in the Badon Gorge' – may very well be a name that was in use at, or not long after, the date suggested for the Battle of Badon and indicated by Gildas. If we judge from the Lincolnshire use, Oder as a place name was in use less than thirty years after Gildas's death. *Caer Odor in nante Badon* is a very strong candidate as the site of the battle.

Caer Odor fits some of the other criteria. It is a potent military position. Whoever held it in the sixth century could command both land and sea routes. Inherent military logic about such places dictates that a strategic site used in one battle will certainly be involved in others. Arthur's *Badon* may have been involved in more than one conflict. Its name or some variation of it should turn up in other battle contexts. We will look at that possibility.

The name *Caer Odor in nante Badon* also suggests that researchers have been wrong in assuming *Badon* is a compound word. In this form it appears to stand alone and complete and that means it is most likely to be a personal name. We should recall that Gildas says *Badonici* and Nennius says *Badonis*. Both are genitives and that means the place, Latin *Mons* or hill, belonged to a person called Badon. The Latin *Badonici* form of the name used by Gildas may imply a Welsh or Irish ending, *ach* (*Badonach*), which would mean the 'people of, or people ruled by, a man called Badon'. Can we find out anything about who this person called Badon was? We need now to look more closely at the Clifton forts.

CONCLUSIONS
1. The discovery made by Leland and Camden introduces a new candidate site for the Battle of Badon.
2. The term *Badonici* indicates a people of a place called Badon or ruled by a man called Badon.

6

THE HILL FORTS OF THE AVON GORGE

The Background – William of Wyrcestre

In September 1481, William of Wyrcestre visited the three Iron Age hill forts in the Avon Gorge. Despite his name, Wyrcestre was a Bristolian also known by his family name – Bottoner. He was the secretary and medical adviser of Sir John Fastolf of Norfolk. Fastolf enjoys an unfortunate and undeserved reputation through Shakespeare's use of his name in his plays about Henry IV and Henry V. Although he was indeed the owner of the Boar's Head tavern in Southwark featured in Shakespeare, Fastolf was also a strong and capable soldier, the Governor of Maine and Anjou, and he had widespread interests all over England. As Wyrcestre went around the country about his master's business, he developed a practice of making a survey of all the towns, churches and places that he visited. He was also an avid collector of, and copier from, old books and documents. He talked to local inhabitants, and set down in writing the orally transmitted legends and stories associated with their city or church. Modern measurements of the churches and other places he surveyed have found him to be an accurate and meticulous observer. He seems also to have been a very competent transcriber of books.

He calculated that the Clifton hill forts (which he called 'camps' because he thought they might be Roman) were about 360 feet (109.7 m) above the dry land by the riverside. About 120 feet (36.5 m) above the dry bank, there was a hermitage dedicated, he thought, to Saint Vincent. The chapel was 9 yards (8.2 m) long and 3 yards (2.7 m) wide, and there was also a kitchen whose dimensions have not survived in a readable form. On the heights above the chapel, there was a very strong *castrum* (Roman camp) which local people told him was founded 'before the time of William the Conqueror by Saracens and Jews', or by a giant called Ghyst (possibly from Welsh *Guieth*, a battle) who threw rocks at another giant called Goram, a resident of nearby Westbury-on-Trym.

Leland, Camden and Aubrey

A hundred years later, Leland and Camden also found the Clifton camps impressive. Camden noted that Saint Vincent's chapel was still there, and that a mighty rock overhanging the gorge was named after the saint. Another famous antiquarian, the gossipy John Aubrey (1626–97), who, as a child, often visited his grandmother Mrs Whitson in Bristol, noted a vast quantity of stones tumbled on the surface of the earth. They were very thickly scattered, but were rather more thickly scattered on the Leigh Down, or western side. Aubrey believed that they had been thus distributed by the earthquake that he believed had created the gorge. In 1668, he reported with regret that they had nearly all gone, broken up by the local people because they were found to make handy and excellent material for the lime kilns. The great overhanging rock and the hermitage had disappeared too, apparently having fallen into the gorge. It may have been blown up by the residents. There have been constant attempts to blow up the ford and other features of the gorge. The rock and the hermitage of Vincent may have been removed by local people who feared them as a hazard to shipping.

Draper's Discoveries

The removal of material by man and nature was halted to a very large extent in the last decades of the eighteenth century by General Sir William Draper (1721–87) who was appointed Conservator of the Downs (and therefore of the 'camps') by the Company of Merchant Venturers, who owned them. Draper's purpose was more economic than antiquarian. Clifton was changing. Starting around 1780, and inspired by the hot wells (warm natural springs) by the riverside, Clifton was transformed from a rough village of small farmers, shepherds and sailors into one of the most fashionable suburbs in Europe. Among the property speculators was General Sir William Draper.

Draper was personally largely concerned with the development of the two roads closest to the Clifton 'camps', Gloucester Row and Sion Hill. In levelling the ground for his buildings, his workmen made discoveries of Roman coins. The coins found dated back as far as Nero but also included the last Roman coins known to have been circulated in Britain – those of Constantius, Constantinus and Valentianus. More interestingly, for those interested in battles, the workmen also discovered some bodies. Although all trace of them has now disappeared, the local Bristol antiquarian G. W. Manby saw and described them at the time. He believed the abundance of bones showed Sir William's site to have been 'a place of interment, after some struggle for the recovery of British liberty'. There was apparently something about the bodies or objects found with them that persuaded Manby that they were the bodies of men who had fallen in a fight. There may have been some artefacts which led him to believe that specifically 'British liberty' was involved in their deaths.

Barrett and Manby

Manby joined another local antiquarian, William Barrett (who published a study in 1789), in researching the broad approaches of the Clifton 'camp', just before much of it disappeared under elegant Georgian terraces (see Fig. 4 in plates). Barrett and Manby also looked at the camps on the western side of the gorge. The South-Western camp became known as Burwalls (which might be *Burh – wealh* – Welsh fort) but that name is of uncertain age. The north-western camp was called Stokeleigh after Leigh Downs, the name for the whole ridge which runs north from the swampy area (now Bristol Harbour) on that side of the river towards the Roman port. *Stoke* means a gathering place – usually for religious purposes – and that might have some significance, as we shall see later.

At Burwalls the antiquarians found four fosses (ditches) and three ramparts. The walls were about 20 feet (6.1 m) wide at the base rising to three or four feet (1.2 m) wide at the top. The camp at Stokeleigh was adorned by a huge wall with a deep fosse at its foot. At Clifton and Stokeleigh they thought they saw signs of buildings within the ramparts. They looked for the hermitage, and found no trace of it, but speculated that it might have been a cave (still there) about half-way up the face of the gorge on the Clifton side.

Seyer and Scarth

Some thirty years later, the sites were surveyed again by Reverend Samuel Seyer and Prebendary Scarth. Seyer confirmed signs of buildings within the ramparts at Stokeleigh, and at Burwalls he estimated the fortified main gate to be 50 feet (15.24 m) wide. Scarth and Seyer, following an observation by Barrett, thought that fire had been used to induce a form of cementation or vitrification within the walls.

Lloyd Morgan

At the end of the nineteenth century, Conwy Lloyd Morgan, Principal of University College Bristol and a founder of the discipline of experimental psychology, was the first truly scientific examiner of the site. He compared the Clifton camps with the vitrified forts of Scotland, and concluded that the fires observed had been incidental and directed to some other purposes than vitrification. Although Morgan didn't say so, the burnt material may be evidence of a battle. Fires were often used to reduce wooden palisades on the top of the stone walls of hill forts in siege situations, and Gildas, our best witness, talks of the *obsessionis* (siege) of Badon. Morgan also noted that Romano-British pottery had been found at Stokeleigh but, although he had tried very hard, he personally had not been able to recover further examples at any of the camps. He also found no further bodies.

Burrow

In 1981 – exactly five hundred years after Wyrcestre had begun the surveys of the 'camps' – the archaeologist Ian Burrow made the first assessment of the 'camps' to modern scientific standards. Burrow believed that, although he could show that it was still protected by double-walled defences, the Clifton 'camp' had been substantially reduced in area by Draper's developments and that it had originally been much bigger than the area he studied. That is confirmed by Heath, who wrote at the end of the eighteenth century that every gulley on the Clifton side was fortified. Although Draper's men levelled much of it, the site outside the area surveyed by Burrow still shows changes of level that may be old fortifications. There are still signs of a substantial 'camp' between modern Gloucester Row and Sion Hill and the edge of the Gorge.

On the Burwalls/Stokeleigh side, Burrow confirmed more accurately the internal structures and the extent of the impressive walls. He also found a wall that ran south-west from the other defences and then turned south for over 200 metres and then west again before petering out. Some earlier investigators speculated that this wall was an incomplete link to the nearby Maes Knoll, which is the western end of the Wansdyke and is visible from Burwalls. The Wansdyke is a wall built about the beginning of the sixth century which runs eastward from Maes Knoll many miles beyond Bath. If Burwalls really was linked to the Wansdyke, it was a site of great military or political importance. That means it and the other Clifton 'camps' may have featured in more than one conflict.

Other Badons?

There is indeed evidence that a place with a name like Badon was a known site of repeated military encounters. The *Anglo-Saxon Chronicle* tells us that Cerdic, Port and his sons Bieda and Maegla moved north from southern Hampshire and seized somewhere called '*Biedanford*'. Later, Cuthwine and Ceawlin defeated three princes with Irish names in battles at Gloucester, Cirencester and a place called *Bathanceastre*. *Bathanceastre* is sometimes assumed to be modern Bath, but philologists object that Bath at that time in Anglo-Saxon would be *Baeth*. The *th* in the middle of the name is the Anglo-Saxon letter *thorn* which is usually transcribed in Welsh by *dd*. If *ceastre* is translated as Welsh *Caer*, we have *Bathancestre* reading as *Caer Baddon*. This *Caer Baddon* may not be Bath but is probably the site of the battle we have been seeking.

A Central Part of a Struggle?

Could a *Caer Badon* or *Baddon* fit into any likely military strategic scheme which might tie the Clifton forts to the Battle of Badon and King Arthur? As we have seen earlier, Harley 3859 (Nennius) tells us of twelve battles fought by King Arthur. Our study so far has shown us a strategic context over a period of years – perhaps even as many as twelve years. We reached the tentative conclusion that we were seeing an account of a struggle over time along a north-south line reaching from the south coast up to the Middle Severn.

This series of encounters should not be seen as border battles between established states. They were more explorations of an area of contention between rival potentates, but they match the claim of Gildas that first the enemy and then 'our countrymen' had the upper hand in a series of conflicts. The Clifton forts lie in the middle of that line. A central position in a speculative strategic scheme, however, is not by itself enough to establish Clifton as Badon. We need further evidence, and the battle list of Nennius may offer a clue.

A Christian Victory?

The eighth battle, at *Guinnion* (Glastonbury), and Badon are both claimed as 'Christian victories'. Arthur is said to have carried the image of the Virgin Mary on his shield in both encounters, and victory was obtained through the strength of Jesus and the Holy Virgin. These claims of Christian virtue may be pious later additions to the text, and we should keep that always in mind. Nonetheless we should raise the question: are there any overtly Christian military signs to be discerned at Clifton?

We can see two possibilities. Both are conjectural and neither is decisive. Anglo-Saxon charters relating to the holdings of West Minster, the abbey at Westbury-on-Trym, show a boundary marker in Clifton (possibly at modern Saville Place) which was called *Sweordes Stone*. Place name studies suggest that this may be the personal name of a man called *Sweord* although no one of that name is known to have ruled or been active in the area, and boundary stones dedicated to one individual for other than funerary purposes are unknown. Irish examples offer a different explanation. North of Dublin, there is a village called Swords. Its name is nothing to do with weapons. It means holy (*sord*). Can there have been a holy stone, perhaps a high cross, on the site commemorating the victory?

There is a possible answer to that question. The hermitage dedicated to Saint Vincent is very odd. Although there is a claim of a 'Saint Vincent' buried in a place of honour at Glastonbury, there is no other dedication to this saint in England in medieval times, and we know of no dedication to him in the Age of Arthur.

Saint Vincent of Lérins, one of the few saints called Vincent who is early enough for medieval, or earlier, devotion at Clifton, is unlikely because Lérins was associated with the Pelagian heresy. Saint David, and other holy monks active in the area in Arthurian times, were reputed to be strongly against Pelagianism. In later times, in the medieval period, any hint of Pelagianism would have invited active persecution. If the hermitage had ever been dedicated to him, and he came from Lérins, it would have been renamed, and yet the Saint Vincent connection has persisted to the present day. There must be another reason why Saint Vincent is honoured – if indeed it was he, or any other saint, who was honoured by the dedication of a hermitage. Was the name preserved because it was not a dedication of a hermitage named after a saint but the marker of a Christian victory over pagan opponents?

We know that broadly around this time the *Rerecross* at Stainmore on the Yorkshire and Westmoreland borders was raised to mark a Christian victory over Eric Bloodaxe. A memorial stone celebrating a Christian victory is therefore a plausible and possible consequence of the Battle of Badon. We know too that the Welsh and the British in the sixth century were greatly taken with the Roman Emperor Constantine – several generations of Cornish kings of this period were named after him. Constantine's mother, Saint Helena, through some confusion that suggested British birth, was honoured as 'Ellen of the Hosts' in Welsh tradition. We know too that, at the Milvian Bridge, Constantine famously saw a sign of the cross or the chi-rho symbol of Christ in the sky, and was told in a vision *'In hoc signo vinces'* ('in this sign, the cross, you will conquer'). We might therefore ask: did the winners of the battle raise a stone to mark the victory of Badon – the *sordes* stone of Saville Place? At the time of the battle a stone, or a cross like the Rerecross at Stainmore, in that position would have lain on the outskirts of the Clifton camp, and would have been exactly at the head of an ancient pathway which descends from the ridge path to the ford. Did it perhaps carry a legend, reflecting, or in some other way similar to, the words associated with Constantine's victories?

The term 'saints' (*sancti*) may have been used to describe persons who had chosen Christ rather than continuing to follow Pagan gods. We might conjecture an inscription, *'In hoc signo saxonos sancti vincent'* (In this sign [presumably that of Saint Mary] the saints [the Christian forces] will defeat the Saxons). If that stone over time lost its top through the fall, or destruction, of the cross element, the part referring to the sign, the words *saxonos sancti Vincent* might have remained.[1] People, discovering the stone and knowing words such *saxum* (rock), *saxeus* (stony) and *saxosus* (full of rocks), may have converted the memorial of the victory over the Saxons into the simple place name which persists to this day – 'St Vincent's Rocks'. Without the stone itself, that must remain mere, albeit entertaining, speculation.

The Case for the Clifton 'Camps' as Badon

The real case for the hill forts at Clifton as the site of the Battle of Badon does not rely on amusing guesses. The importance of the place is declared by the impressive walls and central buildings indicated in all three hill forts by Burrow's modern study, and its strategic location astride a ridgeway, and just upstream from Rome's major port in western Britain. The three Clifton hill forts were reoccupied in the sixth century; we know this from recent archaeology carried out to modern standards of investigation. That modern picture is enhanced by the expert evidence and astute observations gathered over five centuries by Britain's finest early topographers – Wyrcestre, Leland, Camden and Aubrey. The coins and bodies discovered by Draper's workmen, and the burning found by Scarth, add useful details. The more scientific studies of Morgan and Burrow have done nothing to detract from the emerging picture of a place of military importance in the sixth century.

Stone Certainty

There is one further compelling detail. Aubrey's observations may tell us how the battle was conducted. Aubrey tells us of great numbers of widely scattered stones.[2] Gildas, our only sixth-century witness, uses a metaphor to make his religious point. It is drawn from the battles of his time, and it tells us how the stones may have got there: 'Now my two sides are protected by the victorious shields of the saints, my back is safe at the walls of truth, my head as its helmet has the help of the Lord for its sure covering. So let the rocks of my truthful vituperations fly their constant flights.' It is an image drawn from a siege where one party faced an artillery barrage of stones from the other.

It appears that Roman artillery – the propulsion of large stones by an onager, scorpion or ballista[3] or some similar device – was still in use in sixth-century Britain as a siege weapon. Gildas knew personally about bombardments by stones and he may have come under such fire. He seems to have known exactly what to do – place your back to the wall, and rely on your helmet and shield, and those of your colleagues, for protection. He may even have been at the Battle of Badon, and may have expected his intended audience to know that. From the image used by Gildas, we know that such weapons were used; from Aubrey, we may see that they were used at Badon – or at least at Clifton.

A Strong Case

The truth remains: we cannot prove to modern standards that Clifton was where Badon was fought, or even that stone-throwing machines were used there. Draper's bodies tell us some battle was fought there, and, given the status of the site, it was probably an important one. There is also an old tradition of a battle there – between 'Saracens and Jews' or rival giants. It may have been the siege of Mount Badon mentioned by Gildas. For the moment, all we can say with certainty is that the case for Clifton as the site of the Battle of Badon is stronger than any of the other candidate sites proposed and advanced. We should build on the evidence we have so far found and consider *how* Badon was fought, and see if that might illuminate further what we can say about Clifton as the battle site. It may also guide our thoughts about whether or not Arthur the warrior was really involved in the conflict at that particular location.

CONCLUSIONS

1. Three hill forts, a ford, a river, proximity of ridgeways, proof of sixth-century occupation, a site of economic, military and possibly religious importance, a local tradition of a battle, reliable reports of features no longer visible on site suggesting a battle – the Clifton camps tick all the boxes for Badon.
2. There is no indication in the evidence of the presence of Arthur.

7

WHAT HAPPENED AT BADON?

The Background – William of Malmesbury
William of Malmesbury (AD 1095–1143) was the foremost
European intellectual of his day, and he was an avid collector
of books and stories on which he exercised an informed and
dispassionate judgment. At some time before 1140, he made
several visits to Glastonbury where he heard tales of King Arthur.
We don't know what he heard, but he formed the judgment that
King Arthur had been a great man and that it was a pity that he
was remembered only in fables, by which he meant the stories told
by the Welsh. In general, he found little he could use in the Welsh
tradition.

The Welsh Poetic Tradition
William, despite his learning, may simply not have understood the
nature of the Welsh record. It comprised not fables or attempts
at formal history but a wide range of poetic forms. *Forsundud* or
'illumination' verse, for example, was a poetry in praise of princes,
a sort of 'list poetry', or 'hall of fame', in which great men were
listed and important places were linked without much attention to
narrative, or whether the men honoured had even lived at the same
time. It was a way of associating the heroes of the present with the
great ones of the past. What mattered was the nomination in the
lists of the great.

Great men and events were also recalled in *englynion*, short verses, often with a sort of witty or sarcastic final punchline. Sir Ifor Williams found one example:

> Morgan and his men planned
> To drive me into exile
> And burn my lands:
> A mouse scratching against a cliff.

We have no need to assume a real mouse is involved. The irony and sarcasm are not literal, and that is typical of Welsh poetry. It valued the arresting visual image and treasured the wit of the punchline in moving the hearer (they were all recited rather than written down) to bitter tears or to laughter. Bards sought the immediate reaction rather than a recording of men and events in a way which might constitute a history to be studied or contemplated. Above all, no bard was trying to give precise dates, places or even accounts of events and the men who took part in them. They wanted to create an immediate emotional response. If we treat the *englynion* with judgment, however, they may prove to be potent sources of information.

We can see, for example, their social and political effects. The bards and poets who could compose such verses were much feared – sometimes with good reason. In court circles, ridicule could lead to violence and murder. King Arthur himself, for example, was said to have been trained as a 'satirical' poet – satire was the lowest form of poetic training, a sort of education in rhetoric for princes and leaders. He was, it seems, an effective satirist, but could not accept being the subject of ridicule. On one occasion, after he had been wounded in the knee in a fight over a woman, in disguise he joined in a dance of women to gain access to another girl. Hoel, his cousin and the brother of Saint Gildas, made an immediate *englyn* in which he said the dancing of the maidens was lovely – except for the big one with the bad knee. Arthur had him seized, taken away, and executed.

The *Triads of the Island of Britain* (*Trioedd Ynys Pridein* – TYP) are another important source for our quest. They are verses which link three names together – three warriors, three battles, three warhorses – with some common feature that joins them, such as fame or misfortune. Sometimes TYP adds a fourth name that, for good or ill, contrasts sharply with the other three or exceeds their misfortune or bravery. The TYP served as a sort of menu or *aide memoire* for poets. With poets having announced a selection of triads, a ruler or patron could decide which story he wished to hear.

Arthurian material was evidently popular, and seems to form the earliest stratum of the TYP, certainly reaching back far into the sixth century. Unfortunately for our purpose, although the TYP have much to say about Arthur, and his last battle at Camlan, they do not offer any thing very much on Badon.

In any case, we should not expect very hard factual information from the TYP. In general, the Welsh poetic material is allusive, and rather like modern imagist poetry. It can offer a sense of immediacy, with striking 'word pictures' that seem almost filmic. It is as if we are dealing with vivid film clips that come to us with no provenance and no reference in time and place. In the Early Welsh 'imagist poems', we just have the pictures. The poems may make us see what happened, but with very little context; they never aspire to be history, or even the raw material out of which history can be formed. There are no dates and few precise places.

As we have noted, what matters in the Welsh poetic sources is the wit, ingenuity or literary excellence of the story, not its historical truth or relevance. That is why William of Malmesbury, possibly the best historian of his era, found it very hard to use. He dismissed the Welsh tradition as 'fable', and his example has been followed by most historians since. In pursuing our objectives, we can perhaps find a way to use Welsh culture, the Welsh poetic tradition, and thus bring new light to shine on Arthur and his battles.

Writers and Politics

William did not need the Welsh tradition. He had other potentially historical sources to look at, and other political motivations for writing. In AD 1141, William was among the clergy who declared for the Empress Matilda in her wars with King Stephen about the rightful succession to the throne of England. It was a brave thing to do in such a violent time, but was not entirely surprising. Matilda had been his first patron and was the half-sister of another patron, Robert, Earl of Gloucester. Robert was one of the best soldiers of his time, but he was also a learned and interested man, effectively the tutor of the future Henry II, who has the rare distinction of being the only king of England to be educated in Bristol. William's scholarship and independence of mind were beyond doubt, but his skill was always at the service of the emerging Plantagenet dynasty, represented then by Matilda, Robert and Henry II. They effectively commissioned everything that he wrote, and, in the middle of a civil war, they didn't ask for Arthur.

That topic was left to Geoffrey of Monmouth, who wrote a lively and entertaining account of Arthur. The Battle of Badon was, for Geoffrey, a minor part of a swelling imperial theme which saw Arthur conquer Ireland, subdue Iceland and capture Norway and Denmark. Arthur, according to Geoffrey, then subjected to his rule Poitou, Aquitaine, Gascony, Normandy and Anjou – more or less what Matilda and her husband, Geoffrey of Anjou, claimed for themselves and their son Henry.

There are signs that, in constructing his narrative, Geoffrey of Monmouth used some Welsh material. At least part of his account of the battle derives from Nennius. As we have seen, Nennius places the Battle of Badon at the end of a sequence of twelve battles. It was the final victory over the Saxons. According to Nennius, the Battle of Badon was also remarkable for two other things. First, it was a Christian victory inspired by the Virgin Mary and her son Jesus Christ. Secondly, it was won by Arthur alone, who killed 960 men in one charge at the climax of the battle.

The story told by Nennius, however, is not really about the events of the battle and how it was fought; it is about credit for the victory. He gives a reason (Mary and Jesus) that is linked to religion, and, in his own day, to the growing adherence of the Welsh Church to the Catholic Church. He also offers a reason that may be about credit in the sense of the division of spoils and plunder (Arthur alone killed this vast number of the enemy – no one else deserves reward). In Nennius, Arthur's actions were key, and so the victory, in lay terms at least, is his alone. That point of detail either escaped Geoffrey or was not of much use or interest to him.

Telling the Tale – Geoffrey of Monmouth
In looking at literary sources such as Geoffrey or poetic resources such as the TYP for detailed information, we need to follow the suggestion of Kathleen Hughes, made earlier, that we

should accept detail in early documents but not the main thrust of the story, and, in particular in religious writing, any benefits, spiritual or temporal, the story may claim for its hero or his church. Geoffrey of Monmouth clearly used Nennius as a source for some material, but almost all the detail of his yarns came from his fertile imagination, and can be discounted as history. His aim was to produce a story of interest to his potentially helpful, powerful readers. His Badon, which he identified as Bath, sees the siege of a hill fort which ends with a sudden and successful onrush led by Arthur, who then dispatches his friend Cador of Cornwall to pursue the fleeing Saxons to the Isle of Thanet while Arthur goes to Scotland to relieve a siege at Dumbarton.

Telling the Tale – Wace

Wace (*c.* 1110–*c.* 1174), a Jersey-born monk who worked in Normandy, was the next Plantagenet writer to attempt the story of Arthur and Badon. Again, we can look only at the detail. In Wace, the good citizens of Bath close their gates and defend their walls. It is the Saxons who defend the hill fort, and he added a wood but not much else to the scene. Arthur again leads the attack, and Cador pursues the fleeing Saxons to a more plausible location, a place near Teignmouth which is close to the supposed landing point of the Saxons, Totnes.

Telling the Tale – Layamon

The next teller of the tale is a mid-Severn cleric of Irish-Norse descent called Layamon. He introduces a ford into the story. The Saxons were slain in the water so that their armoured bodies bridged the Avon (the river is casually named) at the ford with steel. Layamon uses some memorable language, and introduces images that can only have been based on Welsh 'imagist' poetry. In Layamon's version, for example, Arthur tells his troops that one Saxon leader, Colgrim, is like a goat on the hill trying to fight off the wild wolf. 'I am the wolf and he is the goat; the man shall die.'

He goes on: 'Yesterday Balduf was the bravest of knights but now he stands on the hill and beholds the Avon, how the steel fishes lie in the stream. Armed with the sword, their life is destroyed, their scales float like gold-dyed shields. There float their fins as if it were spears. These are marvellous things come to this land; such beasts on the hill, such fishes in the stream.'

His defeated Saxons 'wandered as the wild crane does in the moor-fen when his flight is impaired and swift hawks pursue him and hounds cruelly meet him in the reeds. Then neither land nor water is good to him, hawks smite him, hounds bite him. Then the royal fowl is doomed on his way.'

This reads like authentic sixth-century source material because it matches Gildas's use of natural imagery to make his point. In Gildas, some Irish invaders are like 'wolves leaping dry mouthed over the fence to the sheep when no shepherd is there'. Roman legions were like a pent-up mountain torrent bursting over barriers to confront the raiders who were 'dark swarms of snakes emerging from the crevices of rocks'.[1] Nature in Gildas and Layamon is brought into play to provide sharp images of the affairs of men. Sadly, however vivid and lively these images may be about battle incidents, using them does not permit Layamon to offer much guidance on the location and nature of the fighting.

Telling the Tale – the *Mabinogion*
For that, we have to turn back to Earl Robert and a book he may have commissioned for the political and linguistic education of the young Henry II. It is a collection of Welsh stories and legends called the *Mabinogion* (for the young man? A primer for Henry?). Henry also had the benefit of the teaching of one Matthew, a Welsh monk. The overt aim was to make him familiar with the culture and languages of the peoples he ruled. He was already fluent in French, English and Latin. The purpose of his Bristol stay was to know the Welsh language and what mattered to the Welsh people. The aim of the *Mabinogion* appears to have been to provide entertaining stories about matters of interest to a king – leading men in battle among them.

The educational plan worked very well politically. After some initial hostilities, Henry II was able to form a relationship with Rhys ap Gruffydd which made him effectively Henry's viceroy in Wales – the Prince of Wales or the Lord Rhys.[2] That brought political and military benefits and may have offered some cultural advantages too. Through Rhys, he may have gained some insights into Ireland and the Irish, knowledge of the Irish language and

Irish poetry as well as the collection of stories prepared for his pleasure and education, the *Mabinogion.*

The *Mabinogion* used to be regarded as a charming and rather unfocussed collection of folk tales, but further study has revealed that its stories are actually sophisticated literary works, which, although they were composed possibly around the time Henry II may have seen them, draw together much earlier material. One of the stories, *The Dream of Rhonabwy*, gives an account of the Battle of Badon.

A Version of Badon

The Dream of Rhonabwy is a three-layered story. The first layer begins with a quarrel between two brothers, Mawdawg (d. 1159) and Iorwoeth. Iorwoeth, dissatisfied with his treatment at his brother's court (the brother was king of Powys), goes off raiding in England. Rhonabwy is one of a number of warriors sent after him to bring him back. Rhonabwy and his companions spend a night in the dreadful, dark, flea-ridden, dung-strewn house of Heilyn the Red. To find rest, Rhonabwy places himself on a yellow ox-hide bed and begins to dream.[3]

The first part of his dream forms the second layer of the story. Rhonabwy finds himself introduced by his guide, Iddawg, to King Arthur who is assembling troops for the Battle of Badon. Arthur laughs at the twelfth-century warriors, implying that they are no match for the warriors he needs for the coming battle. This regret about the standard of soldiers may derive from an old poem, *Pa Gur,* in which Arthur mourns the death of his son and his friend Cei, saying he will not have such warriors again. Within this layer of the story, the passage can be read simply as a satire on the standard of warriors of Rhonabwy's time compared with the fighters of the heroic age.[4]

The second part of his dream gives an account of the Battle of Badon. Rhonabwy is told who the assembling leaders are. There are named commanders from Cornwall and Denia (the Forest of Dean, which Geoffrey mistook for Denmark). There is enormous excitement as warband after warband, led by their famous commanders, join the army, and the great hosting 'descends below Caer Vaddon'. Overall command is vested in Arthur and Owein, who sit down to play a Welsh board game called *gwyddbwyll* (wood craft). *Gwyddbwll* was a game like chess and involved stalking, deception and sudden attack in a kind of mimic warfare.

A series of messengers approach the two commanders as they sit playing. Owein is told Arthur's men are molesting his 'ravens'. Owein asks for them to be called off, but Arthur says merely that it is Owein's move. The message is repeated three times with increasing force and urgency. Arthur remains unhelpful, and Owein orders his page to go where the fighting is fiercest, raise the banner, and let God's will be done. The effect is remarkable. Inspired by the apparently Christian banner, the ravens revive, and inflict great casualties on those who had been injuring them.

The process of message and response is then repeated, only it is now Arthur's pages and squires who are under attack from the ravens. Arthur asks for them to be called off, and Owein says, 'Your move, my Lord.' After the third occasion of message and response, the fighting dies down.

On the face of it, this layer of the *Dream* appears to be a silly repetitious story, and that reputation may have protected it from alteration and 'improvement'. It therefore remains a detailed, unchanged account of how the battle was conducted. By looking at the detail, we can see the outline of a real event.

The word for a raven (*bran*) is also the normal word for a warrior in Early Welsh. The exchanges over *gwyddbwyll* were about men, not birds. Arthur and Owein were pursuing a policy of cunning deception of the kind Gildas (chapter 2) has led us to expect in warlords of the time. The *gwyddbwyll* was not a game; it was the plan for the battle. The plan saw first one, and then the other, stand alone against the enemy, presumably to exhaust the opposing forces. The effect of the banner is a sign of a Christian victory. The three repetitions – the number three is important – signal the age of the original material. Such repetitions are a marker for oral performance of the kind we see in the TYP, and the number three indicates a likely triadic source. That tells us that the story may have originated close to the time of the battle.

The poetic origin of the core material about the battle is confirmed when Rhonabwy questions his guide, Iddawg, about what he has been told. Iddawg replies using two more triads. The first triad names three men 'who took Owein's losses badly', and the second the three men 'who took Arthur's losses hardest'. We should recall that triads about Arthur are from the earliest strand of TYP. This is possibly genuine sixth-century evidence.

Osla the Saxon Enemy

The next section of the *Dream* reveals that the fighting was not between the forces of Owein and Arthur, but between their men and forces led by a Saxon called Osla Big Knife. Osla, we are told, is seeking a truce, and sends Arthur tribute to achieve it. Osla, it seems, is the defeated party, but we don't hear in this story the reason for his discomfiture. There is no repetition of the sudden charge by Arthur which marks the accounts of Nennius, Geoffrey, Wace and Layamon. In *Rhonabwy's Dream*, the fighting just stops with no splendid finale.

What happened is indicated elsewhere in the *Mabinogion*. Osla appears in another story called *Culhwch ac Olwen*. In that story, Osla's nickname is explained by another triad. 'When Arthur and his troops come to a cresting flood, they would find a narrow spot. Osla's knife in its sheath would be laid across the flood and that would be bridge enough for the three armies of the island of Britain and the three off-shore islands with all their plunder.' It appears that a narrow spot on the River Avon, a ford, may really have played a crucial role in the result of the battle. This reads as if there existed, at one time, a savage jest that every time Arthur and his men wanted to cross a river, Osla's dead men provided a bridge of the kind Layamon described poetically, a bridge of corpses, spears, shields and swords. As we will see, it may later have come to be called 'the Sword Bridge'.

The Tide of Battle

The anecdote offers some further information about how Osla was defeated. Osla's knife is named; it is called 'short-broad' with the Welsh word *bronllavyn* attached to it. This may be a scribal error for *bron llanw* (almost full tide). The tidal range at Bristol – the second highest in the world – seems to have played a role. It would appear that Arthur and Owein had devised a stratagem that led to Osla being trapped on the ford as the tide came in.

Tides, of course, are gradual, and only surprise by their speed of approach on level sands, where unwary walkers can suddenly be in danger. Badon, if it was Clifton, featured a river and a gorge. The normal tide there today is the second highest in the world and it is rapid, but not speedy and sudden. To trap Osla and his men suddenly, Arthur and Owein may have needed to create a temporary blockage further downstream at *Abonae* which, when released close to full tide, produced a sort of tsunami that hit the Saxons on the ford.[5]

We may even have, as it were, an 'imagist' picture of it. Gildas (c. 17) uses a vivid image of a large wave to describe such an attack.[6] Gildas is describing a mountain torrent swollen by tributary streams filled with storm water. He says it comes 'thundering as it goes, wells out beyond its channel, back furrowed, forehead fierce, waves – as they say – cloud-high. It foams wonderfully and with a single surge it overcomes the obstacles in its path.' This is not how storm 'overflows' in the mountain streams usually occur. The destructive wave is no small mountain stream. In mountain streams there is commonly a slow build-up that, over an hour or so, becomes a torrent. There is no wave unless the stream breaks through a barrier. Gildas is describing something more abrupt and dramatic than a swollen stream. He is describing a major 'cloud-high' wave, a tsunami, in a narrow channel. It doesn't seem to be something that he has heard a bard sing about, and therefore, for him, forms a 'second-hand' image. He saw this himself, and probably from above, because he could see both the wave front and the streaming lines in the water behind it.[7]

We can say with great certainty that this catastrophic wave was a real event because Gildas describes an effect that has only become understood properly in the last fifty years. Halfway through his image of the 'cloud-high wave', he breaks off to note an effect on human spectators: 'Because of them (the waves) the pupils of the eyes are darkened despite their constant refreshment from the flickering of the eye-lids, when they encounter the lines of the whirling clefts.'

Gildas is here describing the effect on humans of the air pressure-wave which precedes the water-wave of a tsunami which is, in fact, often more damaging than the water itself. Soldiers caught on the ford of the river with a very high water-wave approaching them, and, in the path of an air pressure-wave further condensed and enhanced by the walls of the gorge, would have had no chance. It would be like being hit by a fast-moving invisible concrete wall, and then having a tonne of water dropped on you. If the air pressure did not kill them, they would be drowned. The apparently wild number of 960 dead in one charge given by Nennius and Geoffrey may be more accurate than is sometimes thought.

A Second Badon

Another battle may confirm the 'cunning trap at a ford' scenario. Bede tells us that, in AD 655, at the Battle of Winwaed, Penda of Mercia was defeated because Oswiu managed to drive the numerically superior Mercian forces back into the waters of a river in full flood. Oswiu (who may be a descendant of Osla) may have recalled his relative's misfortune, and reversed the result (although on this occasion Oswiu was the Christian and Penda the pagan). In that same year the *Annales Cambriae* records *bellum Badonis secundo* (the Battle of Badon for the second time). Nothing is known about a battle on the same site as Badon at that time. The Welsh annalist may simply mean that Oswiu at Winwaed used the same tactics as Arthur and Owein had used to overcome Osla at Badon – a sudden, deliberately created flood (devised by a Christian commander) overwhelming a pagan force trapped on a ford or river crossing – a veritable second Badon.[8]

A New Picture of the Siege of Mount Badon

The incidental detail in the two *Mabinogion* stories, taken together, makes it possible for us to regard the Battle of Badon as a major hosting, perhaps a unique assembly of forces. Welsh sources say that Owein had a famous elite force called his 'flight of ravens' which numbered three hundred chosen warriors. Arthur's warband, if it matched other war bands in TYP and elsewhere in Welsh tradition, perhaps numbered more than 400 and even as many as 2,100. We can't come up with a precise number of armed men in the struggle. Other warbands, led by other tyrants and kings, may have been under the command of Owein and Arthur in the fighting, but *The Dream of Rhonabwy* doesn't allow us to say how many of the warbands named there got to Badon in time. The battalions of Cornwall arrived on the third day, and their arrival may have been the signal to attempt to create the killer wave. We can say nothing accurately about the presence of particular warbands and leaders, or the numbers of men involved. In our sources, we see only material from a 'list poem' that includes warriors from several generations before the battle and some who were added long after it.

Picture of a Battle

We can, however, make a coherent, although speculative, picture of the battle, and the fighting leading up to the siege at Mount Badon. It seems that, in a prelude to the battle, Arthur strongly held the north bank of the Severn Estuary. His protecting warbands, placed on the north side of the Estuary, did not move towards Badon until they were certain that Osla was committed in that direction on what is now the English, or Gloucestershire, side of the waterway. It is likely that Arthur had strong forces to the south too – perhaps on the fringes of the great forest[9] – to persuade Osla westwards towards Badon. Arthur may have directly engaged the advancing host head-on from time to time, falling back before it. When they reached the Avon, he may have put up a token resistance in the eastern Clifton fort before crossing the river, and allowing Osla to occupy it.

By the time the armies reach the area of modern Bristol, we may have perhaps as many as ten thousand men situated in three strong hill forts in contention over a river ford, a naval base and a main north/south and east/west ridge-path route. We know enough to say that Arthur and Owein had sufficient men to hold the western forts at Clifton.[10] Osla may have had equal, or superior, forces that held the eastern side from which he bombarded his opponents (Aubrey's stones). The siege is conducted using fire and artillery devices, throwing very large stones up to 3 or 4 kg in weight. There are direct sallies and attacks on the walls over the course of three days and three nights.

On the first day, Osla attacks Burwalls, and almost takes it before Owein rallies his troops under a Christian banner. On the second day, Osla tries his luck with Arthur and Stokeleigh, but its vast walls defeat his onslaught. Even as this is going on, Arthur and Owein are preparing a trap for him. At low water, near *Abonae*, they begin to block the river. On the third day, at low water, they sink several ships in the gap and wait for the tide. Arthur leads an attack on the Clifton forts and then retreats, drawing Osla's men after him. He suddenly turns and charges, disputing the ford with them, and denying them the western bank. They attack in ever greater numbers across the ford, and Arthur draws some of them onto the western bank. At a precise moment, probably in response to a visual signal given from the heights above him, he charges again, pushing them back onto the ford, before quickly withdrawing into Stokeleigh. Then the vast tide breaks through the downstream barrier, and roars up the gorge in a tidal wave, carrying nearly a thousand men to their deaths. When the water subsides to normal high-tide levels, the dead men and their weapons float in the stream in the way described by Layamon.

All this, of course, is merely conjecture, though it does fit the fragmentary details that we can discern in the accounts available to us. Taking it all together, we have a plausible account of what happened at Badon. Proof, however, will always lie beyond us, and we may have gone too far on present evidence. We have, for example, been making two unspoken key assumptions: that Arthur was at the Battle of Badon and was a commander there. Welsh tradition, *The Dream of Rhonabwy* aside, is remarkably silent about Arthur at Badon, and indeed about Badon itself.

So what have we got? William of Malmesbury was the best historian of the twelfth century and he saw material which has not come down to us that convinced him of the historicity of Arthur. We can trust his careful scholarship. We can be as sure of Arthur's existence as we can be about the existence of anyone in the sixth century. The fables William regretted, some points of detail in Geoffrey, Wace and Layamon, and the stories included in the *Mabinogion* appear to show a possible conflict at Clifton's ford and its three hill forts. We have been able to construct a plausible scenario for the battle. If we are to take this further, however, we need to look more closely at the man known as 'King Arthur' and ask some questions. Was he a king? Where did he rule? Was he really at Badon?

CONCLUSIONS

1. Several literary sources tells us a hill fort and a ford were involved in the Battle of Badon.
2. Welsh 'imagist poetry' says defeated dead soldiers floated in the river after the battle.

3. Cunning deception was an element in their defeat and may have involved the manipulation of the river and/or the tide.
4. The defeated commander, Osla, became proverbial and famous for providing a 'Sword Bridge' (the dead soldiers in the river).
5. Other similar battles were remembered and reported in ways which partly confirm the course of events at Badon.
6. Arthur is confirmed as a ruthless, competent and cunning commander of the warlord kind Gildas has led us to expect.

8

THE GLASTONBURY GRAVE

The Political Background

For many years, historians, without much thought or evidence, have claimed that the monks of Glastonbury Abbey, facing a financial crisis and needing to find a new attraction for pilgrims, decided to dig up the body of King Arthur to increase their income. That is simply not true. The motives behind the recovery of King Arthur's body were political, and they came from King Henry II of England.

King Henry II knew a lot about King Arthur. So did his mother, the Empress Matilda, and his uncle Robert, Earl of Gloucester. William Curthose, his great-uncle, the brother and captive of his grandfather Henry I, in terms of descent the rightful king of England, also knew about Arthur. Curthose was held prisoner at Cardiff, where he learned Welsh and read about Arthur. He even may have read something unique about the warrior and king. Cardiff had been seized from its Welsh ruler by Robert Fitzhamon, and, among his spoils, there was a document called *the Roll of the Round Table*. Its capture from *Iestyn ap Gwrgan* is the first mention of 'Arthur's Round Table'.

Fitzhamon's daughter Mabli was married to Robert of Gloucester who succeeded to his father-in-law's considerable Welsh possessions, his courts and his bards, and presumably the *Roll of the Round Table*. Henry II's wife, Eleanor of Aquitaine, lived at Domfront where Chrétien de Troyes, one of the greatest of Arthurian storytellers, may have played as a child.[1] Henry II's family were the patrons of, or otherwise influenced, William of Malmesbury, Geoffrey of Monmouth, Wace, Layamon, Chrétien de Troyes and almost everyone else who laid the foundations of the Arthurian legends we know today. What is sometimes called, mainly in Europe and America, the *Matter of Britain* was in essence a Plantagenet creation, and was under their control and patronage. Even the copies we have today of many of the early manuscripts of writers like Gildas, Nennius and the Welsh Annals were also made at this time, possibly under their direction. There is a danger in that. Chrétien de Troyes says in *Erec and Enide*:

> *Que devant rois et devant comtes*
> *Depecier et corronpre suelent*
> *Cil qui decanter vivre veulent.*
> (There is one law for those who sing
> Before the court of count and king:
> They work a change who sing for gold
> And sale corrupts the tale that's told.)

Writers then, as now, in order to live and to make books, had to keep an eye on the market, and write about what the publisher/patron thought was interesting. It was a time of change, and a new world order was emerging. The remnants of Roman Gaul were moving towards the formation of the nation state of France, and its Capetian kings actually already called themselves 'King of France', although the domains they ruled were somewhat narrower. Large tracts of what is now France were actually held by people like Henry II, or were ruled by independent counts who might do homage to the King of France for their lands, but dreamed of taking a firmer, less impeded grip on what was theirs. The 'Arthur of literature' the Plantagenets caused to be created had a role to play in this interplay of homage and tribute between kings. Plantagenet statecraft may lie behind everything we think we know, or can find out, about Arthur. The Plantagenets may have called an old world into being to redress the balance of the new. We must always be aware that.

Henry II and Arthur
There is, however, little doubt that Henry II had real knowledge that owed nothing to the fertile imaginations and inventions of

his writers. Henry had been educated in Bristol, and may have visited Glastonbury at that time. During his reign, when the Abbot of Glastonbury died, he had refused to appoint a new abbot for a time, and had held the revenues and resources of the abbey in his own hands for several years. He had the linguistic skills to read any document or record the abbey held, and the capacity and opportunity to speak to monks there about traditions they remembered.

How Henry II gained the information we do not know, but he knew exactly where Arthur was buried at Glastonbury, and had several times mentioned it to the monks there. He told the monks that Arthur's body lay between the two 'pyramids' beside the abbey, and that he would be found in a wooden coffin about 16 feet (4.88 m) down. When the old wooden church dedicated to Saint Mary – the oldest and therefore the holiest structure at Glastonbury – burned down, perhaps it was taken as a sign. At any rate, and whatever the reason, not long after the old church was destroyed, the excavation began.

The excavation was intended to make some sort of political or religious statement – perhaps additional penance by Henry for the death of Thomas Becket, or to help in his relations with the king of France, who, at that time, was collaborating with Henry's wife and children in an attempt to unseat him. It might have been an act of penance for the destruction of a holy relic – the Old Church – that was in his care. We don't know now and it didn't matter then. By the time the monks had completed their work, Henry II was dead.

The Excavation

Their excavations had otherwise been crowned with success. At some considerable depth, perhaps even the predicted 16 feet, the monks discovered a large, hollowed-out oak receptacle – possibly in the form of a boat – which served as a coffin. Close to it, or even as part of it, there was a second coffin. Both had been covered by a stone slab, and on the underside of the stone was an engraved lead cross. On one side of this cross was an inscription: *'Hic jacet sepultus rex arturus in insula avalonia'* which is usually translated as 'Here lies buried the famous King Arthur in the island of Avalon'. Elsewhere on the cross, or close to it, was a further inscription which read: *'cum Wenneveria uxore sua seconda'* ('with Guinevere his second wife').

Inside the oak 'coffin', the monks found the bones of a very large man. One shin bone was said to reach the middle thigh of a tall man's leg. Using current physical anthropology systems, we can say that the dead man must have been in life well over 2 metres in height. The head was prodigiously large, and showed ten or more wounds, all of which had healed in life, save one which may have been his death blow. They also found a female skeleton. The plaited golden hair on this body was still intact, but when they touched it, it crumbled into dust. There was no other information. We are left, as the monks of Glastonbury were after the death of King Henry II, to make of the remains of Arthur what we can.

We begin by making an assumption. To pursue our quest, we must choose to regard the body in the grave as that of the warrior and king called Arthur. That may be too much for some people. We really have no way of knowing who the man in the grave was, or of proving that he was Arthur. The identity ascribed to the body by King Henry II and the monks of Glastonbury could be simply a mistake. It could be a fraud. All we can say with confidence is that the body in the grave was widely regarded by people at the time as that of Arthur, and they had more sources of information to hand than we have.

The Pyramids

The grave itself, as revealed by excavation, is unlikely to have been faked by Henry II, the monks of Glastonbury, or anyone else. Fifty years before the dig, William of Malmesbury had noted the 'pyramids'. At that time, they seemed to have been used as grave stones to mark the resting place of the distinguished dead, such as Saint Patrick and Indract, an abbot of Iona. 'Pyramids' are odd structures to find in an English and Christian context, and that suggests that they may not have been pyramids at all. They could possibly have been the bases of Irish-style high crosses. At Oldcourt near Bray in Ireland, a cross's base was discovered that is nearly pyramidal. It is thought to have supported a wooden high cross[2] and has been dated to the eighth century. At Moone in Ireland, there is a large high cross of stone with a taller, thinner 'pyramid base'. It is dated a little earlier, although both bases could have been made as late as the tenth century. The significant fact about both is that, like the Glastonbury 'pyramids', they were engraved. There is no particular difficulty in seeing the 'pyramids' as Irish; Irish monks were thought to be active at Glastonbury for several centuries.

There is no doubt that these cross bases, or pyramids, existed, and at the right period for the excavation. Ralegh Radford, in modern times, re-excavated the site and uncovered the foundations of the bases of the pyramids,[3] and further down he found *cist* graves – that is stone-lined graves – at the right depth. There were signs that a large, irregular hole had been dug and quickly filled in again. Radford was prepared to concede that the cist graves were possibly of the sixth century, and that around the time of King Henry II there had been an excavation at least to the depth at which they were found in his dig.

The Oak Coffin

The hollowed-out oak that formed the coffin is of major interest. In 1972, writing about the Glastonbury grave, Richard Barber noted that hollowed-out oaks had been used since the Bronze Age for burials. The best-known example in England is the 'Gristhorpe Man' who dates from about four thousand years ago. Other examples have been found in eastern England, and some have been found in Yorkshire at the end of a known Trans-Pennine trade route from Ireland.

This Irish connection may be sufficient cause for us to look again at a hollowed-out oak boat found on the shores of Lough Neagh. The dendrochronologist Mike Baillie[4] dated this example, with a high degree of confidence, to around AD 540. It is unlikely that the boat was used, or was intended to be used, for navigation on the Lough. At this time, coracles would be the expected form of military, transport or fishing craft. This partially completed boat may therefore have been intended for ritual use. Although it is not known when this form of burial ceased in the British Isles, it might very well have survived into the sixth century in Ireland, because Ireland was more geographically isolated. There are not enough known examples to say more. Most oak coffins may simply have rotted away. If the oak coffin was a hollowed-out boat, it may be a distinct sign of a pagan burial.

An oak boat-style coffin is not likely to have been forged in the twelfth century when other differently constructed coffins were available. Forgers at that time in any case would have been unlikely to know much about ancient boat burials. An oak coffin of the boat type, however, could very well have survived at Glastonbury if, as the account by Gerald of Wales suggests, it had been placed in the stone chamber found by Radford, or in a stone-lined *cist* grave with a stone slab lintel on top. However, although Irish slab graves are known from the sixth century, in England there are few before the eighth century. Burial in a *cist* grave, either directly or in an oak coffin, in sixth-century England would have been unusual, and may be a sign of an Irish inhumation.

The Double Grave

The double grave, however, is not unprecedented in England around this time. Bede tells us that Abbot Huetbert (*fl.* late sixth century) reburied two of his predecessors in a single coffin divided down the middle. This type of coffin was enough in use for it to have a name – *theca*. A coffin of that type is also unlikely to have been faked. Cist graves too are unlikely products of a fraud. Although some writers, such as Richard Barber, have suggested the finding of King Arthur was a convenient fraud to solve some of Glastonbury's financial problems,[5] the grave, as it was described at the time, has too many details that would have been well beyond the capacity of the monks to replicate for their own purposes. Archaeology at Glastonbury and elsewhere, and the balance of evidence, says this was a genuine burial, made at a time unknown to those who dug up the remains. There are good, detailed, virtually contemporary accounts of the actual excavation by Gerald of Wales and Ralph of Coggeshall (AD 1193). We must conclude that Henry II's information was good, the grave was genuine, and the excavation was carried out, without fraud, in the manner he had suggested. There was no fakery at that stage.

The Lead Cross

The lead cross is more problematic. Leland in 1533 saw and described the lead cross, and Camden published a drawing of it in 1607 (see Fig. 10 in plates). The shape is odd. In the sixth century, as far as we know on current evidence, the 'wheel-shaped' or 'Celtic' cross was used, and the 'cross-shaped cross' didn't develop until around AD 750. The shape of the metal cross indicates that it was made long after Arthur died. The letter forms are not those of the sixth century when Arthur might have been buried, but neither are they of the twelfth century, as we might expect, if they were forged around the time the monks did their excavation. The letter forms look to be of the ninth or tenth century. The material used – base metal or lead – is also unusual, and it was placed on the underside of the slab, which is strange if it was intended to identify the occupants of the oak coffin. Taken together, they point to the Glastonbury grave being a re-interment at some time in the two hundred years before the excavation.

The Inscription

The form of words used on the lead cross appears at first to be conventional. *Hic jacet* ('Here lies') is widespread among early Christian graves in Britain. *Sepultus* is less common but is known from an Anglesey site where a man called Saturnius was buried with his wife under a tombstone dated to AD 530. Other later examples of the use of *sepultus* on stones appear in the north-east of England in eighth-century contexts. So far, so good. There is no evidence of forgery or fraud in the formal part of the inscription.

Arturius

The name *Arturius*, however, raises a lot of questions. It is not Artorius. The last Roman of that name left before AD 300. The Arthur of the grave was not the 'last of the Romans', as some enthusiasts used to insist. The inscription looks as if a Latin ending has been added to the Celtic name *Artuir*; that is about as far as Roman influence goes.

Artuir as a name is recorded in four places in the sixth and seventh centuries. One Artuir, the son of the Irish king of Dalriada, Aidan Mac Gabran, was killed in battle. An Irish tribe, the Dessi, were expelled from Meath and settled in Dyfed in west Wales. Their genealogy reveals an *Artuir* who was the great-grandson of the King Votepor who was denounced by Gildas. The *Annals of Clonmacnoise* say that a man called Mongan was killed in Kintyre. The passage is difficult to translate, but it may mean that he was killed there by Llacheu, son of Artuir, or he may simply have been killed by a stone. Certainly, someone called Artuir is mentioned in the Kintyre incident. In AD 697 a priest called Feredach signed an agreement with the Abbot of Iona – the document reveals that his grandfather was called Artuir. That is about it.

All of the Artuirs we know about have Irish or 'Irish in Wales' connections, and their area of activity or association is with the

Kingdom of Dalriada which extended from northern Ireland into southern Scotland and the Western Isles. None of these Artuirs has any known links with Glastonbury, and we don't know that any of them were kings in any meaningful sense.

It is possible that the Arthur of the grave was not actually called Arthur or Artuir, and we may need to look for another name, his original name. In early Celtic society, it was possible to acquire a nickname, or special name, through appearance, a joke, or courage, or some defining incident. The famous Irish hero *Cuchullin* ('the hound/guardian of Ulster'), for example, was called *Sentana* at birth, and came into his nickname or title by defending (sometimes alone) his native province. Artuir or Arthur, as a name, may have arisen in the same way.

We should therefore consider whether the Arthur we seek might have had a link with the Welsh leader *Aircol Lauhir*, the ruler of Tenby in south-west Wales. The Welsh had a fondness at that time for 'joke names' in list poetry – such as *Nerth map Cadran* (Might son of Strong). Arthur might have been called *Arator map Aircol* (Ploughman, son of Farmer) as a nickname or title. If Arator was just a nickname of this jokey kind, the man our search is leading us to may really have been Erbin Map Aircol, a known warrior who was a contemporary of Votepor and Gildas.[6] The name Artuir may be also derive from a pun on *Uthr* (bear) – one of the kings denounced by Gildas is addressed by that name, but we can't attach that possibility to any known, or likely, individual.

Arthur of Loughall?

There is a further possibility. His name may originally have had nothing to do with Britain. In Ireland *Airthir* was the tribal name of a people living around Loughgall, near modern Armagh – they were the eastern part of a wider confederation known as the *Airgialla* (the Oriel in English). The name *Airthir* means 'eastern' or, applied to a man, 'easterner', and it can become Arthur by well-known linguistic developments. The Cornish expert Charles Thomas noted the term *airthir* on an old map of the Scilly Isles, marking the position of a small island lying south-east of the main islands. It is now called Great Arthur, and it has nothing to do with the king. It is merely descriptive of an eastern location in the same way as the tribal name originally was in Ireland. We also know from studies of the Welsh language by Sir Ifor Williams that the letter 'r' led to the letters 't' and 'c' becoming voiced – represented by the spellings 'th' and 'ch'. The development of the Welsh language tells us that the early version of the name, *Artuir*, became the more familiar one, *Arthur*, in a perfectly regular and well-understood manner.

The idea of 'Arthur of Loughgall' may tell us more. Arthur may have been a leader, the 'king' of the *Airthir* people of Loughgall and North Armagh. There is no particular difficulty in him bearing only a tribal name. Irish warrior chieftains were commonly known only by their tribal names. In, or near, Arthur's time, there was a chieftain called *Coirpre* who bore only the name of his tribe.[7] Today clan leaders in Scotland are still called 'the MacTavish' (the MacTavish of Mac Tavish is the more formal name) or 'the McGregor' (the McGregor of McGregor) or whatever their clan name is. When there is a clan gathering, the leader is addressed simply as 'McTavish', as if it were his personal name. If that is what we see in his name, Arthur may have been an Irish warrior called 'the Easterner' who led one of the constituent tribes of the Oriel. The Oriel were tributaries of the Ulster kings of the Dal Fiatach who dominated the lands around the Irish Sea, the 'Irish Sea Province'. An Ulster hosting could have brought the individual in the Glastonbury grave to England. He may have become an opportunist 'soldier of fortune' or mercenary leader there. He could have been the nominated *dux bellorum* of an Irish Sea Province hosting called by a powerful over-king of the Irish Sea Province.

There is some additional evidence to consider. The reported size of the man in the grave allows us to say, with high probability, that this giant man came from a particular area of Ireland.[8] There was only one place in the British Isles over the last few thousand years that regularly produced people who were giants. That place was the area close to the western and southern shores of Lough Neagh (part of the modern counties of Tyrone and Armagh). Both men and women there have reached heights well over 2 metres because of a gene which has been present in the population for over two thousand years.

The gene, however, produces height because of a malfunction of the pituitary gland, and, if not treated, leads to extreme height and acromegaly (gigantism). Patients today with acromegalic conditions frequently present with mobility difficulties. An acromegalic Arthur who was a successful hand-to-hand fighter is unlikely. However, Elizabethan accounts of the bodyguards of the Earl of Tyrone speak of very tall warriors. Other Irish fighters known in well-documented history – such as Kelly the Boy from Killane in the 1798 rebellion – were very tall. Kelly was reported thus: 'Seven feet was his height with some inches to spare.' That is, he was in excess of 2 metres in height. Kelly was an accomplished and inspiring man on the battlefield. He was not acromegalic, and he was, in modern terms, more like the outstanding very tall Irish athletes who play rugby or Gaelic football today.

Although Arthur's reported height may be persuasive evidence that he was Irish, and from the shore-land territory of the *Airthir* near Lough Neagh, in the end, we must admit that the name on the metal cross of the Glastonbury grave doesn't completely confirm that identification. Of itself, and without the height evidence, the name on the cross really tells us remarkably little about him.

Rex

The next bit of the inscription is also problematic – *rex*. Rulers in the sixth century called themselves kings, but they ruled no large dominions. In Ireland, for example, there were more than 150 kings, and Wales seems to have been no less well provided with monarchs – some of them Irishmen.[9] Some sovereigns were mightier than others, and held sway as 'high-kings' to whom other kings paid tribute. The title 'king' in the sixth century does not help us very much. 'High-king' tells us even less – the term was not used at this early date; it was a later invention.

The general notion of 'kingship' is actually more helpful. Around this period Ireland has better records than England about 'kingship' or 'kingliness', and we can see that Irish succession to the throne was not automatic. The eldest son did not always become the king. Precisely who succeeded depended to some extent on ability within a ruling cousinhood called the *derbfine*. Within the *derbfine*, selection was based on, as one early document puts it, 'elder for kin, worth for leadership, wisdom for the church'. The power of the *derbfine* extended to the selection of abbots, and abbots as much as kings wielded power (*flaith*). Indeed, the word *flaithem* was used more frequently than *ri* (Latin *rex*) in describing the powers of kings. In some respects too, the authority wielded by abbots was greater than that of a king because men and women, on becoming Christian, were possibly more under the control of the abbot than they were as ordinary subjects of the local king. There was often also a tension between king and abbot about the exercise of the powers we would understand now as vested in 'kingship'. As we have seen, some Welsh rulers, such as Maelgwn, solved that dilemma for their subjects by being both king and cleric.

In Ireland, the result of the king/abbot dilemma was that ruling families took care to see that abbatial power was not lightly conferred. At Iona, for example, only two abbots in around three hundred years were not members of the Cenel Conaill branch of the Ui Neill *derbfine* or 'royal family' from which the founder of Iona, Saint Columba, came. The Bible and the Crown went hand in hand, and most powerful kings had a monastery nearby run by a relative. If Arthur really were a king, on the Irish model at least, somewhere behind him there must have been a family group (*derbfine*), and possibly a powerful monastery. If we could find them, we might know who he was.

It is, however, quite certain that Arthur was not always a king. In the largely Welsh records we have, Arthur is most frequently called *dux bellorum*, the battle leader (or *cathmilid* in Welsh and Irish – Ireland also has *toisech*), and the 'battle leader' was not the king. He was simply the leading warrior, the commander in the field. Kingship may have been an honour conferred upon Arthur by much later tradition, perhaps two or three hundred years after his death. In his own day he was a warrior only, and, if he became a king, it was late in his career.

Inclitus

The claim of kingship may not be the only area of doubt. There are signs elsewhere on the lead cross that the inscription may not be all it seems to be. The next word, *inclitus*, seems straightforward at first sight. In Latin it means 'famous'. But Plautus, the Roman playwright, uses the same word in his comedies in an ironic sense. Plautus has a stock character, a boastful and perhaps fundamentally cowardly or stupid soldier that he called '*dux inclutissimus*' (very famous leader), and *Miles Gloriosus* (renowned soldier). Both carry the ironic sense of boastful incompetence in military matters. *Inclitus* means the opposite of what it appears to say.

In the Isle of Avalon

That the sense of the whole inscription may be ironic and contradictory is reinforced by the next phrase, '*in insula Avalonia*'. In Gildas and Nennius, Arthur appears to have won Christian victories at Badon and at Glastonbury. We might expect some reference to him as a 'soldier of the Cross' on his grave, but instead we have *Avalonia*.

Avalonia appears to be the Latin version of Welsh *Aballach*, and is difficult to understand in this context. *Aballach* may have been a legendary king in Wales, and therefore be a male personal name rather than the name of a place or district. *Aballach* is a female personal name in Ireland, and derives from the word for 'apples'. The original Aballach may have been a pagan apple goddess. There is also a male pagan deity with that name, associated with the classical notion of the 'Fortunate Isles' – another name for Paradise. The Paradise referred to was a pagan one, not the Christian Paradise or the Garden of Eden.[10] Does the inscription tell us that Arthur is in Paradise, the island of apples, or in some pagan sanctuary, the Otherworld Island presided over by the Celtic sea god *Manannan MacLir*? None of it seems to be specifically Christian, and some of it may be overtly pagan. On the other hand, it may simply mean he lies in the 'island of holy women' (*Guinnion*). The holy women could be devoted to a Pagan goddess rather following Christ. Either way, there could be a sign of religious disapproval here.

The Second Wife

That may link to the inscription regarding the second body the monks found: *cum Wenneveria uxore sua seconda* (with Guinevere his second wife). This is also not what it seems at first sight. It is not a simple description of his domestic or marital arrangements. 'Second wife' (*adultrach*) in sixth-century Ireland (and we can imagine also in Wales and Cornwall at least, if not in Scotland and most of western England) was a technical term. *Uxore seconda* is a translation of *adultrach* and *adultrach* meant 'mistress' or 'concubine'.

The name assigned to the second and female body is interesting too. The name of Arthur's female consort in literature exists in many forms: *Gvenhvyuar*, *Gwenhwy*, *Guanhumara*, *Guenhuuera* and *Gweenwara* all appear in Geoffrey of Monmouth and in

Welsh sources. In French we have the familiar Guinevere, and in Irish the very different-looking but similar-sounding *Finnabair.* On the Modena Cathedral archivolt in Sicily, her name appears in a possibly Breton or Norman form, *Winlogee.* In all of these tongues, the meaning is the same: it means 'white phantom'. White was the colour of holiness so her name really was a version of the Greek *Sophia* of the Tripartite notion of God (Father, Logos, Sophia). In English, it is 'the Holy Ghost', a name of great religious potency and devotion. There is no sign of this Christian link in the name form chosen for the dead woman in the Glastonbury grave. Where then does this form *Wenneveria* come from?

It may not be a serious attempt to communicate her name at all but a sort of bitter pun. Clerics were not above such nasty jokes. Henry II's mistress Rosamund Clifford, sometimes referred to as *Rosa Mundi* (Rose of the world), was described in one document as *Rosa Immundi* (the rose of filth and impurity). On her grave a rhyming epitaph made essentially the same remark:

Hic jacet tumba Rosamundi
Non Rosamunda
Non redolet sed olet
Quae redolere solet

(Here in the tomb lies the rose of the world, not a pure rose.
She who used to smell sweet still smells – but not sweet)

Guinevere seems to have incurred the same disapproval. In pronunciation in the Welsh of the sixth century, and for some hundreds of years afterwards, medial syllables were dropped. Thus the Early British name Caractacos became Early Welsh Caractacus which moved through Ceretic to Saxon Cerdic. Latin has the word *venus, veneris* meaning 'charm, the qualities that excite love'. The same word was applied to the spring goddess Venus who was identified with the Greek goddess Aphrodite who was overtly sexual. Thus the word Venus, and words derived from it such 'venereal', became associated with illicit sexual activity and voluptuousness. *Wenn(ev)eria* was apparently meant to be pronounced *veneria* and gives a meaning for this version of her name that means something pejoratively sexual.

The meaning of the full inscription then becomes something like, 'Here lies buried the vainglorious so-called King Arthur with his mistress Lecheria in his pagan paradise.' The insulting cross is placed on the lower side of the covering slab, and the oak coffin was apparently placed inside the cist grave or tomb that the stone slab covered. Arthur and Guinevere, wherever they had been buried at the time of their deaths, had obviously been reburied by people who disapproved of them on ethnic, political or religious grounds – possibly all three. The people who buried Arthur and his consort were determined, insofar as the bodies might be discovered and exhumed, that anyone finding him at a later date would know he was not a man to be approved of. Quite specifically, he was not the hero a popular oral tradition may have already created by that time (around the ninth or tenth century). He most emphatically was not a 'Christian Hero'.

Saint Dunstan and Disapproval

Who buried him in this fashion and with such intentions? The prime suspect must be Saint Dunstan, or monks working under his direction. Born in Somerset, Dunstan studied with the Irish monks of Glastonbury, and became a skilled artist, and, perhaps significantly, a metalworker. He would have been capable and competent enough to make the lead cross with his own hands. Forced into exile, he lived in a Benedictine monastery in Flanders, and when he returned to England he adopted the Rule of Saint Benedict, the law code set out for the government of monasteries by the saint. When he was restored to power – he was virtually Prime Minister of England although the post didn't exist then – he set about rebuilding Glastonbury.

The Benedictine Rule he imposed on the Abbey of Glastonbury feared contamination by loose living. The Rule states, for example, if a guest in a Benedictine house was 'lavish or vicious' in his behaviour, he was told to depart and, if he resisted, 'two stout monks were to explain the matter to him'. It may be that Dunstan felt that, at Glastonbury, he had no need for a heroic king whose Christianity and moral standing he doubted. Arthur's remains were removed from wherever they might have been kept, possibly in a place of honour between two Irish high crosses. The crosses were deliberately removed, or not replaced if they had rotted or fallen. Arthur was buried deep, beyond any fear of contamination, outside the new abbey church – not in the place of honour before the altar. Over the site of Arthur's grave, Dunstan piled about 10 feet of earth (3 m), ostensibly to provide better footings for the great new abbey church he was building. He also tried to make sure that no one sought the king's resting place. The story was promulgated: 'Arthur's grave will be for ever unknown.'

Arthur and the Kings

Some sort of record seems to have been kept, and Henry II appears to have come into possession of it – possibly because he refused to appoint an abbot when the spiritual direction of Glastonbury fell vacant. For a time, he kept the resources of the abbey entirely for himself. When William of Malmesbury, Geoffrey of Monmouth, Wace and others had created an interest in the kings of England, and in Arthur, Henry II decided upon a resurrection for his own family political purposes, but he died before his scheme, whatever it was, could come to fruition. His son, Richard the Lionheart, had no interest in Arthur. When placed in possession of what purported to be 'Arthur's Sword', he promptly gave it to the King of Sicily. King Richard's successors were too busy trying to survive to care much for a dead king. So Arthur passed from politics into literature, and the man we can see now is the creation of poets, bards and writers of romance. He is not the sixth-century warrior and he is not the man in the Glastonbury grave.

The key figure in creating the 'Arthur of literature' is Eleanor of Aquitaine, Henry II's queen. Eleanor and her daughter Marie gathered around them a gallery of poets and writers who were proponents of what became known as 'courtly love'.[11] Put bluntly, courtly love was an illicit love affair that was, officially at least, all talk and no action. Poets vied with one another to provide stories – called *lais* and *romans* (songs and romantic stories) – and Eleanor and her court, having discussed these poems, adjudicated on both the merits of the poems and on the actions of their characters. It was a kind of soft-porn soap opera for a courtly ladies' 'Reading Group', a circle where adultery may have been practised but could carry with it, occasionally, fatal consequences.

The favourite characters in the *lais* and *romans* became the people around King Arthur, and, because of the excellence of the writing, the real sixth-century chieftain disappeared, and was replaced by a benign monarch who presided over a court where ladies were beautiful and knights sought their favour by heroic deeds. That image was so powerful that it renewed itself in successive ages, and has continued to excite the imagination of men and women over at least nine centuries. Arthur became a mirror in which men of all ages and many cultures could see themselves. He was no longer real.

Our search for 'the real Arthur' doesn't need to end in the excavated grave of Glastonbury, or in the lovely sunlit court of old Camelot. We may be yet able to discern something of the man Henry II expected to be once again useful as a king, and, beyond him, the man we think may have been involved in the Battle of Badon. Our aim now must be to see if a biography of the Arthur of the sixth century can be constructed from the sparse materials we have to hand.

CONCLUSIONS
1. The Glastonbury grave was not faked.
2. The man buried there may be Arthur.
3. The inscription reveals he may have been an Irish leader from Loughgall and Guinevere may have been his concubine.
4. The inscription otherwise appears to show that he was buried by people who disapproved of him.
5. The 'Arthur of literature' supplanted the 'real Arthur' and was a Plantagenet invention.

9

A LIFE OF ARTHUR

Background to Biography

The 'Arthur of literature' is a creature of the imagination. The king we inherit through the work of all those who were inspired by his story from Geoffrey of Monmouth and Wace, through Chrétien de Troyes and Thomas Malory, to Tennyson and Lerner and Loew, is more emblematic than realistic. He is presented to us as a king conceived and born through magic, who comes to his throne by symbolically drawing his sword *Excalibur* from a rock. He reigns as a brave and benign monarch, sagacious in peace and valiant in war. There are some sorrows to give some rounding to his character. Arthur is troubled, for example, by the love his friend Lancelot feels for his wife, the lovely Guinevere. The manner of his death enriches the picture too. It is tragic, almost operatic. Through the revolt and treachery of his nephew Mordred, Arthur meets his end at the Battle of Camlan. He is borne, dying, from the field by his sorrowing companions. At the edge of a lake, the distraught Bedivere, on Arthur's instruction, throws his magic sword into the waves, whence a ghostly hand emerges to seize and draw it under. The dying king is passed to the care of weeping maidens who convey him to the Isle of Avalon where his faery sister, Morgan la Fay, waits to cure him of his wounds. Arthur is seen no more. But his people wait, generation after generation, for him to come again to inspire their lives, and to save them from their enemies. The life of Arthur, as it has descended to us through art and literature, was an ideal life, and the Age of Arthur, as we have inherited it, was a Golden Age to which men longed to return.

The primitive Arthur, the real man behind the stories, was a different and, on the whole, more believable figure. If he existed at all, he was a sixth-century warrior, general and tyrant. The time he lived in, in as far as we can determine it from the archaeological record, was not a golden age. Arthur and his circle inherited little from Roman Britain. If they inhabited the remains and ruins of the Roman towns and villas at all, they walked homewards through streets filled with rubbish to shelters they shared with their animals. They lived the life of Celtic subsistence farmers and pastoralists, supplementing their income perhaps by some occasional raiding of their neighbours. Their comforts were few and they died young. The life of a man at Arthur's court, if he had one, was conjecturally nasty, probably British, and certainly short.

If we are to recover Arthur, find the real man, we have once again to put all the romances written about him, and virtually all we have ever heard about him, to one side and accept only what we can find of him in the words of those who first wrote about him. In general terms, in trying to discover the life and times of the real Arthur, we have to prefer records produced before AD 1150, that is before Geoffrey of Monmouth in England and Chrétien de Troyes in France began the romantic versions of Arthur's life and adventures. Occasionally, however, Geoffrey, and others who came after him, may unwittingly offer us a detail worth following. Not everything written after 1150 is tainted. We can accept some incidental information, little details seemingly inessential to the story they are telling.

The Birth of Arthur

We begin with his birth. Arthur's father is unknown and his mother's name is uncertain. Geoffrey of Monmouth claimed that his father was one *Uthr Pendragon* who came to his mother's bed by magic. We can discount the magic as a means of procreation, and note that the putative father's name is not a personal name, but a title. It means literally 'terrible paramount chief', and is possibly best thought of as 'prominent over-king'. There must have been several monarchs around at that time who might have merited that description, but we have no means of identifying which one was thought to be Arthur's father. Arthur is one of the few characters in this time who does not bear a name in the form X son of Y. We cannot connect him to a known family.

Geoffrey says Arthur's mother was called *Igerne*, and the pre-Geoffrey Welsh tradition says she was called *Eigr*. Eigr was said to be a daughter (one of many) of a king of Brittany called *Amlydd Wledig*. The name might be Irish *Amlaide*, or an invented name, *an-blawdd*, which means 'terrible commotion'. Neither name has any secure connection with Brittany.[1] The original records pertaining to Arthur may have read *eriugena* (of Irish descent, Arthur the Irishman). The name of his mother may be a scribal error, a learned mistake, or a deliberate and invented falsehood by the monks who made the first written records of his birth.

Monks did alter records. As we have noted earlier, Arthur's name has also been intruded into the ninth-century Welsh genealogy of Dyfed where he usurps the place of *Erbin map Aircol* of Tenby in south Wales, but his name is missing from other versions of the same list. We may have to accept that his origins and parentage were actually unknown, and his family details were supplied later to make useful political connections for rulers, or to gain advantages for monasteries.

The Schooling of Arthur

We may be on surer ground with his birth place, or at any rate the place where he was brought up. The two are not necessarily the same. In the sixth century, boys were often sent to be brought up by a king with whom the boy's parents' tribe had, and hoped to maintain, good relations. The system combined the advantages of fostering and hostage-holding with some of the benefits of a boarding school. Since we cannot recover the names of his parents and the place of his birth, we should look at where he went to school, where he learnt to be a scurrilous bard and an outstanding warrior. We can ask: where was he fostered?

The likely answer to that question is Cornwall. Geoffrey says Arthur was born at Tintagel in Cornwall, and suggests that his mother's husband Gorlois was then at nearby Domellick (*Damelioc*), close to modern St Dennis. Geoffrey may have had some special local knowledge because he mentions the name of Ulphin de Brea, who, he says, held the land overlooking Tintagel. De Brea's continental antecedents are known; he appears to have been a real but very much post-Arthur person, and that may give some credibility to this part of Geoffrey's story. Geoffrey may be repeating a genuine local tradition of a landholding in the name of Brea rather than creating a fiction to fill a gap in his knowledge. We can be sure of one thing: if Ulphin ever held land in Cornwall, he did not hold it in Arthur's time.

The fact is that we have no sound information about who may have held Tintagel around the time of Arthur's birth. A meaning for the name Tintagel might help us with that, but there is no agreement about what Tintagel as a name might mean. Ekwall and Padel were prepared to accept that *Tin* was really *Dun* (a fort) in a possible Irish spelling ('t' for 'd' as in Giltas for Gildas). Ekwall could make nothing of the rest of it, and Padel thought it might be 'the fort of the constriction' (Cornish *Tagell*) because of its narrow entrance. Ralegh Radford and Swanton were attracted by a name found on the island of Sark. It is *Tintageau*, earlier *Tente d'Agel* ('the castle of the devil'). None of them appears to have a considered *Dun na Gaedel* or *Dun na Goidel* (the Irish or raider's fort) although the ninth-century *Cormac's Glossary* says that there were at least two Irish forts in the land of the Cornish Britons. The oldest Cornish name for Tintagel, *Trewarverne*, later *Trewenna* (to which we will later return), may be the best clue we have. For the moment, we should leave place names and stay with Tintagel and see what physical evidence can suggest about it.

Archaeology tells us that Tintagel imported Mediterranean wine and other goods from North Africa, and that there was some pottery from Ireland. It may have been a military stronghold, but is probably best understood as a monastery of the Irish type. Ireland, unlike Romanised Britain, had no significant towns. As the great Irish monasteries developed in the sixth century, they functioned as towns, becoming centres for manufacture, and for the export and import of useful goods. Broken tiles found at Tintagel appear to have come from an Irish monastery at Strangford Lough, which implies a religious or a trading link. Tintagel may have served as the entry port for Mediterranean goods for all of the lands bordering the Irish Sea, 'the Irish Sea Province'. Archaeology says the goods found in numbers at Tintagel are also found around in the whole area of the Irish Sea Province (see Fig. 10 in plates). Tintagel, even if it was a monastery, was really a cultured and sizeable town. If Arthur was indeed born or fostered at Tintagel, his formative years were spent in a rich cultural environment, one of the richest in that regard in the Britain of his time.

The name of nearby Damelioc tells us more about the religious link. The first part of the name is linked with Latin *dominicum*, or *domus* which both evolved to mean a 'church' in the sense of a building devoted to worship. This was a popular, not an official, name, and was in use on the Continent for a short time only (about AD 333 to 450). In Ireland that use continued for perhaps another hundred years. The second element *lioc* means a 'stone'. The whole name means a church built using stone rather than wood or wattle and daub.

In Ireland a *familia* (a network of churches) that signalled its presence by building stone churches flourished for about two centuries from around AD 450. Place names similar to Damelioc, using the Irish element derived from *dominicum, Donagh* (as in *Donagh* [the 'church'] + *more [big]* to form *Donaghmore* ['the big church']), show that it was widespread. It was based initially in lands south and west of Lough Neagh, an area associated with the tribe called the Oriel *(Airgialla)*, a people who included the *Airthir*. This Church spread its influence southwards to the Irish sub-province of *Brega* (which may lie behind Geoffrey's note about Ulphin de Brea – he may have got the wrong Brea). The Oriel paid tribute at that time to the Dal Fiatach at *Dunlethglas* (modern Downpatrick), which suggests that the Church *familia* was linked to Saint Patrick. The monastery most associated with the Ulster kings was the great abbey of Bangor, which may have been the 'mother house' of the *familia*.[2] We can connect this *Damelioc* as a name directly and linguistically to Ireland. The Irish *Annals of Tirechan* mention *Domum Liace Cennani* (Cennan's stone church). The name *Damelioc* is strong evidence that Arthur, if he was born at Tintagel, was born into a Christian, and possibly Irish, society. It may even, conjecturally, be an indication that he was an Irish lad fostered in Cornwall, sent there to learn to be a warrior.

Arthur the Warrior
Arthur certainly grew up to be a warrior – all the evidence points that way – but his status beyond the fact of 'warrior' is always not quite clear. Aneirin, the Welsh bard, used him as a comparison, or 'benchmark' of 'warrior effectiveness'. He says of the warrior *Gwawrddur* that 'he glutted the ravens of the fort but he was

not Arthur'. That is, *Gwawrddur* was a successful fighter, but didn't attain the levels achieved by Arthur. Nennius tells us he fought 'among the kings of Britain but he was the *Dux Bellorum*, the leader of the battles'. The implication is that he led the wars but, unlike some of those who fought alongside him, and whom he commanded, he was not a king. The hagiographies of the Welsh saints refer to him frequently as 'Arthur the warrior' without assigning a rank to him. The twelfth-century poem *Arthur and the Eagle* refers to him as 'chief of the battalions of Cornwall'. In a life of Saint Gildas, Caradoc of Llancarfan calls him *Tyrannus* (a ruler) rather than *rex* (a king). But he did become a king, because Caradoc later describes him as 'the rebellious king' without saying against whom, or what, he rebelled. He also apparently became a supreme commander of the type he seems to be in *The Dream of Rhonabwy*'s account of Badon. The *Black Book of Carmarthen* calls him *amherwdyr*, which is equivalent to the Latin *Imperator*. *Imperator* is normally translated as 'Emperor' but, in this case, may mean no more than 'general', a term equivalent to *dux bellorum*.[3]

Welsh tradition is also somewhat vague about his actual ability as a soldier. Arthur seems to enjoy achievements and victories mixed with real fallibility. On the one hand, he is a successful raider able to reward his followers handsomely; Triad 2 of TYP says he was more generous in the distribution of plunder than the three men who were otherwise the paragons of generosity in Britain. Triad 20, on the other hand, says he was one of the three 'great unrestrained ravagers of Britain'; where Arthur went 'neither plants nor grass sprang up, not for seven years'. This is certainly an impressive, although not a very wise, policy if you want to extract tribute on an annual basis.

The Triads are also critical of Arthur's iconoclastic attitude to the 'talismans of Britain'. Arthur went about destroying these relics, which were thought to protect Britain, because he believed that 'Britain should be not defended by the strength of any one but his own'. This looks like hubris on a grand scale, unless of course Arthur was rejecting the power of the Head of Bran, the Bones of Gwertheyrn, and the Dragons of Dinas Emrys, for religious reasons, in favour of the merits of Saint Mary under whose sign or banner he is supposed to have fought. Alternatively, he may have been determined to make himself the sole source of benefit and protection, and would brook no power, temporal, spiritual, pagan or Christian, over him.

The Triads (TYP) may lead us to question other aspects of Arthur's military career. They contain no hint of the twelve battles listed by Nennius, and the extensive conquests related by Geoffrey. In the Triads, Arthur is not an all-conquering hero. He experiences military difficulties and reverses. He becomes trapped, imprisoned, or besieged, and each time has to rely on his cousin, *Goreu map Custennin* of Cornwall, for relief.

While other early Welsh records provide evidence of further military activity, this too is of an unimpressive kind. In the *Mabinogion*, we have a lot of details about the pursuit of the boar *Twrch Trywth* across most of southern Wales. It seems to have been a real event, and probably did not involve boars (we shall return to the point later). The only feat performed by Arthur himself in that long chase was the killing of an old woman, and he did that from a distance. Elsewhere in the Welsh records, we have a note of Arthur killing a 'hag' and the 'three sisters of *Cribwr Gawr*'. Arthur's reputation seems to be limited to chasing pigs, and killing women – some of them old women.

He has other unheroic qualities. A life of Saint Cadoc reveals that Arthur was out riding with Cei and Bedwyr when they saw a couple fleeing from a group of soldiers. The young man is King (and later Saint) *Gwynllyw*, the future father of Saint Cadoc. The girl is *Gwladys*, the daughter of King *Brychan*, an Irish ruler of central Wales. In the romances and tales written after Geoffrey, Arthur's reaction would be to come to the rescue of the young lovers, to save them from their pursuers and carry them off in triumph to sunny Camelot. In the narrative we have, his first thought is how pretty she is, and his second is to kill the man and to ravish her. It is only with some difficulty that Cei and Bedwyr persuade him otherwise. In other hagiographic tales, Arthur is mean and shifty, and he and his men are often outwitted by shrewd and canny saints who force them to adopt better ways (and give donations and benefits to monasteries).

Although he had a reputation as a 'scurrilous poet', Arthur also exhibits an inability to tolerate opposition, or the application of satirical verse to himself. We have seen that he killed Hoel for one rhyme, and he may have killed his own son, Amr, for another. He drove his friend Cei from his side by bitter remarks couched in a verse, and the breach was so bad that Cei, formerly one of his best friends, refused him thereafter all military aid, even when Arthur was hard pressed.

To say, however, that Arthur was not a completely successful general, that his ravaging was unrestrained, that he was mean, shifty, treacherous, rebellious, bitter and cutting in speech and verse, and even murderous and inclined toward rape, is not to denigrate him. It is to reveal him as a real sixth-century character. Murder, as we see from the condemnations issued by Gildas in chapter 2, was normal in princely society in the sixth century. It was probably a survival mechanism, and the most successful kings may have been those who waded through blood to a throne, and maintained their seat there by the slaughter of friends and enemies alike. As William of Malmesbury, in the twelfth century, said of King William the Conqueror, 'those who are feared by many, must fear many.'

Whatever his methods and moral failings, Arthur in the end seems to have been successful. He became a king, and the most successful warriors of his day thronged his court. He had some claim to lead chieftains from Brittany, Cornwall, west and south Wales, Galloway, Lothian, and perhaps parts of Ireland. Arthur was the focus and the fount of honour, a king generous in gifts of plunder for men who were themselves notably heroic and generous.

The Idleness of the King

Generosity is not the only similarity between the literary 'Arthur of golden Camelot' who has come down to us and the real 'sixth century Arthur'. In both versions of 'Arthur', the king exhibits a marked lack of executive action or capability. The sixth-century Arthur is not much of a hero and does very little himself, and in many of the post-Geoffrey stories, the French and German romances, the literary 'Camelot Arthur' also undertakes few direct actions. In fact, he often does nothing very much at all, leaving the pursuit of monsters, the hunt for the Holy Grail and the rescue of maidens in distress to the knights of the Round Table.

One story about a kidnap provides an interesting comparison. In a tale told in a life of Saint Gildas, Arthur behaves like a sixth-century ruler. When Guinevere is violently seized and carried away by Melwas, king of the Summer Country, Arthur assembles a large army and sets out to devastate the kingdom of the abductor.

A major war is only averted by the intervention of Gildas and the Abbot of Glastonbury. Guinevere is restored, royal honour is apparently satisfied, and, this being hagiography, Glastonbury receives rich endowments.

In continental romances written after Geoffrey, the same narrative is played out with vital differences. Guinevere's presence is demanded by a strange knight, and he is prepared to fight anyone the king nominates for the right to hold her. There is apparently no question of Arthur himself undertaking combat or raising an army. He does nothing. It is eventually agreed that Kay (*Cei*) will take Guinevere to the forest and fight the strange knight for her.

The wisdom of the king's action is questioned, and its foolishness is apparent to all but him. Guinevere herself says softly, 'Oh, if only you knew, you would never, I think, allow me to be led away one single step without opposition.' She makes no comment on his statecraft in entertaining the challenge at all, she shows no resentment in being the prize to be disputed, and she doesn't seem to regard his passivity in the matter as cowardice or indifference.

There are two possibilities: either Guinevere questions his capacity to make any kind of judgment, or she is in a plot to cuckold him. In the version told by Chrétien de Troyes, the mysterious knight defeats Kay. Although he has therefore won her fair and square, when the other knights hear the result of the duel, they ride forth to pursue and punish him as if he had indeed stolen the queen. He is then revealed to be one Meleagrant, son of the good King Bademagu. He is evidently the same man who appears in other tales as Mahleoas, le Sire de l'Isle de Voirre (*Eric and Enide*), Melwas (*The life of Gildas* by Caradog of Llancarfan) and Mellygraunce (Malory's *Morte D'Arthur*).

In other romances written in France and Germany, other abductors appear. In the German *Lanzelet*, the kidnapper is *Valerin* (Gawain), who is also named in in that role in *Diu Crone*. In the French *Le Chevelier de la Charette*, Lancelot sets out to rescue her, but she winds up in his bed. In the Perceval stories, it is an otherwise unnamed Red Knight who seizes her. In *Yder*, the author is forced to invent a second lady of the same name to avoid writing about the queen winding up in a sexual relationship with Yder. In *Sir Launfal* and other later stories, the authors are less squeamish. They say bluntly Guinevere had many lovers.

In Caradog's version, which is probably the earliest, Guinevere is seized and violated (*violatum et raptum*), but in a much later version by the greatest of Welsh medieval poets, Daffydd ap Gwilym, Melwas is not a violent rapist but a daring and successful lover. He is celebrated for climbing up to the queen's bower, and then making off with her, with her willing consent and connivance, to a treehouse built in the green wood. He is a man to be envied and emulated.[4]

Arthurian Morality

If Guinevere is not a free agent in all these adventures, she was a very attractive, but much abused lady. Lancelot, Gawain, Kay, Yder and others in Arthur's court are happy to ride out to rescue Guinevere from a fate worse than death at the hands of Melwas, but are quite happy to allow her to endure it in their own beds. They do not appear to think that what they are doing is going to bring dishonour upon her, nor do they believe that they are being disloyal to their king. With Guinevere before them, they find Arthur is very little in their thoughts, and he seems remarkably unmoved by their actions.

If we assume that the Celtic society experienced by Guinevere and her lovers had not changed very much for about 500 years, and that indeed is what archaeology seems to show, there is an explanation for this behaviour, which means we can believe that something like the original abduction, or willing departure, of Guinevere took place. The Roman historian Dio Cassius, writing about the wars of the Emperor Severus, introduces a 'princess' – said to be Pictish – from the British Isles. This lady makes a spirited reply to strictures by the Emperor's wife, Julia, on the morality of her homeland. She says that customs in Britain are superior to those of Rome. Women in the British Isles openly consort with the best men of their tribe, while Roman matrons commit adultery in private and secrecy with the vilest of Roman men.

There is other evidence too. Julius Caesar says that in Gaul and Britain the Celts had ten or a dozen wives held in common (*uxores habent deni duidenique inter se communis*). St Jerome (AD 347–420) in his letter to Oceanus (Letter LXIX) urges a responsible attitude to marriage 'unlike the Scots (the Irish) who have a 'a community of wives and no discrimination of children,

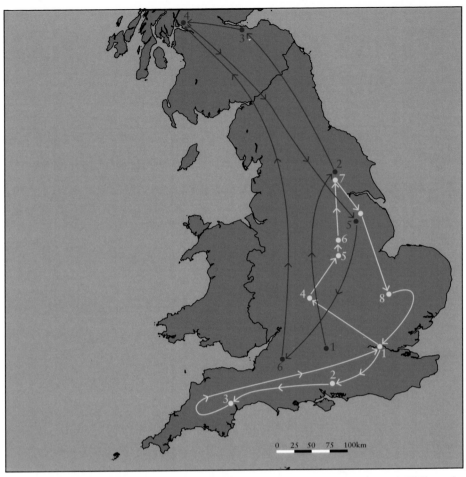

Fig. 1. The campaigns of Arthur (according to Geoffrey of Monmouth) and William the Conqueror. Arthur (red) set out from Silchester (1), relived sieges at York (2) and Lincoln (5) before winning battles in Scotland at Edinburgh (3) and possibly Dumbarton (4). William (yellow) set out from London and pacified the south-west via Winchester (2) and Exeter (3) before returning to London. He then set out for the Midlands, dealing with opposition at Warwick (4), Leicester (5) and Nottingham (6) before 'harrying the North' from York (7). He then put down Hereward the Wake in the fenlands near Cambridge (8) before returning to London. He ended his campaign of suppression with another visit to York.

The two campaigns are similar. Geoffrey was certainly wrong about Edinburgh and may have been wrong about Dumbarton. Dumbarton was called *Alclud* (*Aracluta*, *Arecluta*) and that is usually assumed (and not just by Geoffrey) to mean 'Dumbarton Rock', an impressive fortress on a high outcrop on the shores of the Clyde. There was, however, more than one *Alclud*. In a poem linked with the name of the Irish Saint Feock (*Fiacc*) there is a story which is basically about the marriage of St Patrick's sister Liamain to King Restitutus of Brittany. We are told that 'Patrick (and his family) all went from *Ail Cluade* over the Ictian Sea southwards to the Britons of Armorica, that is to say to the Letavian Britons; for there were relations of theirs there at that time.' The story exists because the marriage produced St Germanus of Man. The information about the trip is incidental, which gives it some credibility as fact. The poem assumes that any reader would know that *Ail Cluade* is the natural port of embarkation for any crossing of the Ictian Sea (the English Channel or La Manche). *Ail Cluade* could be anywhere on the south coast of England from Portchester to Penzance. If we seek a similarity to Dumbarton Rock, we may prefer St Michael's Mount, which was still on the mainland coast then and not isolated in the sea as at present.

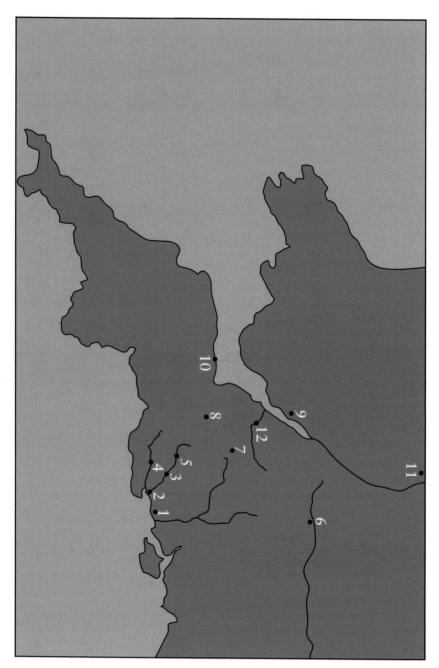

Fig. 2. **Arthur's English campaign: the battle sites.** 1. Christchurch. 2. Wareham. 3, 4, 5. Battles on the Frome, Stour and Trent, Piddle and Divelish. 6. Swinford-on-Thames. 7. Penselwood. 8. Glastonbury. 9. Caer Leon. 10. Carhampton. 11. Leintwardine. 12. Clifton, Bristol. The strategy followed appears to be similar to the campaign of Vespasian – going up the Dorset rivers towards Ilchester subduing the territory held in pre-Roman times by the Durotriges and the Dobunni and the Silures. Only battle 11 is an outlier. Note the importance of river systems.

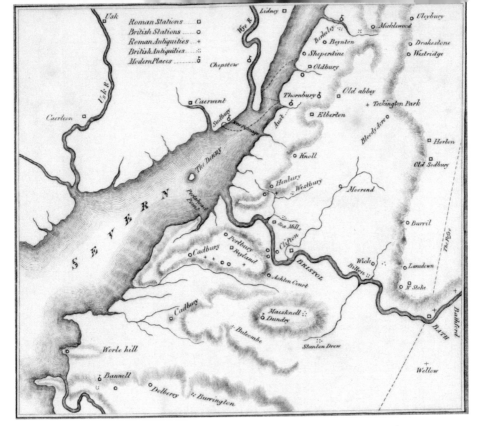

Above: Fig. 3. British and Roman stations around Bristol.

Right: Fig. 4. Camps around the Avon Gorge relative to the site of the modern suspension bridge.

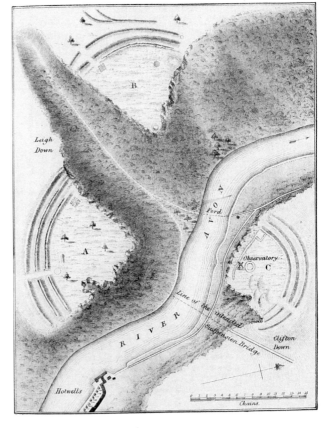

Above and below: Figs 5 & 6. The site of the Battle of Badon; eighteenth-century views of the Avon Gorge by Chatelin.

A. The Abbots Kitchin. B. His Lodgings. C. S.t Josephs Chappel. D. The Town Church. E. the Abby Church. F. the Tower. G. S.t Marys Chappel.
H. Edgars Chappel. I. the Choir. K. the Cloysters. L. the Hall. M. the Monks Lodgings. N. the Almery.

Above: Fig. 7. Prospect of Glastonbury ruins in 1723.

Right: Fig. 8. Glastonbury Abbey c. 1500. (Drawing by F. Bligh Bond RIBA)

GLASTONBURY ABBEY: VIEW OF INTERIOR FROM NORTH TRANSEPT,
as it probably appeared circa 1500. The drawing is based upon historical data,
but the arch and column in the foreground are assumed as an artistic license
in order to obtain the desired perspective.

Above: Fig. 9. Glastonbury Abbey today. The plaque marking Arthur's grave can be seen in the foreground. (Courtesy of Steve Slater)

Left: Fig. 10. An image of the cross found by Camden on Arthur's grave at Glastonbury.

This page: Figs 11 & 12. The habour entrance of Porth Clais in Pembrokeshire where Baetan landed his army to start his dreadful civil war with Arthur. In storm conditions it was a difficult port to enter and the Romans built a harbour wall. Modern boats aside, the harbour sheltered by the wall is still very much as Baetan and Arthur would have seen it. (© Pembrokeshire Coast National Park Authority)

This page: Figs 13 & 14. The island of Skye, where Arthur is said by some to have died. (Courtesy of Will Herman)

Above: Fig. 15. The Preseli mountains. The scene of perhaps two battles with Baetan is unchanged from Arthur's time. (© Crown copyright (2018) Visit Wales)

Below: Fig. 16. The rugged terrain of Tintagel, where Arthur was likely brought up. (Courtesy of Jeff Pardoen)

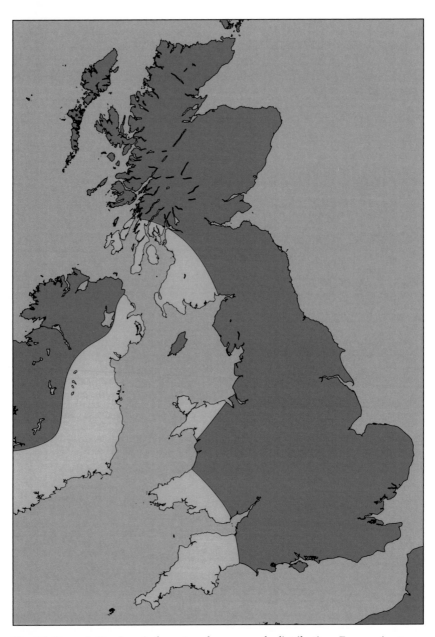

Fig. 17. **Baetan's Empire: sixth-century luxury goods distribution.** Four major types of luxury imported wheel-made pottery have been found in sites around the Irish Sea Province. Such expensive wares can only have been imported and sold on to other more remote users in the context of seas free of pirates and lands where robbers were not feared. There is a high degree of coincidence between the distribution regions found by archaeology and the regions reported in documents to be under the control of Baetan MacCairill. The types are: (a) fine red tableware, some marked with the Christian cross; (b) large storage jars (*amphorae*) from the eastern Mediterranean, used for oil, wine and dried fruit; (c) grey bowls and dishes from Aquitaine made to look like silver; (d) rougher pots and other kitchenware, also from Aquitaine.

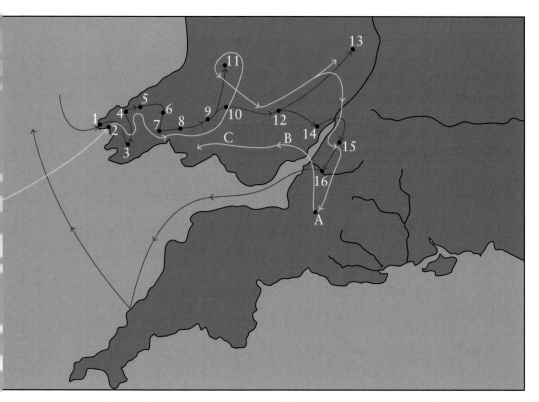

Fig. 18. **The Welsh campaign: Arthur's war of independence**. 1. Baetan (red) lands at the old Roman port of Porth Clais (nr St David's). 2. Arthur (yellow) lands at St David's and sets off in pursuit. 3. Baetan defeats a defensive force at Milford Haven and moves back north. 4. Arthur misses him and pursues him to the Preseli Hills (nr modern Newport). 5. A battle on the River Nevern. 6. A battle at Cym Cerwyn. 7. A battle at Peluniawf between the mountains and Laugharne. 8. A battle on the River Tawy (nr modern Carmarthen). 9. A battle in the Amman valley (nr modern Ammanford). 10. A battle at Lwch Ewin (unlocated); Baetan splits his forces, Grugyn leading some men north into Ceredigion. 11. Arthurian forces surround and kill Grugyn and all his men. 12. A battle south of the Brecon Beacons and Black Mountains after which Baetan again divides his forces. 13. Baetan's northern force is destroyed at Ewas (south of modern Hereford). 14. Baetan wins battle at the mouth of the Wye (nr modern Chepstow). 15. The battle of Camlan. Arthur confronts Baetan at Cam in modern Gloucestershire. Baetan and his surviving forces reach Abonae and Dun Baetan (nr modern Bristol). They find ships there and depart for Ireland via Cornwall.

A. Arthur is taken to Glastonbury for medical treatment and expels Henwen (St Bridget?). B & C. Arthurian forces pursue her but she is protected by Cornish armies led by, among others, Tristan. Neither Arthur's force nor cunning prevail. She returns to Ireland.

The campaign leaves Arthur in control both spiritually and politically in Deheubarth (modern Pembrokeshire, Carmarthenshire and Ceredigion), Somerset and much of modern Wiltshire, Dorset and Gloucestershire. He has become in effect a king but because of his wounds he cannot function as a king.

SOMERSETTENSIS
Comitatus. Vulgo Somersett shyre
Qui olim pars fuit. BELGARVM.

Flatholms Insul

Steprholm Insul

VSELLA EST

Parlok bay · Mynhead · · E Quantok head · Rullis · Betstall point

Oure · Culber · Parlok · Selwortiey · Dunster · Watchet · Lyttoke · Stokland

Ex more · Lackum · Weston Curtenay · S.t December · Denysford · Kilton · Strenxten · Stokgurcy

Steke pero · Timberccombe · Terhamten · Old Cleve Willyton · W. Quantek heade · Housford · Nettherstowy · Dotlington

Ex Flu: · Ex forde · Cuccombe · Luxbore · Withicombe · Samford · Quantok · Bicknaler · Over stowey

Barle Flu: · Withihill · Leighlande · Nettlecombe · Combe · Tullis · Alphin

Welthpole · Exton · Trebore · M.onkefilver · Stokegomer · Laurandedward · Bagvore · Brumfelde

Wynsford · Bruntton regis · Withihill · Bruntenrafe · Laurandedward · Combeflarye · Cethlafton

Haukeridge · Vpton · Hewifle · Clathworthye · Tollande · Bufshops · Kynsfen

Duluerton · Heddan beacon · Lediard · Naylet

Danfwick Flu: · W. Anfte · Bittescombe · Chipstable · Fyfehcade · Naylet · North

Tuchen · Skilgate · Palington · Witelescombe · Preston · Hethfeld

Molland · E. Anfte · Combe Bushton · Murbath · Stowley · Miluerton · Okie · M. Harrene

Langhrigde · Exbridge · Petton · Baddleton · Nynheade · Hillbufsby

Highly · Difford · Clayhanger · Langford · Raitesford · Bradford · Welington · Trall

Bauton · Punton · W. Buckland · Poumford

PARTE · Ashbrittell · Margaret Churne · Samford

OF · Holcombe rogus · Blak don hill · Amblesley

DEVONSHIRE · Canons lydge · Burlescombe · Chumbstanten

Clay haydon

1 2 3 4 5 6 7 8 9 10

Christophorus Saxton descripsitt. William kip sculp:

Steokland

Previous spread: Figs 19 & 20. Christopher Saxton's map of Somerset, early seventeenth century.

Above: Fig. 21. A Preseli bluestone sculpture of the *Twrch Twryth*, the legendary boar inextricably linked with Arthur and Baetan. The sculpture sits outside the visitor centre in St David's, Pembrokeshire. (© Pembrokeshire Coast National Park Authority)

Left: Fig. 22. The Pictish symbols are about forty in number and their purpose is unknown. They are found mainly in eastern Scotland and are thought to date from the sixth century (the Age of Arthur) to the ninth century. Some have Ogham writing associated with Ireland and others feature Christian symbols. The Pictish symbols depict recognisable birds, fish and animals. The exception is the so-called Pictish Beast or Pictish Swimming Sea-elephant. This animal corresponds in many ways with the *Cath Palug* or *murchata* of Welsh and Irish tradition.

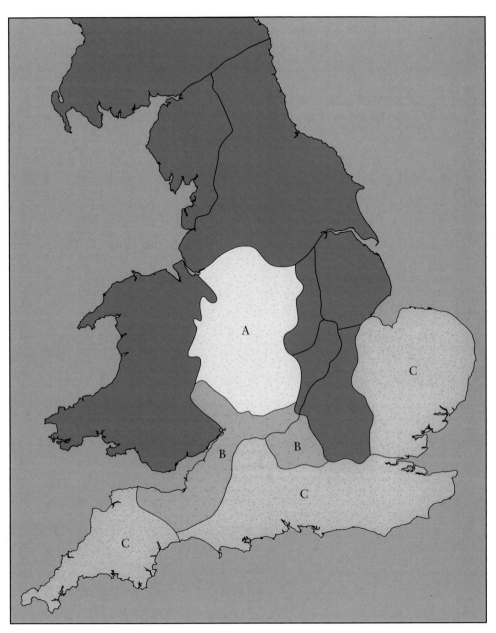

Fig. 23. **The last of 'Arthur's Kingdom'.** About twenty years before the Norman Conquest, it was still possible to discern the old boundaries that had evolved from the sixth-century kingdoms of the warlords like Arthur and the first real kings like Penda. The land of England was divided in to 'earldoms'. There were alliances among the earls built on family connections. The north-east Midlands, formerly Mercia, was held by Leofric (A). Sweyn held what may have been Arthur's kingdom in the south-west Welsh Marches and Somerset (B). Godwine held what had been Gewisse or Wessex (C). His son Harold held what had been East Anglia. At the time of the Norman invasion, the family of Earl Godwine had been placed in charge of about 80 per cent of the kingdom of England.

Fig. 24. '*Morte d'Arthur*' (the death of Arthur), a ceramic tile designed by John Moyr Smith (1839–1912) for Minton, part of a set of twelve designs based on Tennyson's *Idylls of the King*. (Author's collection)

nay more, do not have or are not aware of any semblance of matrimony'. Lives of the saints reveal that, in Welsh and Irish tradition, famous returning warriors of the sixth century, and, to their embarrassment, newly arriving saints like Saint David, were greeted by dancing naked women. Life and morals were different then. Guinevere's behaviour, and that of the men and women of Arthur's court, has to be seen in that context.

Explaining the Glastonbury Grave

The tales we have been examining were the stories of Arthur and Guinevere that were inherited by Saint Dunstan. Dunstan did not have the work of Geofrrey and Chrétien de Troyes before him, because they were then more than a hundred years in the future. There was nothing to mitigate, or redeem, or throw a romantic light over, the stories of the Welsh tradition. He knew nothing of the smiling sunlit world of Camelot, and its handsome knights and lovely ladies. Dunstan faced the unvarnished truth of a sixth-century king who was inclined to rape and murder, thought nothing of killing women, and allowed his wife to consort with any man she liked. Faced with tales of a murderous and capricious king and his much-loved (to say the least) queen, Dunstan, or someone else at Glastonbury, applied the Benedictine standards of the twelfth-century Church to the sixth-century court. Dunstan and his Benedictine monks would allow no occasion, or chance, of contamination. They buried Arthur and Guinevere deep, and away from the place of honour before the altar, with a hidden inscription describing the reason for the decision. 'Here lies a boastful king with his paramour in the pagan paradise.'

That should not be seen as a disappointment, or a slur on a famous king and his lady that we may regret; it is a proof that an Arthur once lived, that fairly accurate stories about him were current three or four hundred years after his death, and that they still had the capacity to move men who heard them. It is a strong indication why he was buried so deep, and it is evidence that the lead cross in the grave may very well be genuine; it says succinctly what people of Dunstan's time thought of Arthur. It may be proof of a sort too that Dunstan, or other people of the time, thought that the bones they were burying were indeed those of Arthur and Guinevere.

The Death of Arthur

We have examined where Arthur was born and how Arthur lived. We should also ask: where and when did he die? Welsh tradition is adamant that he was seriously wounded at the Battle of Camlan, and was carried to his sister Morgan Le Fay[5] for treatment. He did not die on the field at Camlan. The precise place, time and manner of his death are mysteries.

One persuasive possibility is revealed in the far north. Adomnan (AD 624–704), Abbot of Iona, wrote a life of his predecessor in that role, Saint Columba, which includes a story that may be about Arthur. For Adomnan, the most important part, or point, of the story illustrated the ability of Columba to find water for baptism almost anywhere. When water for baptism was required, Columba had the knack of finding, or creating, wells, springs, and even rivers at will. This story began as *dindshencus*, the explanation of place names. In this case the place name to be explained is a river on the Island of Skye called *dobur Artbrani* (the water of Artbran).

Adomnan tells us Columba foretold the arrival, baptism and death of a good old pagan man called Artbranan, and an hour later a little ship arrived bearing just such a passenger. The old man had been a leader of men, the *primarius* of the cohorts of Geon. The saint baptised him. Shortly afterwards he died, and the river was named his honour.

We know from Nennius that Arthur was not always a king. In Welsh tradition mirrored in the TYP, and the lives of the Welsh saints, he is usually called 'Arthur the warrior'. The Welsh word for a warrior was *bran*. In a perfectly straightforward way, 'Arthur the warrior' becomes *Artuirbran* in Welsh. Medial syllables dropped out in the sixth century. *Artuirbran* would, also in a perfectly regular way, result in *Art (uir)bran – Artbran*. The suffix *-an* which occurs in some texts may be a diminutive of affection. *Geon* may be a simple scribal mistake, known from other examples, of 'n' for 'r'. *Geon* is Gower in south Wales, or it may be a mistake for *gawr* (a warrior).

Arturbran in Cornwall

There are more points to consider, and to look at them we have now to return to Cornwall. The earliest place name for Arthur's birth place, Tintagel, as we have seen, is *Trewenna* (first written down as *Trewarverne*). Nearby, there are similar names – St Keverne and

Port Gaverne. The earliest written form of St Keverne is *Sanctus Achebranus*. The great Welsh scholar Sir Ifor Williams noted that round letters, such as 'o', followed by 'r' lead to aspiration of 't' to 'th' and 'c' to 'ch'. We can see examples of that sound change in Cornwall. Cornish historian Charles Thomas has drawn attention to a place name, *Bechiek*, in 1319 which kept changing: *Brethiel* 1336, *Brethyoke* 1389, *Brechiek* 1390. *Achebran* could therefore change to *Athebran*, and scribally the letter 'o' or 'a' could attract and absorb the letter 'r' in written forms. *Achebran* can thus be easily be derived from *Arth(ur)-bran* (Arthur the warrior).

Tintagel (Trewenna), St Keverne and Port Gaverne, it appears, are all place names recording the name of Arthur in the form we see in the Columba story. The place names give us a location (*Tre* means place), a port, and a holy site associated with Arthur. It is a connection not previously remarked upon. That unexpected link gives credibility to Arthur as a genuinely historic person, to the place of his education in Cornwall, and to the story of his death.

Another early poetic record offers a kind of confirmation. It is called *Berchan's Prophecy*, and purports to date from AD 574. The Berchan of the title was an Irish abbot who was regarded as one of the leading four saints, prophets, and poets of Ireland (the others being Patrick, Columba and *Mo-ling*). Who he was and when he lived is not known, but Patrick and Columba are both sixth-century figures or, in the case of Patrick, possibly somewhat earlier. *Mo-ling* of Ferns is a seventh-century figure. The real Berchan, if there ever was one individual, is likely to have been not much later than *Mo-ling* and could have been much earlier. The text of the poem was clearly written by at least two authors a long time after any real Berchan. It is in Middle Irish which term refers to the Irish language as it was from about AD 900 to 1200. For ease of reference, we will refer to the poem as 'Berchan' as if someone of that name had indeed written it.

Berchan's poem is meant to be a prophecy made in the sixth century about Irish and Scottish kings and the events of their reigns. Since it was actually written between AD 900 and 1000, Berchan was able to solve the problems inherent in political forecasting by writing his prophecies after the event, which tends to lead to 100 per cent accuracy in predicting outcomes. His basic idea was to establish his accuracy about past events, and project that reputation onto predictions about the real future. He covered himself in both directions by wilful obscurity which makes him difficult to use, or even to understand. He is, however, a witness of some value because his essential purpose demanded that the reader was able to confirm, from his own knowledge or from other books, that what Berchan said about the early strands of his prophecy was true and accurate. The belief in, and the effectiveness of, Berchan's prophecy for events genuinely yet to come depended on the truth of what he had said about things that had already happened. For us, that means what he says may be a statement about Arthur likely to be independent of both Geoffrey of Monmouth, and, possibly, of the Welsh tradition. It was the truth about Arthur as people in the time covered by Berchan (AD 900–1000) commonly believed it.

Berchan tells us (verse 118 *et seq.*): 'He is the first man who will arise in the East, a dart will glance from the shield's edge, with whom will be wanderers, his grey men, a rider of the swift boat which will seek Ireland in one day. Thirteen years (one after another) he will fight against the Pictish host. He will not be king at the time of his death, on a Thursday in Kintyre.'

Here we can see glimpses of familiar information. The first man (*primarius*) in the east (*Airthir*), a complicated pun in Gaelic on '*do bhile sceith*' and '*do bhile scaith*' about the shore of Skye and the edge of shields, a campaign of twelve or thirteen successive battles, grey men (monks?), and the fact that he is not a ruling king at the time of his death in Kintyre. It looks like a reference to Arthur, and may confirm the Columba death story. We can disregard the Picts (although some of them were part of tribal federations in northern Ireland); they were perhaps the only people the Berchan authors knew that anyone might want to fight on a long-term basis. In any case, they may not be Picts at all. The term used is *chruidthnechaibh*, and Irish *Cruithne* is merely a version of Early British *Pretannia* and Middle Welsh *Prydein*.[6] In the sixth century, it is the name of the whole island of Britain, not the meaning of the limited areas of modern Scotland it later acquired. On one hand, this may be a reference to Arthur's long campaign in England, perhaps on this evidence battles fought *against* Romanised Britons (*chruidthnechaibh*) and Saxon auxiliaries. On the other hand, it may simply illustrate that an author contributing to '*Berchan's Prophecy*' knew the account given in Nennius, and repeated that story with the additional anecdote, which his readers might know to be true, about a famous king and warrior, who was no longer a ruler, dying in Kintyre.[7]

There is one crucial detail in the Skye *Artbranan* death story related by Adomnan, which contains within it a matter we may be able to confirm. Columba, who spoke Irish, Latin, Welsh (Brittonic) and some Pictish, had to explain the Gospel to the old Pagan man through an interpreter, and that drives us back to the body in the Glastonbury grave. If we make the assumption – and, as we have acknowledged earlier, for some people it will be too large an assumption – that the tall man in the Glastonbury grave was Arthur, we can say some accurate modern things about him which appear to be borne out by the *romans*, the legends, and the accounts like Berchan that are difficult to use. We may be able to discern the 'true Arthur'.

Arthur the Idle King – a Diagnosis

We no longer have the bones of 'Arthur of Glastonbury' – they were lost during the Dissolution of the Monasteries – but we can make some useful guesses based on the reports of Gerald of Wales and others. According to Gerald, the monks who exhumed him noted the massive head and the injuries it had suffered in life. The injuries reported to Arthur's head will have had consequences for him and his court, and modern medical research can clarify what they may have been.

Studies show that the incidence of 'right-handedness' in mankind throughout history has been about 90 per cent. Studies of right-handed people today show that around three-quarters of them are 'strongly right-handed'. We have no reason to think that this incidence has changed over the centuries. About 80 per cent of warriors armed with sword, battleaxe or other weapon in the sixth century would have strongly preferred to use their right arm to strike in conflict. That means that a head wound caused by a blow struck in battle between two warriors facing each other is likely to have caused damage to the left-side front of the head. Such a blow will damage the frontal lobes of the brain, perhaps specifically the left-front area of the brain (Broca's area). Damage in this area causes a condition called 'Broca's aphasia' – patients with that condition can understand what is said to them, but cannot articulate a reply. Only their immediate family knows what they want to say. In other words, they need a translator – as the old man in Skye did.

There are other consequences of repeated head trauma. Movement can become impaired, and control of the emotions can be lost. Brain-damaged patients can become unreasonably jealous, or violent and lacking in restraint in social behaviour. They may initiate inappropriate behaviour, or fail to inhibit it. They can develop a high risk of making sexual assaults. At other times, and, as their condition progresses, they can become withdrawn and neglectful of themselves and others. They can seem impassive, uncaring about the life of those around them. They become like the Arthur in both the sixth-century accounts and in the stories and romances after Geoffrey of Monmouth. They become violent and rapacious, and then, later, become inactive and uninvolved socially. If the wounds to his head have been correctly reported, there is, and can be, no doubt; Arthur must have spent the last years of his life as either a shambling, mumbling, incoherent, withdrawn shadow of himself, or as a violent, unpredictable, dangerous, possibly obsessional man, a potential threat to all who came into contact with him. He may have been both at different times.

The evidence of the Welsh traditions and the romances that we have been looking at both seem to suggest that this is exactly what happened to King Arthur. His ravaging was unrestrained, and he went around killing women, and perhaps even his own son. Then he withdrew into himself, and did not notice when men fought duels over Guinevere. At the end, he could not tell Saint Columba that he had been a Christian hero at Badon, and was baptised as a 'good old pagan'.

The Strange Sixth Century
There are two last points to make before we leave our attempt at Arthur's biography. First, we have found, in looking at the life of Arthur, that careful use of sources, even the romantic stories, employing only incidental details, can reveal something like history, although of course nothing is proved. Secondly, we have been often reminded by what we have found that we are dealing with the sixth century, and it was a very different place, not only from our time but also from the time of people like Saint Dunstan. It is certainly different from the imagined world

of Camelot. The social customs of that time occasionally surprise, and sometimes shock us. There is one more sinister example of that to think about before we focus again on Badon and other battles. We need to look at Guinevere.

Guinevere

Guinevere was not the mother of Arthur's children – his sons were grown-up men, warriors in battles when she was around, and we know nothing at all about the names and lives of their mother, or mothers. We have seen stories of Guinevere's life and her lovers, and we may now be able to say something about her death.

The monks who excavated the grave at Glastonbury found that her golden hair was still intact when they opened the coffin, and that means she was young when she died (perhaps no more than thirty). Arthur, on the other hand, was old (perhaps sixty-five or seventy) when he died at the feet of Columba, Abbot of Iona, in Kintyre, a long way from Glastonbury, about AD 564 or shortly thereafter. He was initially buried by his friends under a cairn of stones, but the cairn site in Skye was controlled by Iona. From about AD 570, the *familia* of Iona seems to have controlled Glastonbury too.

It was a persisting link. Indract, Abbot of Iona, was buried at Glastonbury, and Saint Patrick, whose remains in Ireland came under Iona control not later than AD 575, and possibly a decade earlier, may have been reburied there.[8] The monks of Iona may have developed theories about the history of Glastonbury that made them think it a place of unusual holiness and sanctity, and make them wish to have some closer relationship with the place, while retaining for their monastery the leadership of the *familia* (the loose federation of churches and monasteries headed by the Abbot of Iona). The *familia* of Iona may have decided to build a new church, or enhance something already existing at Glastonbury, perhaps not very long after Arthur died. They may have discovered who *Arturbran* was by then. It is possible that they exhumed Arthur's body, and carried it to Glastonbury for reburial between two high crosses to confer local political or spiritual prestige upon the new venture. When their abbot Indract was killed by Saxons during a pastoral visit, Iona elected to bury him at Glastonbury rather than bring him back to Iona. That was a big decision. Monasteries and abbeys then drew spiritual power from the bodies and possessions of notable leaders, the men and women whom we might now call saints. Such advantage would not be lightly surrendered. As we have seen, they also may have repatriated the remains of Saint Patrick, returning him to his native region[9] to add sanctity to their new building.

Iona had a custom which it followed in making new buildings. When Columba arrived there in 564, and wanted to build his monastery, he demanded and got a human sacrifice. The monk *Odran* volunteered. He died or was killed, and was buried somewhere in the foundations. That may have been Guinevere's fate. The real Guinevere possibly ended her life as a victim of an old pagan custom practiced by Christians. We know that she died when she was young because her hair was not yet grey. We know she was placed in a joint coffin made of a hollowed-out oak tree [10] with Arthur, who died when he was old. She may have been killed and placed beside the bones of Arthur to interpret for him wherever he had gone, and to sanctify the new structure.

That is, but should not be seen as, shocking. It may even be what we should expect. Christianity then was a very thin cloak on the pagan ground. We should not forget that druids continued in Ireland well into the eighth century. Life then was not at all like the romances where Guinevere was the glamorous queen of golden Camelot. Her fate as a sacrifice is another message of the excavated grave of Arthur to set beside the metal cross and its strange inscription.

Arthur's Kingdom

We may now have some faint outlines of the figure of the 'real' Arthur, but we still have to find out how Arthur became a king, and what were the consequences for the people he ruled if he did indeed become a brain-damaged, withdrawn monarch. We have to turn now to the consideration of another sixth-century king to tell us how Arthur found a throne. We may also find out how Badon got its name.

CONCLUSIONS

1. Arthur was educated in Cornwall and has associations with the Tintagel area.
2. He was a well-known, but not always successful, warrior and may have become a king.

3. He could not apparently rule effectively because of his wounds.
4. He may have died on Skye and was not then regarded as a king, holding only at that time the title of Primarius (First Man) of Gower.
5. Guinevere may have been buried beside him as a sacrifice.
6. The evidence points to a pagan Arthur who, if the Berchan reference is valid, fought *against* the Britons, or at least some of them.

THE MAN WHO WAS BADON

The Background – the Figure of Melwys

To pursue our quest for Arthur and his acquisition of a kingdom, we need to look again at the king of the Summer Country, the putative lover of Guinevere and the man with many versions of his name: *Melgwas, Melga, Melvas, Maelgwas, Maelwys, Maelyf, Maelluf, Maeluma, Maheloas, Meleagant* and *Mellygraunce*. There is little doubt that all the names refer to the same person (whom we shall call Melwys to avoid confusion), and that this person had many links with King Arthur. Geoffrey of Monmouth tells us this man Melwys was 'king of the Picts'. A seventeenth-century Welsh poem, which contains much older material, hailed him as 'a Prince of Alban' (the whole British mainland). To Chrétien de Troyes in *Lancelot* he was *Meleagant*, the Lord of Goire (Gower), and in another poem, *Erec and Enide*, Chrétien names him as *Maheloas*, the Lord of 'the Isle of Glass' which William of Malmesbury identified as Glastonbury.

Thomas Malory, the knight who wrote *Morte D'Arthur*, is the only person who places him outside the West Country. For Malory, he was *Mellygruance*, who lived in or near London. Malory was mistaken; his man was not a different person, and he didn't inhabit a different locale. Malory only knew that Melwys (*Mellygruance*) had seized Guinevere as she went 'a-maying near Westminster', and he had then carried her off to his castle some 7 miles away. Malory had never heard of West Minster at Westbury-on-Trym, founded as a monastery at least as early as AD 716. (Its religious foundation transferred to Ramsey in Huntingdonshire about AD 974. A college persisted there until late medieval times.) In ignorance of an alternative West Minster, Malory imposed a three- or four-day horseback journey, in excess of a hundred miles, on the fleeing *Mellygraunce* and his captive if they were to reach the Summer Country (Somerset) where *Mellygraunce* was supposed to rule.

There is no need to locate *Mellygraunce* in, or near, London. In fact, Glastonbury is not quite seven *leagues* (27 miles) from Westbury-on-Trym. The fact that Malory made the mistake shows that, at one time, there was a common source for the story of Guinevere's abduction which Malory and Chrétien de Troyes and others all used as the basis of their *romans*. That source is lost beyond retrieval, but the common ground in all the stories permits us to make a clear identification. Malory's *Mellygraunce* is the same man we meet in the other stories; he is the king of the Summer Country and his castle, if he had one, was at Glastonbury. He would have been on his own land with his captive once he had used the ford under the hill forts at Clifton, or swum his horse across the River Avon. He may not have had to reach Glastonbury. Melwys may have had some sort of home, or even a 'castle' (whatever that may have been in the sixth century), only about 3 miles from Westbury, near modern Bedminster in Bristol.[1]

We have no reason to disagree with the great Welsh scholar Sir John Rhys, who said Melwys was a Scot (an Irishman)[2] or a Goidel (a raider) who ruled for a period at, or near, Glastonbury. He may very well have had other territories, such as Gower, and a kingdom in a Pictish region of Scotland or Ireland. It does not matter a great deal. What matters for us is the name of his father.

Bademagu

According to Malory, the father of Melwys is one *Bagdemadus*. This man is strongly linked with people in Arthur's circle in the romances. For example, when the Lady of the Lake puts a spell on Merlin and confines him under a stone, it is *Bagdemadus* who tries to release him. He is also associated with Lancelot. Lancelot, although he has a quarrel with Melwys and may even have killed him, is recruited by the daughter of *Bagdemadus* to fight against the troops of the king of North Wales. The sister of Melwys was obviously a persuasive woman, and her father must have been an impressive man.

Chrétien uses substantially the same story. His Melwys (called *Meleagant* on this occasion) is the son of King *Bademagu* and he is king of Gorre (Gower). In Chrétien's story, *Bademagu* is even more impressive. Although Lancelot has come to attack his son, *Bademagu* binds up his wounds, sustained crossing the 'Sword Bridge' before *Bademagu's* castle. *Bademagu* offers him safe conduct and a warm welcome. His reproofs to his own son Melwys are couched in terms of honour and good sense. His treatment of the kidnapped Guinevere is marked by the same good sense and propriety.

Bademagu's family and retinue also behave well. Knights who throng his court are treated with great respect, and give it in return. When the kidnapped Guinevere takes her leave, she has been so won over by her stay that she pledges her service (and that of her Lord, Arthur) to *Bademagu*.

Descriptions of *Bademagu's* castle in Chrétien reveals that it is a well-protected place. It is guarded by a bridge of unusual construction which runs under the water of an occasionally torrential river. In the real world, it can only have been a fortified ford of some kind. *Bademagu's* fortress is also approached by a narrow stony passage that leads to a 'Sword Bridge'. According to Chrétien, it is so narrow and sharp that Lancelot is wounded crossing it. We, however, may choose to think that Chrétien has not fully understood, or had imperfect sources about, the bridge. It may be the 'sword bridge' famously formed by the dead soldiers of Osla Big Knife. Other topographical details suggest that, in the real world of the sixth century, and leaving aside any talk of pavilions, palaces and castles, *Bademagu* occupies a substantial hill fort by a gorge, perhaps even the hill forts of Clifton. The topography fits quite well.

Baetan

Welsh tradition enables us to identify him. In the Welsh story *Culhwch ac Olwen*, Melwys appears as Maelwys, son of Baeddan. Many years ago, the great Welsh scholar Sir John Rhys spotted that this man must be the same man as *Bademagu* and *Bagdemadus*. The name *Bademagu*, Rhys said, should be read taking scribal methods into account. In Old Irish script the letter 'u' was sometimes a scribal error for a double 'L'. The letter 'g' in the king's name was really a 'q' with a stroke through its limb, and a small letter 'I' placed above the 'q'. It was scribal shorthand for *air*. Rhys was confident that *Bademagu* was the written form of the name of a known and important Irish king, Baetan Mac Cairill.

Baetan Mac Cairill was king of the Northern Irish *Dal Fiatach*, who were the dominant kin group among the *Ulidians* (the Men of Ulster) which comprised the *Dal Fiatach*, the *Dal Riata* and the *Dal nAriade* (who may have been Pictish and Melwys may have been their king). The original tribal homeland of the *Dal Fiatach* was around Armagh, but they lost that to another federation of tribes called the *Airgialla* (the Oriel), among whom the *Airthir* were a prominent group. The *Airthir* (Eastern) were so called because they formed the eastern part of the Oriel, and their territory may have extended around both sides of the southern half of Lough Neagh, and up to areas close to the modern city of Belfast. During the sixth century, perhaps about mid-century, the Oriel, who had previously paid tribute to the *Dal Fiatach*, switched their allegiance to the Ui Nialls (O'Neills) who held north-western Ulster. The Ulidians had a capital at *Dunlethetglas* (at or near modern Downpatrick) and, using their powerful fleets, they compensated themselves for any northern Irish losses they may have had by becoming the dominant power in the lands around the Irish Sea, the 'Irish Sea Province'.

This conquest of the Irish Sea Province made Baetan a very important monarch with many other kings subservient to him. Even the Ui Nialls were prepared to admit that Baetan was, or had been, high-king of Ireland (he and the great leader of Ireland against the Vikings, Brian Boruma, were the only two rulers who were not of the Ui Nialls whose names appear in the lists of the Irish high-kings compiled by Ui Niall historians).

Elsewhere, Baetan is hailed as king of Ireland and Britain (*ri Erenn ac Alban*). *The Book of Lecan* says that Baetan received tribute from Munster, Connacht, Skye and the Isle of Man. He received hostages from the powerful king of Northern England and part of Scotland, Aedan MacGabran. He is said to have cleared the plain of *Manau* (the land skirting the Firth of Forth) of Angles, and to have contended – apparently successfully – with them for the city of *Iudeu* (modern Edinburgh).

An 'empire' of these dimensions is confirmed archaeologically by the distribution of pottery and other trade goods of Mediterranean origin around the Irish Sea Province (see Fig. 10

in plates). In the difficult and politically chaotic sixth century, some power must have provided the security to make that trading relationship possible. Baetan's is the only name to appear in that role in the records that we have. Berchan tells us, 'After that a king from the north takes the sovereignty. He will be high-king of Ireland, not a tawny boastful one. By him will every tribe be drained. He will be king of Alban in the east, a king who wins three battles in the east, three fatalities in Alban. By him are collected into his presence the relics of the saints of Ireland. He will rule strongly for twenty-five years and die of disease in his stronghold at Larne.' Apart from his military triumphs, Baetan was clearly a Christian monarch.[3]

Baetan's sons were active in his wars. *Fiachna Lurgan* 'obtained authority over Alban', and made expeditions to *Dun Guaire* and *Ratho Guali*.[4] *Ratho Guali* remains to be identified, but the great Welsh scholar Rachel Bromwich thought *Dun Guaire* might be *Inys Wair* which, she believed, was either Lundy Island or the Isle of Wight. There is some evidence that it was the Isle of Wight. A now-lost Irish poem about *Fiachna* says *Dun Guaire* was in England (*saxonnaibh*). Lundy may have been seen at the time as Welsh, Cornish, or attached in some political way to a 'kingdom of Somerset'.

Baetan in Hampshire?

There is some further information which offers a degree of confirmation. Bede and the *Anglo-Saxon Chronicle* (which seems to be based only on Bede for this information) assert that the 'Jutes and Saxons' came into southern Hampshire and the Isle of Wight in the first two decades of the sixth century led by Stuf, Wihtgar and Port. Port's sons, Bieda and Maegla, were also active in the invasion. Beyond the gossip from Bishop Daniel of Winchester to Bede (on which Bede's own account is based), there has never been any evidence from archaeology, or anywhere else, to suggest a Jutish presence in Hampshire and the names of the supposed conquerors of the area do not make sense. Most scholars who have looked at this problem believe that these names derive from a Roman harbour (port, that is *Portum Arduni*)[5] and the name of the people of Wight (*wihtgar*).[6] Only Stuf appears to be a genuine personal, and possibly Saxon, name. The evidence in the *Anglo-Saxon Chronicle* about an 'Anglo-Saxon and Jutish conquest' of Hampshire appears to be no more than Stuf and nonsense.

There is one significant and additional point in the *Chronicle* account. It mentions three names of men who are not Jutes or Saxons. Cerdic is known in Welsh records as *Caradawg Strong-Arm* and 'Bieda and Maegla' are likely to be Baetan and his son Melwys. That may lead us to look again at *Port*. It may be not the Roman port but Welsh word *Porth* which means 'help or assistance'. Rachel Bromwich notes that it is used in Welsh contexts to mean 'an army of assistance'.[7] That in itself poses a problem of interpretation. We can see 'an army of assistance' as either as 'a mercenary army' paid to assist, or 'an auxiliary army' called in to help some existing force. Either way, we can reasonably conclude that it places Baetan and his son Melwys in charge of an army in southern Hampshire, the same army which, Bishop Daniel and the *Chronicle* authors thought, made a successful conquest of the whole region. The *Chronicle* story may be an independent account of the twelves battles of Nennius, which we have speculated took place in this part of England.

The possibility of a hosting active in Hampshire, drawn from the widespread domains of Baetan in the 'Irish Sea Province' and modern Scotland, may enable us to throw some light on the Jutes Bede and Bishop Daniel believed were a part of that enterprise. The only evidence of a Jutish presence archaeologically in the South Hampshire area is a possible change in some pottery styles. Even that is controversial, and remains to be securely linked with precisely identified Jutish material. As matters stand, it is only evidence that pottery styles varied.

Bede's 'Jutes' may more plausibly be troops from Edinburgh – men from the 'city of Iudeu' could readily be transformed, by the 'd' and 't' sound change we have mentioned elsewhere, from 'Judeans' into 'Juteans' or 'Jutes'.[8] If that is what lies behind Bede and the *Anglo-Saxon Chronicle* accounts, Baetan's power in England extended to (or possibly extended from) the Hampshire coast. It may also have reached to the mid-Thames at Silchester near Reading, and to Uttoxeter on the River Dove, close to watershed between rivers that flow to the Irish Sea and those who find their way to the North Sea. In both locations, Irish *ogham* memorial stones have been found. Ogham stones were boundary markers. The Irish buried their dead on their borders. Anyone who crossed the graves was in effect 'crossing a Rubicon'. It was an act seen as a declaration of war.

The regions apparently delineated by novel borders, marked by ogham stones, were not some new conjectural Irish claim on the land; they are a marker for an area traditionally raided by the peoples of the Irish Sea. The areas identified were within, and in some cases followed, the older borders of the Roman provinces of Britain. The Scotti (the Irish) and the Picts had long raided western Britain, even in the time of the Romans, carrying off booty or tribute in Roman silver.[9] In the 360s they had erupted into a major insurgency called by the Romans the 'Barbarian Conspiracy', which the Romans, with some difficulty, managed to contain.

The peoples from the areas involved then were still around at the beginning of the sixth century, and raiding Britain from time to time was part of their economy. Like the Saxons to the east and north of England, they could see opportunities, and some of them may have been invited by the Britons as 'protectors' (as we see in the title on the Votepor memorial). The territorial claims, and indeed the wars, of the Irish and the Judeans (who are in Welsh tradition named as 'the Men of the North') should be seen, like the 'invasion of the Saxons', in the context of indigenous leaders and rival warrior elites claiming territory in areas where both Roman domination and Roman protection were no longer available to the resident population. For Baetan MacCairill, they were a campaign to extend the trading area of the Irish Sea Province, and to increase the number of leaders and peoples forced to pay tribute to him.

Baetan's 'Empire'

The territories around the Irish Sea that already paid tribute to Baetan were extensive. *The Book of Lecan* notes, 'There are many score miles between *Dun Baetan* and *Lethet*; long land, wide sea are to the West between us and *Imlech Ibair.*' *Imlech Ibair* is modern Emly in Tipperary where there was a major monastery, and *Lethet* is modern Downpatrick, which was Baetan's capital. *Dun Baetan* is not currently securely located by scholars but appears to have been in Britain.

Dun Baetan

The name *Dun Baetan* is worth looking at more closely. *Dun* is a fort, but because forts were on hills, and in Ireland on headlands (promontory forts) jutting into the sea, it was often translated as 'head' (*Pen* in Welsh, *Ken* in Irish), or by the Latin term *Mons* (which can be a hill or a mountain). We have already seen a battle at *Biedanheafod*, and we know that the 't' in Irish regularly changes to 'd' in English and Welsh contexts). Biedan and Baetan seem to be the same word. *Biedanheafod* uses the Saxon word for 'head' *(heafod)* possibly to translate *Mons, Pen, Ken or Dun*. It may mean, or be, *Dun Baetan*.

There is some further information worth our consideration. In *Domesday Book*, which surveyed all of England, we find that the name for the manor based at Westbury-on-Trym and including Clifton and its 'camps' was *Sineshoved* (in modern English *Swinehead*). Baetan's personal name translates from Irish as 'boar'. *Dun Baetan*, *Sineshoved*, *Biedanheafod* and the Latin *Mons Badonis* mentioned by our sole contemporary witness Gildas are apparently all the same place. *Biedanford*, mentioned in the *Anglo-Saxon Chronicle*, may also refer to the same place. We can perhaps now ignore the various candidate sites involving Bade + a hill fort, and the assertions about the city of Bath as a site for the Battle of Badon.[10] We can now say, with reasonable confidence, that we know the personal name involved. Baetan MacCairill is the man who gave his name to the Battle of Badon. It was an encounter at *Dun Baetan*.

The Battle of Badon
That fact tells us quite a lot about the Battle of Badon. We can confirm, with some certainty, that it was likely to have been a 'Christian' victory. Baetan was a Christian, a 'collector of relics of the saints'. We can also see that Badon was likely to have involved considerable forces. Baetan had the capacity to call to his hostings men from all around the Irish Sea Province, Scotland (*Manau*) and substantial parts of western and southern England, and south Wales. The many assembling war bands described in *The Dream of Rhonabwy* may be rooted in fact.

Baetan may have called them all from their various kingdoms and territories, and he may have been actively trying to unify them into one force, a sort of 'grand army' of the kind we see some centuries later with Scandinavian *micel here*, a force that could undertake the conquest of all, or most of, England. Gildas, in writing his sermon, may have been acting in Baetan's interests by regretting the civil wars after the Battle of Badon, and urging, on pain of divine wrath, the kings and chieftains of Britain towards co-operation. If Gildas was Baetan's abbot, he was assured of protection from the murderous kings he courageously condemned. If Baetan succeeded in welding them together, the Christian faith Gildas believed in would be promoted throughout the whole Irish Sea Province, and, perhaps, throughout all Britain. If he could persuade the warband commanders to some kind of brokered peace and collaboration under Baetan, Gildas could win countless souls for Christ. There was a strong reason for Baetan and Gildas to work together.

Arthur the *Dux Bellorum*

And what of Arthur? Although Welsh tradition is – *The Dream of Rhonabwy* aside – almost silent about his association with the Battle of Badon, Arthur appears, in the sources we have been looking at, to have been Baetan's *cathmilid*, *toisech*, *dux bellorum* or battle commander in the battles listed by Nennius and at the Battle of Badon. Baetan, as a powerful over-king, could have compelled other kings to serve under Arthur's command. A position as Baetan's commander would have made Arthur possibly the most powerful soldier of his day, a man deserving proper remembrance in authentic history, as William of Malmesbury said, rather than in the fables William had found, and regretted, at Glastonbury. Arthur's success and the plunder he had won, or was entitled to, should have made him one of the richest men of his time too. Badon was a convincing victory, and the whole former Roman civil province of Britannia Prima lay open before him after the victory there. Yet, after Badon, Arthur had still not become a king. Why did that not happen? Why did Baetan not reward his general with a kingdom?

CONCLUSIONS

1. The man who gave his name to the Battle of Badon was Baetan MacCairill, king of the Dal Fiatach, leader of the Ulidians, and an over-king who dominated the Irish Sea Province.
2. Baetan could command men for his hostings from many kingdoms and territories.
3. Baetan had the power to appoint Arthur as his *dux bellorum* and to make kings serve under him.
4. Baetan had an army in southern Hampshire, and it may be this force that carried out the twelve battles of Arthur's English campaign.
5. Baetan did not make Arthur a king.

THE WELSH CAMPAIGN: THE REBELLION OF ARTHUR

Fake News in the Sixth Century

Baetan MacCairill was a king well served by poets. When, after his death, his Irish, Scottish and northern English kingly rivals met at the Convention of Drumcett (near modern Limavady), they talked about the attention he and the Ulidians had received from poets and bards, and about the 'lying fables' the poets had constructed about him. They considered a proposal to banish the bards from Ireland to prevent the transmission of what they saw (but did not use the words) as 'Ulidian Fake News'. It was one of the first recorded collisions between politicians and the news media, and it ended in an uneasy compromise. The bards could stay, but they must not include Baetan in their repertoire of heroic tales.

In the end, the attempt to impose a total silence about Baetan did not fully succeed. The building of his reputation turned out to be wider, and more long-lasting, than the work of the Irish bards who sang, or didn't sing, his praises under threat of banishment. As we have seen, in the twelfth century, when the achievements of other Irish monarchs had faded into the mists of time, Baetan was still presented attractively in the romances and early histories. Geoffrey of Monmouth, for example, identified him as Sir Bawdeweyn of Bretayn, one of the leading knights of Uther Pendragon. In Chrétien de Troyes and Thomas Malory, he is a wise and tolerant ruler who honours and respects the knights who come to his court. He is every inch a king, and a model for princes to follow, more or less the reputation that was later to be assimilated into King Arthur himself.

The Duties of King and Commander

In the sixth century, Baetan was a powerful king, and Arthur was only his 'battle commander', *dux bellorum*. In Irish society, the Latin *dux bellorum* may be translated as *toisech* which denoted the head of a tribe (*cenel*) in his capacity as the leader of the warband of that kin, who could be deputed by an over-king to lead wider forces in battle. There were important and necessary roles for the over-king in association with this kind of subordinate. It was a legal agreement. The over-king could not reject (*etech n-aire*) or repel (*essain*) his vassal. He had to make the payments due to his underling (*rath*). The under-king or commander, for his part, had to give hostages who would pay with their lives if he broke faith. Trust, and guarding against possible betrayal, were at the heart of the relationship. If the over-king broke his agreement, the under-king could offer his service to another over-king, and the result would be war. He could, of course, also betray his over-king, and assert his independence.

The Ungenerous Monarch

There is some indication that Baetan may have invited this kind of betrayal and disloyalty by failing to perform his part of the bargain. Unlike the literary creation *Bademagu*, the real Baetan was not, it seems, a generous monarch. He may well have denied Arthur and others their share of the spoils of Badon, the payment or *rath* due to them. *The Book of Lecan* records complaints against him:

> Although I have come from fair Ruath Cruachan with my tributes, my face is long after dinner in the castle of Baetan, Cairill's son.
>
> Although I have come from Skye. I have come twice and three times guarding jewels that have changed their colour, the Scot is very cold.
>
> Fifty, sixty are under the water between Man and Ireland; nine have gone to heaven, dreadful is their pilgrimage.
>
> Though I have come from the mountains of the Alps (probably *Alban*, Britain) I saw many hardships. I gave much silver and gold, without receiving honour.

Baetan appears to have demanded tribute which involved hazardous voyages, or very long journeys by those pledged to serve him, but failed to share the plunder brought before him as custom and law demanded. We have earlier seen that Arthur, the real Arthur, not the literary creation, could not tolerate satirical verses that slighted him. He would allow no talisman or power before him; everything good had to come from him. He was not a man to be insulted, diminished or disregarded without reacting violently. Faced with Baetan's coldness, it seems that is exactly what he did. He betrayed his trust, and he became the 'rebellious king' Caradoc of Llancarfan mentions in a life of Gildas. Using the pretext of an invitation to assist an Irish province, probably Munster, he assembled his warbands from many parts of Britain, Normandy, and Brittany, and attacked Baetan's homeland, Ireland. That attack, and the response that it invited, turned into a war fought right across south Wales and western England.

The Boar War

We know more or less what happened because an account of the campaign occurs in a yarn about pigs in the *Mabinogion*. The tale of *Culhwch ac Olwen* offers us a story about a famous boar called *Twrch Trwyth*. Both *Twrch* and *Trwyeth* mean 'boar' and *Trwyth* is linked to the Irish word *Triath* which is also a boar. But *triath* has another very specific meaning in Irish. It means 'king of a Fifth', one of the great historic divisions of Ireland.[1] Any king who merited the title of *triath* was, if not a high-king (the term wasn't used then), certainly a very important ruler. A prominent king of this kind, who was also called 'boar', can only be Baetan.

Baetan's son Melwys bears a name that may mean 'pig',[2] and 'Pig, son of Boar' is just the sort of name Welsh poetry delighted in. We are told that *Twrch* himself was the son of *Taredd Wledig* which means the ruler (*wledig*) of Tara (*Taredd*), which was emerging then as an important royal site, and later became the seat of the Irish high-kings. There can be very little doubt that the tale of *Twrch Trwyth* is a story about Baetan; the *Mabinogion* offers us a plausible account of Arthur's war of independence against his Ulidian master.[3]

The War of Independence

The story begins with Baetan dealing with some sort of rebellion or failure to pay tribute in one of his domains. There may have been a religious or doctrinal element in the conflict. When Arthur arrived, the clergy there begged for his protection, which suggests that this is Munster, where Church leaders had already begun to follow Roman practices much earlier than in other parts of Irish Christianity. Arthur apparently intervened, and, after several days of fighting, suggested mediation to settle the matter. This was a sensible, and not unprecedented, move. We know Gildas, for example, had avoided wars, notably at Glastonbury, by bringing the parties in the conflict together. On this occasion, *Grugyn*, a son of Baetan and in command of the army, sent back a scornful message of defiance. Meanwhile, Baetan himself set out for Britain to take advantage of Arthur's absence by launching some sort of punitive expedition.

He landed at Porth Clais on the headlands that form the most westerly point of modern Pembrokeshire. It is a small place today, but it boasts a pier that may be Roman. It may have been a major port in the sixth century, big enough to allow Baetan to disembark a sizeable force. His army having landed, Baetan moved south, and defeated a defensive force near Milford Haven. His aim may have been to deny Arthur any ports if he returned from Ireland. When Arthur heard what had happened, he did indeed come hurrying back. The returning Arthur landed at St David's, and found that Baetan, possibly having heard of his return, had passed him, moving north. Arthur showed his strategic grasp: he cut off Baetan's route back to his ships, and began driving him eastwards.

Baetan moved to *Preseleu* (modern Preseli), a small range of mountains in modern north Pembrokeshire. There was apparently a skirmishing campaign along the ancient ridge path now known as the '*Golden Road*', which for thousands of years had been the traditional route used by travellers to and from Ireland. Arthur's men maintained the pursuit. Baetan turned and fought a battle on the River Nevern, which flows into the sea at Newport. Although Arthur lost several of his leading warriors, and the battle was indecisive, he succeeded in his strategic objective of driving Baetan away from the coast.

The next encounter was at *Cwm Cerwyn*, still in the Preseli mountains, near some ancient settlements marked by cairns which still are present on the scene. There, turning at bay, Baetan again killed some of his leading opponents, but without actually gaining a decisive result. Baetan was wounded in this battle, and began to move south away from the mountains.

Arthur himself caught up with Baetan at *Peluniawg* between the mountains and coastal Laugharne, but after a struggle lost him again. Baetan advanced to the mouth of the River Tawy, where again he stood at bay to stop his pursuers. Again, Arthur lost leading men but Baetan was forced further eastward, and Arthur's forces lost touch with him around *Glyn Ystun* which is thought to be at the junction of the Amman and Loughor Rivers. Baetan was still moving eastwards, and was caught again by another Arthurian force in the Amman valley, north-west of modern Swansea, possibly at Ammanford. There several of his sons fell in the battle, and Arthur's army too lost more leaders. Again, neither side could achieve mastery.

Arthur's own troops caught up with Baetan's forces again at *Llwch Ewin* (Lake Ewin) where, in later years, there was a castle (*Castell Luchewein*) which may have been the strong point disputed. The chase then moved to the River Tywi. At this point Baetan divided his forces, presumably to confuse the pursuit, or to attempt to place a strong force behind the army of Arthur. *Grugyn*, the commander of the second group, led it northwards to a stronghold called *Din Tywi* in Ceredigion where he became surrounded. After a bloody battle in which many men on both sides died, *Grugyn* himself was slain. His entire force lay dead with him.

Baetan, unaware of their fate, again split his forces. Another of his war bands went rapidly towards the east, and may have reached what is now the English border before they were caught by Arthurian forces in a region called *Ewas*, south of modern Hereford. There Baetan's men were all killed.

Baetan himself had moved quickly along the Welsh coast to Chepstow, and the mouth of the Wye (*Aber Gwy*) where he won a brief encounter. He may then have marched to the head of the Severn Estuary near Gloucester, and seized Arthur's putative 'capital', Cirencester. Our sources don't tell us that, but it is clear that Baetan seems at this point to have succeeded in crossing, unopposed, the broad flood of the Severn Estuary to the English shore.

Arthur meanwhile, having sustained many losses and confessing himself tired of the pursuit, sent to Cornwall and Devon asking for more troops to join him at the mouth of the Severn. He was apparently now ready to stake all on one final encounter. Baetan, chased from river valley to river valley in Wales, and having lost about two-thirds of his men, now called up men who were his tributaries in England, and assembled a new force. His aim was to get to his ships at the Roman port on the River Avon below the fortress of *Dun Baetan* (modern Clifton). If he could reach the ships, he might be able to go to Cornwall, and find new levies there among his loyal supporters. Further reinforcements might decide the issue in Baetan's favour. Arthur may have been well aware of that, and that is why he was prepared to risk all in one final pitched battle. If Baetan were to reach his allies, and indeed if he was to survive, he too would have to put all on this one throw of the dice. The stage was set for the final Battle of Camlan.

Uncertain Sources

Before we look at Camlan, we should perhaps pause to remind ourselves that the evidence for the Welsh battles of King Arthur, his campaign against Baetan as we have been describing it, rests on a very fragile base. Our sources are uncertain. *Culhwch ac Olwen* gives us a narrative about pigs and piglets which are very probably, but not certainly, to be identified with Baetan and his sons. Nothing about the battles in the campaign and their outcomes is definite. There is a considerable level of uncertainty about locations too. Not all the place names – even the river names – mentioned have survived unchanged, or changed in ways which allow us still to recognise them. The river Tawy in *Culhwch ac Olwen*, for example, is likely to have been not the river now called Tawe which reaches the sea at Swansea (*Abertawe*), but a river, rising in the Brecons, called *Lyn y Fan Fawr*.

Lessons

There are elements of conjecture in it all, and, like any conjecture, it can be either right or wrong, or just plain misleading. The events we have, as we have them, are not history, but they tell a tale, and that tale is, and was intended to be, instructive. The *Mabinogion* (and therefore the story of the boar hunt) was compiled for the education of the young King Henry II. Baetan's failed attempt at suppression of revolt, and the nature of an insurgent leader determined to bring down everything, were both things a young ruler might need to understand. Henry II could learn by these examples. The Welsh campaign was meant to illustrate Baetan's miscalculation, and Arthur's ruthless and obsessive character. His main virtue a military leader, the maintenance of a strategic aim in the face of setbacks, had become a stubborn refusal to change tactics or direction.

As far as Arthur the warrior is concerned, it is that broad picture of a man in his context that matters, to us and to Henry II, not the precise location of obscure battles. The broad picture is of an impulsive, but focussed, tyrant leader, undeterred by vast losses of men and materiel, pursuing a confused and costly campaign, carried out unrelentingly, and against custom, over a short time period, perhaps no more than a couple of summer months. During that short time, very many great, honoured and famous leaders died in battles in which, we are told in *Culhwch ac Olwen*, Arthur's forces went 'from disaster to disaster'. Overall, the Welsh campaign of Arthur is a lesson about pyrrhic victory.

The danger of a pyrrhic victory for rulers was illustrated by Baetan too. Baetan seems to have fared little better than Arthur. Two of his armies, both led by his sons, were totally destroyed. No one survived those encounters. Baetan himself was wounded, and forced to return to Ireland, his English lands possibly placed beyond recovery for years because of his heavy losses. His punitive expedition had led to an avoidable and vast civil war that ignited the whole of the west of England and south of Wales. It was so dreadful that it could only be remembered in later centuries with tragic and ironic black humour. The deaths of heroes became a boar hunt that went wrong, a vivid metaphor for a conflict that was not necessary.

Henwen

There is a related story which also involves a pig hunt, and which may have carried some lessons about religious leaders for the young king. In this tale, Arthur and his men pursue a female pig called *Henwen* (old white). White animals in Welsh tradition are usually regarded as magical, especially if they have red ears.[4] *Henwen* was not a creature that deserved persecution. She was what is called a 'culture hero' – a person, or entity, who conveys benefits to the community. The *Mabinogion* account seems rooted in two triads which suggests an early date for the information we have about her. In Gwent, *Henwen* gave birth to a grain of wheat and a bee; in Pembroke, she produced a grain of barley and a bee; and, at *Lleyn* in Arfon (*Gwynedd*), a grain of rye[5]. In a second triad, she then produced offspring that were less obviously good for communities: a wolfcub, an eaglet and, at Llanfair in Arfon, a 'kitten' which became the *Cath Palug w*hich fought with Arthur's men.

There are signs of resistance to Arthur in the matter of *Henwen* in other triads. In TYP 26, we have the 'three powerful swine herds of Britain' – *Pryderi*, *Drystan* and *Coll*. *Drystan* is the Tristan who wooed Isolde (*Essyllt*), and while all three men seemed to have been involved, *Coll* was the special protector of *Henwen*. When Arthur assembled a large army, and tried to destroy her, she escaped with *Coll* across the Bristol Channel from *Penrhyn havstin yg kerniv* (Penryn Austin near the present Severn Bridge, *Kerniv* here having the original meaning of the whole western peninsula of England rather than just Cornwall). In south Wales, she brought blessings of grain, bees and honey to the people, before giving rise to further opponents of Arthur. Arthur's men pursued her with the same determination with which they had followed Baetan, and that tells us she was important.

Who was she? *Hen* means old and *Wen*, the second element in her name, means 'white', but also was adopted by some saints as a name, and acquired the meaning of 'holy'. *Finnian*, one of the greatest of Irish saints, is one example. Her name therefore may mean 'Old holy woman', or 'female saint', and that may lead us to suspect that she may be Saint Bridget (whose Glastonbury centre was called *Beckery* [beekeeper's island]). Bridget herself, or one of her immediate successors, may be the real individual concerned.

Whoever she was, she was important, or served someone important – possibly Saint Mary, because *Henwen* is often associated with places called *Llanfair* (Mary's Church). She attracted deep loyalty. The Triad 26 tells us her protectors could not be deceived, forced or by stealth persuaded to give her or her offspring up. Try as they might, Arthur and his army could not prevail. If *Henwen* were a reverend mother with some assistants, the anecdote reveals Arthur not just as a man trying to usurp a king to whom he owed loyalty, but a tyrant trying to remove a whole religious way of life, and ensure that all power, spiritual and temporal, came from him and him alone.[6] We have noted this characteristic earlier. Arthur may have been determined to uproot the Christianity that Bridget, under Baetan's protection, had planted at Glastonbury. The pursuit of *Henwen* could be construed as anti-Christian enterprise, or a betrayal of a faith previously defended in arms at *Gwinnion* (St Mary's victory) and Badon.

Betrayals and Consequences

Betrayal seems to be at the root of this aspect of British history. Geoffrey of Monmouth and his successors, in creating the 'literary Arthur', were aware of betrayal as the major cause of the Battle of Camlan. Their Arthur is pursuing a military campaign in France when, in the hour of his triumph in the foothills of the Alps over the Romans, and other fanciful opponents, he hears that his nephew Modred (*Medrawd*) has seized both his queen and his country. Guinevere appears to be a willing participant in the venture. Arthur returns post-haste, and gathers a loyal army to regain his losses. Modred assembles troops to hold what he has won. The two great forces meet in the shock of battle at Camlan.

Celtic heroes are ranged on both sides, and friend fights friend, and brother, brother. Many famous names meet their death, and, at last, Arthur is able to kill Modred (*Medrawd*). He is then borne, dying from his wounds, from the field by the sorrowing Bedivere, one of the last Knights of the Round Table to survive. Bedivere,[7] on the king's instruction, throws the famous sword *Excalibur* into the mere, and hands over the king to his sister Morgan le Fey and her maidens, who convey him into the mists of Avalon to cure him of his wounds. It is a picturesque ending to a tragic opera, and the whole tragedy rests on the initial betrayal.

Welsh tradition, before and outside the creation of the inventive Geoffrey, remembers Camlan as one of the famous 'Three Futile Battles of Britain'. Triad 84 in TYP is rather misogynist in attributing women as a cause, if not *the* cause, of Camlan and the other two battles – *Godden* and *Arfderydd*. The Battle of *Godden*,[8] Triad 84 says, was caused by 'the bitch, the roebuck and the plover' – possibly translations of the actual names, or titles, or nicknames of an individual female rulers, or the wives of rulers. *Cun* (hound or guardian), for example, is frequently applied to male warriors as all, or part of their name, or as a title.

'Bitch' may be simply be a female equivalent of *cun*, and does not necessarily carry the modern pejorative implications. The Battle of *Arfderydd*[9] was caused by the 'lark's nest', which, although it has baffled redactors and critics for a thousand years, is almost certainly a reference to female anatomy (*mons veneris*). In Irish folksong, up to modern times, it is 'the swallow's nest' [10]. We might construe it broadly as 'femininity' or 'femaleness', or 'behaviour typical of women', although it might also simply be a fight over the sexual favours to be granted by a woman to two rival men. In such disputes, the cause of the differences between the men is not infrequently attributed to the woman.

According to Triad 84, the dreadful Battle of Camlan, King Arthur's last battle, was caused by a quarrel between Guinevere and her sister *Gwenhwyfach* (little Gwen). There is no information about the nature of the quarrel, nor indeed about the younger sister[11] but it appears the queen was struck by her sister. Whatever the detail, Welsh tradition asserts Camlan began as a trivial dispute among women, rather than a political or military betrayal by warriors.

On the other hand, sex and gender may have nothing to do with it. The war could have been spiritual or doctrinal in origin, or arose about a dispute over the headship of a monastery, or other religious institution. We know from Gildas that there were such disputes over the spoils of office. It may be a dispute about the headship of a community of holy women in which Arthur backed one candidate and Baetan another. The betrayal may have been in origin only a failure of loyalty, or respect, due to the holder of a religious position.[12]

There is no early evidence of a political betrayal by *Medrawd*. The *Annales Cambriae* (the 'Annals of Wales' in Harley 3859) says simply, 'AD 537 – The Battle of Camlann in which Arthur and *Medraut* fell (537 *an Guieth Camlann in qua Arthur et Medraut corruerunt)*.'[13] *Medrawd* is otherwise known as an exemplary fighter. The *Annales Cambriae* entry doesn't record which side he and Arthur were on, whether they were opposed to one another in the fight or fought on the same side. Guinevere is not mentioned in this context with either of them, but all the later sources are unanimous is seeing Camlann as a useless and unnecessary conflict. It was a battle fought for a trivial cause that could have been settled. That may take us back to Arthur's original offer of mediation in Ireland.

Two Betrayals

The need to show loyalty in both directions seems to lie at the heart of the matter. In the scenario we have preferred, Baetan may have withheld payments (*rath*) due to Arthur, and Arthur, possibly prompted by Guinevere, who thought Baetan's failure in the required generosity was an affront to her personally ('a slap in the face'), decided to assert his own power in the lands he had brought into Baetan's domain. In effect, in modern terms, he declared independence. That was a challenge Baetan could perhaps have solved by a simple reaffirmation of status through the donation of plunder, or the award of a titular kingship, but he chose to take it as a wider challenge to his authority. Thus, his attempted limited punitive expedition into south Wales turned into a major war in which both he and Arthur demanded much of their followers. As Arthur blocked his passage to his ships, in Gloucestershire at the church by the River Cam (*Camlan*), both leaders threw everything into the fight, and both sides suffered great losses. In the end, Baetan broke through, found his ships, and made his way to Cornwall, and then to Ireland.

Arthur the King

As we have seen, in the Welsh campaign, Arthur's excellent military virtue – maintaining a strategic focus (driving Baetan away from hope of assistance) in changing circumstances – became something more like a personal obsession. Despite the heavy losses his forces sustained, he went on pursuing Baetan long after it made sense in military terms to do so. In the end he was prepared to risk everything on one final throw of the dice. Even then the outcome was uncertain. At the final battle, Camlan, Arthur was thought to be the victor, but he was carried wounded from the field of Camlan, and placed in the care of his sister, Morgan. His wounds appeared to be fatal, but he may not have died. He may have become the shambling, incoherent Arthur the warrior (*Arturbran*) that we have found who came, years later, to die in the presence of Saint Columba in Skye.

If he did not die after Camlan, Arthur certainly retired. It is clear that the battles in the Welsh campaign against *Twrch Trwyth* were his last in effective command, and that Camlan was his last real active engagement as a front-line warrior in a battle. It appears, on the slight evidence we have, that the Welsh campaign from the shores of Dyfed to the banks of the Cam was the war in which, by throwing off his obligations to Baetan, Arthur the warrior really became King Arthur. As we shall see, he did not function as a king, and his rule was neither unchallenged nor attended by success.

CONCLUSIONS

1. Arthur betrayed Baetan and attacked Ireland but after a short while sought to end hostilities peacefully.
2. Baetan betrayed Arthur by denying him a fair share in plunder and launched a punitive action in south Wales in response to Arthur's attack.
3. The two actions caused a fiercely contested civil war that ended at the dreadful Battle of Camlan with Baetan fleeing to Ireland and Arthur carried, seriously wounded, to Glastonbury.
4. Arthur's men expelled an old and holy woman and her followers as a part of the war.
5. Arthur perhaps ended the war as a victor and may have become a king, but his wounds may have left him unable to rule.

12

KING ARTHUR AND THE RIVAL CLAIMANTS TO HIS THRONE

Rivals for a Crown

Finding out what happened in western Britain after the Battle of Badon and the *Twrch Trwyth* campaign is not easy or straightforward. One matter – we cannot call it a fact – stands out. Arthur had, by his prowess and ruthless and obsessive pursuit of Baetan, won a kingdom because he had, at least for a time, excluded the Irish king from western England. It was too much to expect that Baetan would accept the result of the campaign; there would in time be a reaction. In the meantime, by about AD 540, Arthur had come to rule a sizeable territory from modern Pembrokeshire in the west to the borders of modern Oxfordshire in the east, and perhaps as far south as the Channel coast. In England, it comprised most of what had been *Britannia Prima*, one of the richest provinces of Roman Britain. It was a considerable achievement.

Clearly, other warlords and military commanders, having seen or heard of Arthur's success, may have thought they too could follow his example, and carve out a land, a throne and a people. We may therefore suspect that there would be wars and contentions, partly resulting from his success and his kingdom; new challengers for his domain would emerge.

That, in fact, is what we see. New wars waged by ambitious men began. Arthur himself, however, took no part in the military events that followed Badon and the *Twrch* wars. When he was challenged for his kingdom, and as he faced odd, unlikely and bizarre claimants to his crown including a sea monster, the king of the Africans, and the first Celtic king of the West Saxons, the defence of his lands was conducted by surrogates.

The Sea Monster

Let us take the sea monster first. In the late twelfth century in France, a man called André wrote a poem called *Romans de Francois* in which he related a story he didn't believe. It begins in the French of the time:

> *Rimé ont de lui li Francois*
> *Que bote fu par Capalu*
> *Li réis Artur en la palu*
> *Et que le chat 'ocist de guerre*
> *Puis passa outre en Engleterre*
> *Et ne fu pas lenz de conquerre*
> *Ainz porta crone en la terre*
> *Et fu sire de la contrée.*

(The French have made a poem about him, that King Arthur was pushed by Capulu in the bog and the cat killed him in war, then passed over to England, and was not slow to conquer it – then he [the cat] wore the crown of the land and was the lord of the country.)

This section of the poem concludes:

> *Où ont itel fable trovée?*
> *Mençonge est, Dex le set, provée.*

(Where did they find such a yarn? It is, God knows, a proven lie.)

Where did they get such a story? It apparently came from Wales. The *Capalu* is the creature known in Welsh tradition as the *Cath Puluc* ('spear-headed animal' but sometimes called in Welsh sources '*Palug's cat*'). In Ireland, it was called *murchata* (sea-cat), and in Scotland, famously and recently, it was, and still is, known as 'the Loch Ness Monster'.[1] It is not a bog animal as André thought; that derives from a linguistic confusion involving words in Welsh for a 'spear' and in French for a 'bog'.

Recent commentators have dismissed the reports of these animals as crude devices to increase the tourist trade, but they turn up widely in early stories long before, indeed centuries before, the invention of tourism. In the sixth century, Saint Columba encountered the Loch Ness animal, and Cei and other Arthurian warriors fought *murchats* in Welsh and Irish locations. Cei and his companions met one at Anglesey (perhaps the one that originated with *Henwen*) which had slain 'nine score warriors' before they managed to kill it. The Irish hero Finn killed another one at Dublin.

In Ireland, traces of the animals survive as elements in place names incorporating the element *peiste* – (as in *Lig na peiste* near Derry), an Irish borrowing of Latin *bestia*. *Bestia* is the equivalent of 'cat' which means, in this context, simply 'animal'. In Wales, they are remembered in the common name for *potentilla anserina* (silverweed). It is *Palf y Gath Balug* – the paw of *Cath Palug* – a description of the leaf form.[2] These creatures also occur on the engraved Pictish stones as the symbol known as the 'Pictish swimming sea-elephant' (see Fig. 22 in plates). The function of the Pictish carvings is probably emblematic; that is, to denote the name of a person or a tribe. It is hardly likely that any tribe would accept being nominated by a sobriquet drawn from an imaginary beast. The Pictish symbols otherwise all show recognisable real animals and fish. It would be strange if only one of them, the sea-elephant, was mythical. If the tribal name existed, then so did the beast. We know that the animals did become associated with tribes. In Ireland, the *murchata*, or 'sea-cat' became used in the sixth century to form the tribal name Murchada, and it lies behind the personal name of a man called *Muirchertach MacErc* (or *Mac Muiredaig*).[3]

There is a degree of confusion about this man. If his father was *Muiredaig*, he was of the Ui Nialls of northern Ireland, but some records say he was the son of a woman called Erc and that his father was Baetan. Alternatively, he may have been simply Baetan's son with no named mother. He seems to have had a definite connection with Baetan. Whatever the truth of that, he is a credible military figure who won many battles in Ireland, and was remembered as a high-king of Ireland (although that term was not in use in his day). He may be the 'sea-cat' we are looking for.

Muirchertach may have tried to extend his rule to England. A tenth-century Welsh poem called *Pa Gur* tells us that Cei, one of Arthur's men, went to *Mon* (Anglesey) to fight the 'sea-cat'. As we saw earlier, nine score (180) men fell in the engagement, and Cei claimed victory. That might be not an accurate report of the outcome. Cei was said to have returned with a broken shield which is sometimes construed as a sign of defeat. Another fragment tells us about a 'speckled cat and her strangers causing uproar in Mon'. The word for strangers here (*hagyfieithion*) usually means 'young men who have come to a court seeking a military reputation'. It has the sense of 'followers', 'clients' or, pejoratively, 'hangers-on', and 'companions'. We might see it best as meaning a 'freelance warband'.

With men like these 'strangers', men hungry for plunder, behind him, Muirchertach may have been given the task of regaining the losses of his father, Baetan, in England. He may very well have done exactly what André's rhyme says he did – launched an attack on Arthur, had a quick military success and set himself up as the ruler of (some at least of) Arthur's domains.

Any success Muirchertach may have had didn't last. His end was rather spectacular, and very much the stuff of myth and legend. He put away his Christian wife, and took up with a sorceress called *Sin* (storm). She told him he must never say her name. When, commenting on extreme weather, he did so accidentally, he was drowned in a vat of wine, burnt by fire, and a roof beam fell on him. We can take it that, after all that, he was no longer a threat to Arthur.

Odor

The next man to offer a challenge is a person who is called, in various versions of his name, Oder, Yder, Odran, or Odroc. There are several persons of that name around in the sixth century, and whatever the spelling and regardless of suffixes like -*oc* and -*an*, it may be clearer to think of them all as Odor.[4]

Odor may have had to come to England to find a kingdom or found a dynasty. *Cormac's Glossary* tells the story of the *Deisi*, a whole Irish tribe who were expelled to south Wales, and remarks about the Irish in Britain, 'It is from them is the race of *Crimthann* over there.' *Crimthann Odor* may be the *Crimthann Mor* who, Cormac says, ruled in 'Glastonbury of the Gael' although that Irish ruler in England is more likely to have been *Crimthann Mor Mac Fidaig*.

Neither of these Crimthanns encountered Arthur, but his co-commander at Badon, Owein, may have been king of an

Irish tribe centred on Clogher and called the *Ui Crimthann*. The tribal name means a 'cunning fox or wolf'. Their king Owein's name may mean 'leader of the oxen' – not the animal, but a tribe with that symbol. Iron oxheads have been found by archaeologists at Clogher which borders on the lands of the *Airthir*.[5] While Owein is an entirely feasible co-commander with his Oriel neighbour, Arthur, at Badon, we have no information that suggests he ever rivalled Arthur for a kingdom in England. Although Owein of Clogher may have held land in Wales, if he ever ruled in western England, it was not a throne he arrived at by deposing Arthur.

The Odor (*Yder*) of the French romances is more engaged with Arthur. In Chrétien's *Lancelot*, his heraldic device is described as a 'stag issuing from a castle gate', which was an old heraldic device representing Ireland. In a commentary inserted by an unknown hand into William of Malmesbury's account of Glastonbury, he is named as Ider or Yder, and his father is named as Nuth (Irish *nith* [wound], or *Nia* [champion/warrior]). Arthur treats him in a treacherous fashion. He and Odor agree to go together to slay three giants who are troubling the ordinary people. The giants are based at a place called the Mount of Frogs (*mons ranarum*) which may be Brent Knoll or Glastonbury Tor. Arthur deliberately delays his arrival, so that Odor faces the giants alone. Odor kills them, but is badly wounded, and is carried to Glastonbury, apparently dying.

John of Glastonbury (who flourished around 1350) has a variation. The key encounter in his version is held at the Mount of Spiders (*in monte de Areynes*).[6] Another French story called *Yder* picks up the story after the fight with the giants, and tells us that Odor was taken to Glastonbury to have his wounds cared for by holy women there. The person who led the curative effort there was Guinevere. One thing led to another, and a love affair between them developed. The author had to invent a sort of parallel Guinevere to maintain the queen's chastity by attributing her loose behaviour to the other Guinevere. While this Odor may have made a conquest of Guinevere, there is no suggestion that he in any way overcame Arthur.

His father Nudd offers more information. He may be a god – the god Nodens who has a Romano-British temple at Lydney in Gloucestershire. In the French poem *Yder*, Nudd is called *Nud* or *Nus D'Alemagne*. We should not too readily assume that this name means he was German. There is an estate in Cumbria called *Dalemain*, situated just a few miles west of Penrith at the junction of the Eamont and Dacre rivers. The name *Dalemain* is of uncertain antiquity, and it was a military site; it featured a pele tower (guard tower) in the twelfth century. It may also have been a place of political importance in the sixth century. It was certainly important religiously quite soon afterwards – Bede records an important monastery nearby at Dacre in AD 731. It is possible that the name derives from *de la main* (of the hand) and refers to the Irish Nudd of the Silver Hand, or to the name by which he was known in Welsh, *Lludd Llaw Erient* (Lludd of the Silver Hand).[7] That doesn't seem to lead us towards a rival for the throne. Neither Lludd nor his son Odor appear to have threatened to unseat Arthur.

Odor of the *Airthir*

There is, however, another speculative meaning of Dalemain that we should explore because it brings us to probably the strongest and most likely Odor of all. *Dal Emain* may mean the Irish tribe (*Dal*) of Armagh (*Emain Macha*) and represent a name for an overseas territory of the people of that place. They were, as we have seen earlier, called the *Airthir*, and their king at the time was one *Odor Caech* (Odor the 'squinty' or 'one-eyed').[8]

This Odor was a noted warrior, and his nickname may not just have referred to his sight. Although there was a story about a bee sting[9] depriving him of the sight of one eye, *caech* may mean something like 'dissembler, a man who might appear to be looking in one direction but actually had his eye on something else'. In some records, there is also a reference to *Baetan Caech*. It is hardly likely that bees were attacking more than one Irish king, so the figurative meaning is to be preferred, at least in Baetan's case.

Baetan, as his over-king. would have been in a position to seek the participation of *Odor Caech* in his wars. If Baetan asked him to attack Arthur, the wily *Odor Caech* may have looked in two different directions at once. He may have offered the help of his warband to Arthur in dealing with opponents (the giants of the Tor who, through a confusion possible in the Welsh language, may have turned from 'warriors' into 'giants'). He found, however, Arthur's late arrival at the encounter with the giants showed him also to be devious, and not to be trusted. Odor may therefore have chosen to pursue ambitions elsewhere. Whatever the reason, *Odor*

Caech of the Oriel abandoned any interest in England he may have had, and seized the kingship of the Dal Araide which had been held by *Fiachna Lurgan*, the son of Baetan. He then extended his reach across the sea into north-western England. Odor of the Oriel was simply not interested in attacking or deposing Arthur. He was interested in carving out a larger kingdom for himself, and his choice fell not on south and south-western England but on Ireland, Scotland and northern England.

Caradawg

There can, however, be no doubt about the dynastic and royal intentions in the west of England and Wales of another claimant – Caradawg. His name appears widely in the sources as *Caradoc, Caradauc, Coroticus, Cereticus, Carados, Careticus, Ceretic, Keredic, Kyriadoc, Karadues* and *Cerdic*. *The Dream of Rhonabwy* says that he was Arthur's chief adviser and first cousin, but that may always have been an uneasy relationship. Triad 18 in the TYP tells us Caradawg could never endure a *pennteulu* (warband commander) over him. That may be due to a talent for insubordination, or to a feeling that he was superior socially (whatever that may have meant in the sixth century) to almost anyone he might meet.

Caradawg was very well connected. His father was *Lyr Lledyeith* ('Lyr half-speech', which suggests a foreign origin, or some sort of ethnic mix in parentage). He may have been *Lyr Leth-ri* ('Lyr the joint-king' although who the other 'half-king' may have been in that scenario is unknown). *Lyr* seems to have ruled in the Isle of Man, and in the area around Edinburgh. That makes him a powerful man with possible access to widespread and profitable plundering opportunities at a time when the noblest prospect a warrior from Scotland saw was often the high seas that led him to England.

Caradawg had important links by marriage. Triad 71 in the TYP says that his wife was *Tegau Gold-Breast*, the daughter of *Nudd*, king of the North, who may be also the man who was a god in Lydney. Triad 1 says Caradawg was the chief elder (*ben henyf*) of all Britain. He personally ruled in Cornwall, and Breton tradition makes him (in the *Life of St Padarn* and in the *Livre de Carados*), the founder and ruler of a kingdom centred on Vannes in Brittany.

Caradawg's standing did not depend entirely on his connections or inheritance. He was also one of the leading warriors of his time.

Triad 18 names him as one of the three 'battle horsemen of Britain' and his horse was called, because of its prowess, 'battle-splitter'. Like Baetan and Arthur, Caradawg was a king with several courts, wielding power in many lands, stretching from modern Scotland through Cornwall to Brittany. He could call many men to his hostings.

It was inevitable in the aftermath of Baetan's discomfiture in the great *Twrch Trwyth* campaign that he and Arthur should become rivals. Geoffrey of Monmouth tells us of one *Keredic* a 'fomentor of discords, hateful to God and to the Britons also', which suggests that it may have been doctrinal religious disputes as much as territorial ambition that divided them. Whatever the reasons, it was a long-lasting rivalry. Ranulf Higden in his *Polychronicon* reports that 'men rede in somme cronykes that Cerdicus fought oft with Arthur and yf he were overcome, he aroose up eft strenger to fyghte, and atte last after six and twenty yere of Cerdicus comynge, Arthur was wery and gave hym Hamshyre and Somersete and called that countrye Wessex'.[10]

The King of the Africans
The Wessex dimension is where the king of the Africans comes in. Geoffrey of Monmouth tells us that the Saxons revolted against Caradawg (*Keredic*) and sent to Ireland for Gormund, Godmund or Godmundus, king of the Africans, to come to help them in their wars. Gormund arrived with a huge fleet and an army of 160,000 men. He drove Caradawg from city to city, and eventually penned him up in Cirencester. He destroyed that city by fire and pursued Caradawg across the Severn into Wales.

Gormund then did something very strange. He was, without doubt, victorious in his war, and was able to distribute much plunder to his troops and his friends, but he went further. He divided the territory he had conquered into two main areas. The first part, Somerset and Hampshire, went to the Saxons, and the other part, Wales and Cornwall, he assigned to the Britons. Arthur at that time seems to have been settled in Gower, or at least relocated there. Geoffrey of Monmouth was in no doubt that it was Gormund's war that destroyed the power the Britons had gained after the victory of Badon.

We can supplement, and partially verify, Geoffrey's imaginative account from other sources. William of Wyrecestre noted that

Arthur had been crowned at Cirencester. In occupying that city, Caradawg had seized a place that was important to Arthur, and that may lead us to think that it was Arthur, and not the Saxons, who sent to Ireland for Gormund. William also gives us an anecdote about Gormund's siege. He says Cirencester became known as the 'city of the sparrows' because Gormund set fire to the city by tying burning straw to the sparrows. When the birds returned to their nests in the city, they ignited the rooftops of the houses.[11]

If Arthur was indeed the person who sought help against Caradawg, that may help us to identify Gormund. Arthur is unlikely to have sought aid from Baetan or his successors among the Ulidians. He may very well have approached the man who was their chief rival on both sides of the Irish Sea, Aedan MacGabran. Aedan was king of the Dal Riata (one of Baetan's old fiefdoms) which gave him lands in County Antrim in Ireland and in Scotland. After the death of Baetan, Aedan met with the Irish King Aed at the Convention of Drumcett, and they agreed between them how hostings of troops from both sides of the sea would be called in future; basically, Irish hosts for Irish wars and British hosts for wars in mainland Britain. Aedan thus was able to extend his power over northern England as far south as the Humber Estuary. He was also one of the northern figures who had chosen to name his son Arthur. That means he knew and admired Arthur.

This Son of York

If the rules confirmed later at Drumcett had come into force, or were already followed as an informal or convenient custom, a campaign in England by Aedan to sustain Arthur required an English hosting. That is what seems to have happened. Aedan chose a man from Yorkshire to lead the fight against Caradawg, and it is easy to see how Geoffrey mistook him for the king of the Africans. Nennius tells us that *Cair Ebrauc* was one of the cities of Britain, and we can confidently identify that as the Roman city of York, *Eboracum*. The name continued into Saxon times as *Eoforwic*. *Eboracus* (man of York) is known as a personal name, and turns up in the Arthurian romances attached to the father of the famous (in opera at least) Parsifal, *Effrawc*.[12] Any man from York could be called *Eboracanus*. The letter 'b' by this time was being pronounced as an 'f' or a 'v'. *Eboracaunus* could thus easily become '*Efricanus*', and a king of York thus transformed into a king of Africa, *Africanus*.

We can find the commander's personal name in a Yorkshire context too. In the Hundred of Weighton, close to the modern town of Market Weighton, is the hamlet of Godmanham. The earliest recorded form of the village name is *Godmunddinggaham*. That name breaks down into three main elements. *Ham* (a village) *inga* (a people) and *Godmund* (a personal name). It translates as the 'village of Godmund's people'.

Godmanham is a dependency of the multiple estate of Everingham (the village of Eofor's people) which incorporates the personal name *Eofor* (a wild boar), or relates to the city of York. There really is very little difficulty in regarding Gormund of York as Godmundus, king of the Africans, a man with a duty to come to the hostings of Aedan MacGabran. He is not a figment of Geoffrey of Monmouth's rich imagination; he is entirely credible as the successful opponent of Caradawg and the nominated defender of injured Arthur.

That leaves another question: why, having won, did he apparently dispose of his conquests? There is a possible answer: he may have contracted leprosy. He made what arrangements he could for the conquered lands because he too could no longer lead an army or rule a country. He retired into the religious life in a hermitage, perched high on a rock at Roche in Cornwall where he lived out his days as a recluse in the care of one devoted daughter. *Gomunda* is remembered there, not only as a leper who had been a famous warrior but also as a man who left the wars to become the patronal saint of the church and the parish.

Caradawg's Kingdom

Caradawg seems to have accepted Godmund's dispensation. He succeeded one Maglo (*Melwys*) as king of Somerset and, with his son Caurdaf (*Krowda*, *Creoda*), set about increasing his grip on his kingdom by a series of engagements with unknown foes.

We can make some useful guesses about his territory because boundaries have a great resilience over time. Some modern estates still follow the borders of their Roman villa predecessors. If we judge by the ancient boundaries, it appears Caradawg's kingdom followed closely the boundaries of the dioceses of Worcester, Bath and Wells, Salisbury and Winchester which, in turn, closely match the provincial borders of Roman Britain, *Britannia Prima* (see Fig. 23 in plates). He did not dispute his western and northern boundaries; his ambitions were to consolidate what he held, and to expand to the east. The *Anglo-Saxon Chronicle* says it was around the mid-century that he *feng to rice* (began to rule) in the area that became known as Wessex. Caurdaf, his son, was succeeded by Cynric (*Cunorix*, Hound-king or Guardian-king in Irish)[13] Some accounts make Cynric the son of another famous warrior, Ceawlin.

This Ceawlin was very active in campaigns in the upper and mid-Thames area, and contended with Aethelberht, king of Kent, as far east as the London area. He also defeated three leaders (with names that occur, or are closely paralleled, in the regnal lists of the *Airthir*) at Gloucester, Cirencester and Bathanceastre. His allies in his wars appear to have been Saxon leaders called Cuthwine and Cutha. Cutha was killed in a fight in Oxfordshire and, although he took great plunder in that encounter, Ceawlin is reported to have been expelled, and 'left in anger for his own people' after Cutha's death. That suggests he may have been fighting in some sort of mercenary or auxiliary role. He may have tried to reassert himself the following year, but was unsuccessful. He died with Crida (*Caurdaf*?) in a great battle at Adam's Grave, a large tumulus a few miles east of Devizes.

His opponents on that occasion, according to William of Malmesbury, were a combination of Britons and Saxons. Some years later, the Saxons moved their capital from Dorchester-on-Thames to Winchester. Under Caedwalla, they started to use the term 'West Saxon' to describe themselves as a people. Previously their leaders – Caradawg, Caurdaf, Cynric and Ceawlin – had led an elite warrior group called the *Gewisse*, and for a time that term was used interchangeably with Wessex as the name of the kingdom. *Gewisse* may descend from the idea of the Roman *comitatenses* (elite guards or mobile field army), or it might be a translation of the Irish *fianna*. It could also be a version of *Hwicce*[14] which meant a 'guardian war band' and became a tribal name for the people of the area that corresponded to the great early diocese of Worcester, and who became the Mercians.

Exactly when and how these new 'kingdoms' in the west defined themselves remains obscure. What we know is that the territories in the southern part of 'Arthur's kingdom' adopted the name of

Wessex in the reign of Caedwalla. Caedwalla, according to Bede, was the first among the rulers of that country and people to be a Christian. We might add that perhaps that may only have meant a 'Christian' as Bede understood it. Caradawg, and his sons and grandsons, may well have been 'Celtic Christians'. While he had some regard for Saint Aidan and Iona, Bede simply didn't recognise Irish or Welsh Christianity in England.

Whatever their religious beliefs and affiliations, the accession to power of Caedwalla brought to an end the rule and adventures of the men who had known and fought with, or for, Arthur, men like Caradawg, Caurdaf and perhaps Ceawlin. After the death of Ceawlin, no more Irish names appear among the Saxons. Caedwalla's accession also ended the interest of Irish warrior elites in England. Baetan and his sons were dead, and Arthur himself fades from history.

Western England, Wales and Cornwall were never an 'Irish Empire'. Whatever power the Irish Goidelic (raider) warlords like Arthur, and the raiding warrior elites (*fianna*) who backed them, wielded in England was temporary, and was always an incomplete hegemony. It began about 500 and was over by 580. The Irish had started well, but they failed in the end to establish themselves as they did in Scotland, where they conducted an incursion which was every bit as successful as the Anglo-Saxon arrival in England. In Scotland, they, like the Anglo-Saxons in England, also changed the name, language, religion and culture of the country they occupied.

The 540 Event

The Irish, however, didn't lose England because of the successes of King Arthur in the Welsh campaign, the victories of Gormund or the triumphs of Caradawg. The Irish Sea Province ruled by Baetan collapsed, and the Irish leaders who followed him lost their power, because of a natural event. The precise nature of the event has not yet been established and it has scarcely been studied. It is clear, however, that something catastrophic happened. Tree-ring studies by M. J. Baillie in Ireland reveal that, around AD 540, there was a distinct temporary climate change. Trees didn't grow. Some oaks around Lough Neagh took twenty-five years to return to normal growth. Studies elsewhere confirm that it was a hemispheric event. Tree growth was restricted right across the whole northern part of the earth. Such a phenomenon is usually caused by the eruption of a super-volcano somewhere around the world. Large quantities of material block out the sun and affect the weather. Crops do not grow, water supplies fail, and human and animal populations are seriously affected. The acidic debris of a volcano which may have caused this 540 event has not been found in the Greenland ice cores,[15] and that has led to a search for an alternative cause.

Clube and Napier have speculated on the effect of a body such as an asteroid or a meteor hitting the Earth.[16] On land, it would have an effect equivalent to the simultaneous explosion of many nuclear bombs. In the Tunguska incident in 1908, an object of the kind they conjecture hit a deserted part of Russia and knocked down trees for 60 square miles around the impact site. Clube and Napier suggest that an ocean impact perhaps would cause a greater disaster as giant tsunamis swept towards populated sea coasts, and a large plume of dead sea creatures and salt water rose high into the sky, again blocking out the sun.

That is what appears to have happened in AD 540. A triad not normally considered part of the TYP survived by chance in a Latin version found in the Exeter *Chronica de Wallia*:

> These are the kingdoms which the sea destroyed. The kingdom of Teithi Hen, son of Gwynnan, king of Kaerrihog. That kingdom was called at the time Realm of Teithi Hen. It was between St David's and Ireland. No one escaped from it, neither men nor animals, except Teihti Hen alone with his horse; afterwards all the days of his life he was weak from fear.

> The second kingdom was that Helig, son of Glannog, it was between Cardigan and Bardsey, and so far as St David's. That land was very good, fertile and level, and it was called Maes Maichgen; it lay from the mouth of the Ystwyth to Llyn and up to Aberdovey. The sea destroyed a third kingdom: the kingdom of Rhedfoe son of Rheged.

We can add another. A *cantref* (district) belonging to Gwyddno disappeared beneath the waves in western Wales. There were similar changes in Cornwall, and a region there called Lionesse may have been lost. The Scilly Isles became a group of islands rather than one place, and a forest was drowned beside St Michael's Mount in Cornwall. Maelgwn, king of Gwynedd, was found dead in the church of Rhos without a mark on him, apparently the victim of noxious gases from the boundary layers of the sea. A contemporary report found in a French library says there was plague in the water. The Byzantine historian Procopius described an island place called *Brittia* which seems to be western Britain. While life in the east of the island went on as usual, in the west of the land, Procopius says, nothing could live – men, birds, trees and crops all died. Anyone venturing into the area died immediately.

It was a disaster from which there could be no easy or quick recovery in sixth-century Britain. Even today, nations with access to international help and the best efforts of modern science take years to recover from tsunami events. In the sixth century, it took two or three generations, and some of the effects on language and culture and the land and the seas were profound, and are still with us today.

The sea remained disturbed for some time, but eventually found new shores and returned to something like what men were used to. One Irish annal entry reads, '*Muirgielt capta est.*' 'The madness of the sea has been constrained.' While the sea may have returned to normality in appearance, beneath and within it fish stocks were unlikely to be back to normal because the food chain had been disrupted. That meant communities dependent on the sea for food would perish. Nothing much grew in the fields. Even today, tree cover in the western counties of England is still notably less than it is in the East. There were no birds to help plants germinate and spread.

People dependent on the land for food were not better placed than the folk by the seaside. The literate, luxury-loving population denounced by Gildas disappeared. The peoples who traded luxury goods from the Mediterranean and Aquitaine around the Irish Sea Province stopped their voyaging. Some of them may have migrated to Armorica to found the land and people of Brittany.[17] Languages like Welsh and Cornish changed abruptly from inflected tongues (like Latin) to the less structured versions, the uninflected ancestor tongues of modern Welsh and Cornish. Merlin (*Llawawg*), Sweeney (*Suibne*), Lailoken (*Laleocen*) and other famous bards, who kept in their minds the oral traditions of history, law and poetry of their nations, went mad. In the great Irish monastery of Bangor,

Saint Comgall ordered the keeping of annals and written records (*eraicept* – that which should be remembered), so that history would not depend on the ramblings of men who had lost their wits. In any case the language changes made much that was remembered incomprehensible. Men could no longer understand their own written and spoken history, and their heroes, like Arthur, became the central figures of incoherent fables. An anecdote associated with one *Cadyryieth* tells us about bards chanting a poem which, 'apart from *Cadyryeith* himself, no man there understood except that it was about Arthur'.[18]

There was a religious response too. People had seen for themselves that Gildas had been right, and he became justly celebrated as a true prophet. The mass destruction seems to have followed his prophetic sermon by only a few years at most, and may have been almost immediate. The merit of his prophecy seemed to indicate that the Last Days were at hand. The Irish looked in Isaiah and saw that they should urgently take Christ's message to all those who had not heard it, wherever they might be found. Led by men like Columbanus, the traditional raiding peoples became evangelists and they set out in ever increasing numbers to evangelise the world, raiding and colonising now for Christ.

There were political effects. Baetan and Muirchertach died immediately. A Ulidian army was destroyed by an earthquake. In the uncertainty and confusion, Baetan's unwilling tributaries, rivals and other enemies seized their chance. His remaining sons were killed in battle in the 550s, and in 560 his great monastery at Bangor and his fortress at Dunlethglas were looted and destroyed. In 564 Melwys, an old man by then, was forced to carry Columba of the Ui Nialls ashore through the waves in Iona as a sign of submission.[19] In 575, at Drumcett, the spoils of Baetan's Irish and Scottish empire were divided up among his rivals and former tribute bearers, and the poets who remembered, recorded and recited his deeds were threatened with expulsion from Ireland if he were mentioned in their songs and poems.[20]

In Britain, as we have seen, Arthur lived in a sorry confused retirement in Gower while Caradawg and others who had served Baetan set about creating a new kingdom in what became Wessex. They probably went on behaving very much like the Irishmen, Welshmen, or Cornishmen they were, but by the time the *Anglo-Saxon Chronicle* was written three centuries later they had become naturalised Englishmen, or, at the very least, West Saxons. The Battle of Badon was forgotten, along with the great internecine campaigns they had fought in. Their once substantial pageant of men and affairs, their towers, palaces and their temples had faded, and left not a track behind. They are now such stuff as dreams are made on. When we dream of them now, we do not envisage the ravages, battles and betrayals of the violent sixth century; our dreams now are shaped by the imaginations of writers like Geoffrey of Monmouth and Chrétien de Troyes, and we see only golden Camelot. We do not see the wily, violent, amoral chieftains who held sway in the sixth century. Above all, we find it hard to discern the figure of Arthur, warrior and king, and to understand the battles that made him famous, and the dreadful civil war that brought him in the end to a kingdom of his own.

CONCLUSIONS

1. Arthur may have become a king in the western half of Britain but he did not reign and left no trace of his rule.
2. When others challenged for the right to rule his 'kingdom', they were opposed by surrogates like Gormund of York, not by Arthur himself.
3. The only challenger to have left a mark was Caradawg, who became king of Wessex and thus heir to Arthur in England.
4. The remaining signs of an Irish or Goidelic (raider) attempt at hegemony in the south and west of England and south Wales during the sixth century were lost in the mysterious event of AD 540.
5. That vacancy of record cleared the path for the establishment of an 'Arthur of literature'.

13

THE QUEST CONCLUDED

Lessons

What have we learnt from our quest? King Arthur has, for many years, been regarded as a hero who led the oppressed Britons in a series of defensive actions against the invading Saxon hordes. His twelve battles were all victorious, and he thus preserved British liberty for perhaps another two or more generations because the vile Saxons were pushed back eastwards to their strongholds, or even back to the countries from which they came. If that were true, it would be sufficient to make Arthur one of the most important British warrior kings ever to have led his countrymen in time of peril.

But it is not true. In our study of the archaeological evidence, the literature and the legends, we did not find that mighty king. The real sixth-century Arthur, the warrior, the true Dark Ages king, as we have found him, albeit faintly and with a great deal of speculation, is a warlord. He is very like the Anglo-Saxon warlords who imposed themselves on eastern England around the same time at which he was active in the west. He appears to have been Irish and Goidelic (that is, a raider). If the Berchan reference to a '*primarius*' who fought an opponent for thirteen years really is a reference to him, Arthur fought against, not for, the Britons. He may not have won all his battles, but he fought with some success, and may have come to rule about a third of the landmass of England. However, perhaps because of his war injuries, he has left little trace of his reign as a king in the west. We can nonetheless put together now some sort of picture of this man, Arthur the king and warrior, as he may have been in his time, what we may call 'the real sixth-century Arthur'.

The Triumph of the Raiders
The sixth century can be read as a time when those who used to raid Roman Britain in the time of the legions – the Saxons on the east coast and the Irish and Picts on the west – continued their activity, and found very little resistance, perhaps none. Both groups of raiding peoples found decreasing amounts of portable booty. It was inevitable that they might choose to stay, or even be invited to stay by Britons who preferred taxation with peace to the random chance of rapine. Whether it was a submission to force or an economically driven choice, there is no doubt that in eastern England (and we would say also in western England) the defenceless Britons fell into the power of the warlords. In that respect, Arthur was a man of his time, not different in any marked way from Ida of Bernicia and other unnamed Saxon leaders who emerged at the same time.

Arthur of Loughgall
We know nothing at all of the antecedents of Ida, but Arthur appears to have been born in the last decade of the fifth century at, or near, Loughgall in Ireland, and died, after a confused old age, in Skye. He was educated in Cornwall in leadership arts like rhetoric (satirical poetry at that time) and the profession of arms. As a young man, he became a warrior in the great hostings of the Ulidian king Baetan MacCairill, who ruled the Irish Sea Province. Around the second decade of the sixth century, he emerges as a leader in a campaign in southern England by a mercenary or opportunist army drawn from around the Irish Sea Province in a hosting called by Baetan MacCairill. In that army, Arthur was Baetan's *toisech*, his *dux bellorum*, and he led Baetan's tributary kings from both sides of the Irish Sea, from Wales and from Scotland, in wars that may have lasted more than ten years.

Arthur's Opponents
In their conduct, aims and objectives, the wars that the Irish and their allies were engaged in were very much like the military adventures of the Saxons who established, about the same time and apparently by the same methods, a substantial grip

on northern and eastern England. Arthur's main opponents appear to have been Saxons from the eastern Midlands of England, the forerunners of what became, under Pybba and Penda, the Kingdom of Mercia. At the Battle of Badon, these 'Proto-Mercians' were led by Osla Big Knife, who may be part of the family of the later Christian king, Oswiu, who contested control of the English Midlands against Penda. The direction of the contention between Arthur and the Irish and the Proto-Mercians over time was north/south (or north-east/south-west) rather than the rather binary east/west contest envisaged in the old and discredited 'Britons *versus* Saxons' contest. Both armies may have been fighting not only on their own behalf but in the interests of a Brittonic population which seems, from archaeology, although the documentary evidence is silent, still to have been present in the land. Britons may have been among his opponents in the years of his early success, but in his later years, Arthur appears to have been engaged against Caradawg and other leaders in what were manifestly 'civil war' quarrels over captured territories.

It is true that the success of the 'warlike Arthur' may have set a limit to Saxon (or proto-Mercian) expansion for two or three generations, but that was almost accidental. The real significance of the battles of Arthur's English Campaign, and in particular of the siege of *Mons Badonis*, is the one that Gildas gave it: wars against the external enemy (non-Britonnic armies) to the north-east ceased, but relentless civil wars among the Goidelic warlords of the west (Cornish, Welsh and Irish) continued. The significance of Badon is that it marked the watershed between the two kinds of warfare. Arthur's remaining battles, such as the Welsh campaign, were fought as part of civil wars, and they were fought only in the west.

Arthur the Pagan?

Arthur, as he appears in Harley 3859 (Nennius), seems to be a Christian hero, but that is late, and possibly tainted, evidence. The Arthur we have seen is more like the tyrants Gildas condemned. He is violent, and he doesn't draw the line at sacrilege. In story after story, he appears opposed to the Church, and is bested by canny saints who outwit him and frustrate his ambitions. If we have identified *Henwen* correctly, he hounded a Christian leader from her monastery. He may also have destroyed her shrine or church at Glastonbury because we see, about twenty years after the expulsion of *Henwen* by Arthur, that Saint David and Saint Paul Aurelian (*St Pol de Leon*) found it necessary to undertake extensive restorations there.[1] That may lead us to doubt that he ever fought under the banner, or sign, of Saint Mary. The Arthur we have seen is a self-reliant man who wants his followers to rely on his wisdom, guile and strong sword arm rather than pagan talismans or divine assistance, delivered through the power of saints, even Saint Mary. We must also enter a doubt that Arthur, or anyone else in the sixth century, ever fought under the banner of Saint Mary (Mother or Magdalene).

If King Henry II was correct, and the body in the Glastonbury grave was that of Arthur, we may question which religion, if any, he may have followed. Dunstan, or whoever buried him at Glastonbury, regarded him as a pagan. To those who made the Glastonbury grave, Arthur was a vainglorious military man to be consigned to his last resting place in a pagan style in a hollowed-out oak boat with his paramour Guinevere beside him, either as a human sacrifice or as a help, or translator, in whatever afterlife he might be going to. Those who brought an old and dying Arthur the warrior to be blessed by Columba also thought he was a 'good old pagan'. If he was indeed *Art(ur)bran* of Skye, his Christianity arrived only on his deathbed.

The Historical Arthur?
Much that we have found – 'Arthur of Loughgall', 'Arthur the warlord', 'Arthur the pagan' – may be uncongenial to some people. That is not entirely surprising. All statements made about possible history in the Dark Ages are contentious, and we have recognised from the outset that it is impossible to prove anything, or to write history as it is written about better-documented or witnessed ages. Pursuing a quest about Arthur is like undergoing a Rorschach 'inkblot' test. People see in very different ways the same limited number of shapes (the same few documents and the same inconclusive archaeology). In reviewing these sparse inkblots of potential history, they find responses that are often more culturally determined rather than proceeding from analysis or reasoned surmise.

The fact is that trying to formulate an analysis of what may have gone on in the sixth century is always difficult, about King Arthur or anyone else. A leading scholar of Saxon Britain, Nicholas Higham, writing about his own views on the emergence of the Saxon kingdoms of eastern England in the sixth century, or a little later, says, 'There are dangers in this analysis, of course, since it rests on a conjunction of archaeological evidence, which is contemporary but difficult to interpret, with written comment which is predominantly later.'[2] That has been our problem in our quest in the west. We may take some comfort that Higham concludes that even imperfect analysis nonetheless allows an exploration of 'how things may have happened'.

Guy Halsall, another historian who is an expert in this period, is less accepting and more forthright. He regards any quest for Arthur as fruitless. He says, 'To pretend to have provided answers sought by that romantic quest from the surviving written sources is downright dishonest.' Halsall suggests that we should shape our questions to the evidence that is at hand, and then we might find plausible answers.

In this study, we have done what we can with what is currently available to us. We have honestly declared that our hand is weak, and we have played it as a weak hand, unlikely to win many unchallenged tricks. We have shown our reasoning, and we have made no extravagant claims about our conclusions which are, at best, tentative and open to challenge. To do otherwise, and say nothing, to refuse to attempt to interrogate the sixth century and some surrounding decades, would be to accept a sullen and unresponsive silence in the record about substantial time periods over some two, or perhaps even three, centuries that shaped, at the very least, southern England, and perhaps had a wider and more important long-term national and international effect. We should not admit defeat at the first shot.

It is legitimate to wonder, for example, why this man, Arthur, comes down to us with his name essentially unchanged (*Artuir, Arthur, Art(ur)bran*) while so many of his contemporaries – Baetan, Melwys, Caradawg, Caech (Kay), Muirgen Liban, and Guinevere – have many versions of their names, and indeed become difficult to recognise because of the changes in name form. Arthur appears to be in some way pre-eminent. His name is unchanging. That alone suggests he must have been a historical figure, and an important one at that. Our best guess is that he was indeed 'Arthur of Loughgall', a successful raider from Ireland, born about AD 495 and who died around AD 570.

Other Arthurs

For those who continue to find that unsatisfactory, other Arthurs are available. Anyone can respectably take a position that suggests a different Arthur from the pagan warlord 'Arthur of Loughgall' we have found. It all depends on how we see the very restricted good sources (Gildas and Saint Patrick) and interpret the enigmatic evidence of the archaeology; these are the 'Rorschach inkblots' we all have to look at, and they are very limited in number and in kind. We can only offer our best guesses, how they strike us. We cannot prove anything about Arthur to modern standards. Researchers can even assume, quite properly, in the logic of Halsall's position, that he never existed, or, if he did, that he is not worthy of our conjectures.

A Breton Arthur

That arid view has not won unanimous support. Many versions of Arthur have emerged. Geoffrey Ashe, for example, suggested a Breton king who might be Arthur. This man was called *Riothamus*, and his name appears to mean 'Supreme King'. He was, according to some pedigrees, a prominent member of ruling clans in *Domnonia* (Devon). He flourished as a king around AD 460, and that is really much too early for most of the other data we have about Arthur and his circle. There is no record of any battles won by him in Britain. His Breton career also raises some doubts. We only know – and even this is rather uncertain – that he took an army from Britain to combat Germanic opponents in Brittany, and apparently succeeded. He suffered some reverse not long after that, and we hear no more of him. He was neither a successful warlord nor a dominant and long-lasting king. He is an unlikely Arthur.

Arthur of Devon

There is another Dumnonian Arthur. He was said to be the grandson of Constantine, the king of *Corneu*, which can be Cornwall, or the whole western peninsula. There are three kings who match that description: Erbin, son of Constantine; Gerient, grandson of Constantine; and Cado, the great-grandson of Constantine.

Although Arthur's name replaces an Erbin (*Erbin Map Aircol*) in one genealogical list, and the spiritually aware will see significance in the Old Church of Glastonbury catching fire upon St Erbin's Day, there is no other source that indicates a real relationship between Arthur and the Dumnonian dynasty.

Arthur of Cumbria

In the middle of the nineteenth century, W. F. Skene proposed a Cumbrian Arthur, and there is some merit in that suggestion because Welsh tradition may be thought to support the idea of Arthur as one of the 'Men of the North' (*Gwyr y Gogledd*) whose story may have been relocated in Wales. Norma Lorre Goodrich took up the idea, and used late medieval sources to suggest a link between Arthur and the Kingdom of Rheged. Rheged, however, only became prominent two or three generations after Arthur, and Goodrich has had few followers for her imaginative suggestions.

A Yorkshire Arthur

There also has been little support for a man called *Arthwys* who ruled in the English mountain region of the Pennines. While the battles described in Harley 3859 (Nennius) may well have taken place in the north, this man was at least a generation earlier than the time in which we think King Arthur lived. He may, however, be connected in some way with another *Arthwys* who ruled in Yorkshire, and who was closer to Arthur's time. There is almost nothing that connects either of the two *Arthwys* with the other stories that have come down to us about Arthur.

Another Irish Arthur

One of the 'Irish Arthurs', who lived a generation or so after our 'King Arthur of Loughgall', has also been put forward. He is Arthur, son of Aedan MacGabran, king of Dal Riada, the kingdom that spanned the North Channel to include Antrim and parts of Down in Ireland and Ayrshire and the Edinburgh region of modern Scotland. This Arthur was killed in battle with the Angles, and, if he ever ruled anywhere, it was probably in Scotland. He cannot be connected with the battles of Nennius, or the Welsh campaign. He is simply too late, and in the wrong place, for credibility.

A Roman Arthur

Beram Saklatvala saw an Arthur who was the 'Duke (*Comes*) of Britain', and the last champion of the Roman cause. His Arthur was a Roman cavalry officer who fought to preserve a national unity bequeathed by the departing legions. He also asserted Roman virtues and the Christian religion though his chosen and preferred battlefield weapon, the mounted soldier. Saklatvala created his Arthur by an imaginative combination of Roman history and the knights of Malory. There is no evidence of any such connection in the sixth century, and the figure of Arthur thus created may owe more to Dryden's *King Arthur* – Arthur as the epitome of the English nation – than to any early record. Those who find Saklatvala's Arthur attractive note that there is an early record of a Dalmatian general serving with the Roman forces in Britain in the second century. His name was Lucius Artorius Castus. He was active in Britain and Brittany, but seems to have left no progeny bearing his name in either place. Any connection between him and King Arthur in the sixth century is extremely unlikely.

A Saint Who Was Arthur

Finally, we have another *Arthwys* who does perhaps have some credibility. This man ruled in Glwyssing and Gwent in south-east Wales, and is thought to have lived in the seventh century. Two amateur historians, Baram Blackett and Alan Wilson, argued that he really lived in the early sixth century in *Cernyw* (south-east Wales) and not in *Cerniw* (Cornwall). They put forward some ideas about the location of his grave. The identification of Arthur and Arthwys was also followed by Barber and Pykitt, who suggested that Arthwys of Glywssing retired to Brittany, and became known there as Saint Armel.

Armel was the son of Hoel, which makes him the nephew of Saint Gildas, and one might have thought that that relationship might therefore be more open and explicit in Welsh tradition. If it is there, it is not obvious, and that may lead us to doubt the connection. There is, however, no doubt that a Saint Armel existed. He still has a shrine called Saint Armel des Bochaux near Rennes. Nothing is known of any extensive military career he may have had under that name before he became a monk, and the identification is very conjectural, but he is certainly of the right period. He is thought to have died around AD 570.

The Glamorous Arthur

That such a multiplicity of Arthurs should exist is a witness to the point Higham made; there is archaeology of the time but it is difficult to interpret. There are documents but they are written between three and five hundred years after the time of King Arthur, and reflect their own times more than his. There is another problem. The stories, *romans* and poetry about the warrior king of the twelfth century were written by some outstanding authors, perhaps among the best ever at their craft. Their vivid imagination has proved stronger than the scant 'truthful' data we have been able to identify. In searching for Arthur the king and warrior, that glamorous portrait has proved to be seductive. Men (and some women, like Norma Lorre Goodrich) have looked at all the material available, and used it to find an 'Arthur', but may have relied too heavily on the later medieval narratives. The Arthur who emerges from that approach is quite clearly not a man who could have been successful in the harsh world of the sixth century.

The Continuing Quest

Hard as that is for anyone who loves, and is inspired by, the 'Arthur of literature', the glamorous ruler of sunny Camelot, it should not deter people from trying to find out for themselves more about King Arthur. It is a quest in which anyone can now join. With the advent of the internet and the digitalisation of many library holdings, the search through all the material, whether early or medieval, no longer takes months or years spent in arranging inter-library loans, seeking permissions to make personal visits to distinguished collections, and procuring accurate translations of texts in different languages. With the right skills and a good computer, an interested person could review all that is known of King Arthur, in the primary sources, in the course of an afternoon. The later medieval stories and references might take only a few days more. All that is needed is the interest and the determination to persist.

New Arthurian researchers may also find that they need a thick skin. Fresh discoveries among the inkblots are often sharply criticised. Enthusiasm in this field is rarely welcomed. All the past proponents of other Arthurs have honestly and sincerely read what there is to read. With some ingenuity and, at times, naivete, or guided by their own situation and times, they have reached conclusions different from those we have adopted. That is fair enough. We can all reach our own conclusions about Arthur, and we may, or may not, persuade others to our view. That is the nature of quests for King Arthur. Caxton, the printer and publisher of Malory's Arthur, was perhaps the first to realise this point. In his preface to *Morte D'Arthur*, he said, 'For to give faith and believe that all is true that is contained herein, ye be at your liberty.'

We cannot make people accept what we have found as 'true'. They are at liberty to accept or reject it. We can only declare how we conducted our quest. We have looked at the hard, contemporary evidence – the archaeology of post-Roman Britain and the distribution of artefacts in the Irish Sea Province, and the sparse words of several passages in the text of Gildas. We have considered the battle list of Nennius in Harley 3859, dated about AD 800–820, and the accounts of the Welsh campaign and the expulsion of Henwen in *Culhwch ac Olwen*, which are about two or three hundred years later. We have noted the remarks about Arthur the warrior in the lives (*vitae*) of the Welsh saints (from around AD 700 onwards). We have reviewed the legends and the Arthur who appears in the *Triads* (from about AD 700 onwards). We have studied the man in the Glastonbury grave and concluded, wrongly or rightly, that he was Arthur the king. With modern medical science to guide us, we were able to make some accurate remarks about his medical condition, and we may have detected in the yarns and stories of the *Matter of Britain* about King Arthur that this diagnosis is confirmed by his reported behaviour. We have otherwise tried to avoid the 'romantic Arthur' created from the twelfth century onwards. While we have accepted some details from the medieval *Matter of Britain*, we have left to one side the main figure of Arthur portrayed there. We have also discounted a reading of history that insists Arthur was a British hero defying evil invaders.

We did not come to this task with some pre-existing Arthur in our heads, and that may have been an advantage. With no pre-existing theory to support, we have been able to discern, albeit faintly, a sixth-century Irish warlord with a commitment to Christianity that was at best dubious. We can say that we have seen a warrior who became a king. In that limited sense, our quest is ended. But, of course, any quest for Arthur, or indeed any search for new perceptions about the Dark Ages, is never ended.

A new archaeological find, a lucky strike by a person with a metal detector, the revelation of an unsuspected hoard of silver or gold, a chance discovery in the re-cataloguing of a library, or perhaps even the unexpected exhumation of the bones of Glastonbury, may all turn up new information that would lead us to revise our opinions.

Otherwise, in searching the sixth century, we can only make a current approximation, our best guess at the moment, but we must stand ready to evaluate anything new about the past. We may need to change our opinions if new data, or new answers, found through the application of modern science, become available. A quest in any case is rarely about the answers; a true quest means that we have to keep on asking questions, new and better ones. We may not, we will not, perhaps we cannot, prove the truth about King Arthur, but we can entertain and educate ourselves and others in making the attempt. The quest for Arthur, warrior and king, can go on, and there is no end to it. It is its own holy grail.

AFTERWORD

THE RECEPTION OF NEW THEORIES

People putting forward their own thoughts and discoveries about the controversial King Arthur, and speculating about events that may have surrounded him, with the hope that they might at least find some guarded acceptance, should be encouraged by the words of J. B. S. Haldane:

> I suppose the process of acceptance will pass through the usual four stages:
>
> (i) This is worthless nonsense.
> (ii) This is an interesting, but perverse, point of view.
> (iii) This is true, but is quite unimportant.
> (iv) I always said so.
>
> *Journal of Genetics* Vol. 58, p. 464 (1963)

There is another version which may owe something to the famous rhyme about Benjamin Jowett, Master of Balliol (1817–1893).

> First come I. My name is Jowett.
> There is no knowledge but I know it.
> I am the Master of this College.
> What I don't know, isn't knowledge.

The alternative 'Jowett' version of the rules of acceptance in academic circles is:

1. If this were true, we would know it; we do not know it, so it isn't true.
2. This may be true, but has not been proved.
3. This may be proved, but it is not significant.
4. We all know this, and it does not require re-statement.[1]

APPENDICES

In the main text of this book, I have from time to time in the interests of clarity and brevity left out detailed argument and so, lacking that detail, some readers may be sceptical about particular conclusions that I have reached. They may think, for example, that I have assigned Arthur himself to the wrong time, and require more information to be persuaded about the methods by which I reached my view of his historicity and the period in which he may have flourished. Others may have searched the main text in vain for my views on cherished stories in the penumbra of Arthur, the 'Sign of Saint Mary', or, perhaps, their favourite parts of the Arthurian myth such as 'the sword in the stone'. For the sceptical reader, and those who are merely curious, or want to know more detail about some matters in the Arthurian hinterland, perhaps to identify a topic they might wish to pursue themselves, here are five appendices which may help.

APPENDIX I

DATING IN THE SIXTH CENTURY

Copying Errors

Dating events and people in the sixth century is difficult because all the sources we have for that period (with two exceptions) are material copied in the ninth century, or later, from earlier records that no longer exist. Most of the copies we have of the ninth-century documents are artefacts made around the twelfth century. Until Caxton introduced printing to England, all copies were made by hand, and each time a copy was made the text changed.

The men who made the copies had reasons to write what, and as, they did. They were not trying to make an accurate copy unchanged from the original. They were trying to elevate the status of the family of the ruler who commissioned the copy, or assert the antiquity of their monastery to give it more power and prestige, so they omitted some things and added others. They also made errors through misreading, carelessness or misunderstanding.

Much of the early material was kept in annals. Annals were not continuous narratives, but long lists of events, written in columns, of the deaths of saints and the exploits of kings. Dates and events could be placed in the wrong column, and later silently corrected in an entirely erroneous way. The result is that some rulers can appear to be active over very long periods – well over a hundred years. Kings were sometimes, without much regard for actual dates or likelihood, given fathers or mothers for political reasons, or were drawn into the orbits of greater heroes, or saints of greater holiness, for prestige. Their affiliations and families were sometimes changed to remove facts that had become inconvenient. To use and understand the early sources we must adjust the material, trying as much we can to recover the original date or the original source.

This is a somewhat arcane skill, and generates its own academic controversies. I had no wish to enter that scholarly battleground. To work out what may have been happening in the Age of Arthur, I formulated my own methods, and reached my own conclusions. This note is an attempt to explain how I arrived at conclusions about *when* things happened.

The *Annals of Ulster*

My examples are drawn from the *Annals of Ulster*. If we ignore the religious entries pertaining to saints and abbeys, the *Annals of Ulster* offers several strands of secular stories: information derived from the Roman historian Marcellinus; information from Ui Neill sources about the Irish king Aed Ainmire and his ally on the other side of the Irish Sea, Aedan MacGabran; and information from bardic sources about Baetan and the Ulidians, the Men of Ulster. There is too a core of observations of the natural world. All have been woven together with the religious information to form an unspoken narrative – propaganda if you like – rather than the bare factual record the *Annals of Ulster* purports to be.

We can distinguish strands where material has been misdated. Material relating to Aedan MacGabran is wrong by about eighty years. He can't have taken the Isle of Man in 504 as an active warrior aged at least twenty, and again in AD 582 or 583. We can estimate a *floruit* date for him, through Bede and Adomnan's *Life of St Columba,* of around AD 580. It is evident that some 'Aedan dates' are out by eighty years. We call that the 'Aed 80'.

The *Annals* tell us that Fiachna Lurgan, son of Baetan, was a victorious warrior between 563 and 616. But we know from *St Columba's life* written by Adomnan, supported by Bede, that neither Baetan nor his sons, that is, the Ulidians, were powerful at the time of the Convention of Drumcett which is fairly securely dated to AD 575/576. The hegemony of the Ulstermen must be earlier than that. The dates pertaining to them seem to be misplaced by forty years (the Ulidian 40).

Modern accurate tree ring studies reveal that hottest summer in the sixth century was AD 560. The hottest summer noted in the *Annals* is AD 589. There appears to be a thirty-year discrepancy (the Natural 30).

Impact of Date Change: Aed 80

496 Fall of Dunlethglas, Baetan's capital, becomes 576 (about the same time as the kings assembled at Drumcett sliced up Baetan's 'empire'). That seems more credible than a date where Aed and Baetan were either not yet born or were infants.

Impact of Date Change: Ulidian 40

563 Baetan leads an army (which apparently included Ui Nialls as mercenaries or tributaries) becomes 523 (which is consonant with what we know of the relative importance of the Ulidians and the Ui Nialls early in the sixth century)

574 Victory by Fiachna, son of Baetan, becomes 534

578 Return from Man (*Reversio Manu*) becomes 538

581 Death of Baetan becomes 541 (perhaps in 'the 540 event')

594 Fiachna's victory in Man becomes 554

601 Ulidian army struck by earthquake in Bairchu (south-east Ireland) becomes 561 (this may be wrong still – see note on the *Annals of Wales* below)

602 Fiachna's victory becomes 562

606 Slaying of the sons of Baetan becomes 566

610 Death of Maelumai (Melwys, son of Baetan) becomes 570

616 Sack of the monastery of Bangor becomes 576 (that is just after Drumcett, or possibly at the same time)

Impact of Date Change: Natural 30

564 Great wind becomes 534

573 *Muirgeilt capta est* (the mad sea is constrained) becomes 542

576 Abundance of nuts becomes 546

Impact of Date Change: The Welsh 130

The *Annals of Wales*, which is thought to be based on an Irish original, covers some of the same events but appears to have suffered from the same thirty-year displacement as the natural events plus a hundred years. In the Welsh record the correction shows:

676 The rising of a star seen throughout the world becomes 536

682 A great plague in Britain becomes 542

683 A great plague in Ireland becomes 543

684 A great earthquake in the Isle of Man becomes 544

689 The rain turned to blood in Britain, and in Ireland milk and butter turned to blood becomes 549

More Misplaced Events?
Another *Annals of Ulster* entry, possibly affected by the same earlier copy as the Welsh record, plus ten (that is 140) says: 684 (corrected to 544) the death of children began, and *Loch nEchach* (Lough Neagh) turned to blood.

685 There was great windstorm and an earthquake in Ireland (corrected to 545) which may be the same one mentioned in the Welsh Annals, or the one that destroyed the Ulidian army in south-eastern Ireland. Fiachna Lurgan's victory in Man and the 'slaying of Baetan's sons' may also need further correction to 532 and 536 respectively.

Summary of Revised Events
These revised dates for events are consistent with modern scientific evidence of a possible 'impact event' in 540 plus or minus ten. The proposed sequence of events goes like this. A new star appeared in the middle 530s – possibly a comet. Shortly thereafter there was a great windstorm (as in the Tunguska event in Russia), and an earthquake was experienced in south-east Ireland and the Isle of Man. Then children died, and rain and lakes turned to blood. As vegetation recovered, there was an abundance of nuts (a normal biological response by nut-bearing bushes and trees to a 'threat'). Sea conditions returned to normal levels and conditions, but we have no information on fish stocks. There was a 'dearth of birds' that may be part of the same natural event.

Political Consequences
Political consequences, known from other sources in the period 540 to 576, confirm the shift in power indicated by the date changes. After 576, Aed Ainmire and Aedan MacGabran were the dominant leaders in the northern part of the Irish Sea Province.

This fits the picture that we have seen earlier emerging from the study of the literature in the main chapters of the book. We can perhaps even derive detail otherwise missing. It may be, for example, that the *Reversio Manu* (the return or retreat from Man) and the slaying of Baetan's sons reflects, or was part of, the *Twrch Trwyth* campaign.

The 'corrected annalistic dates', the literature and the tree-ring science give us a plausible sequence of dates for the events of the sixth century. We should, however, always remember, and constantly be aware, that even the most plausible argument does not constitute 'proof'. For anything approaching 'proof' we need either new documents and/or more archaeological data. Thinking about *when* things may have happened, however, may direct our thoughts productively as we seek to find out *what* may have happened.

APPENDIX II

THE 540 EVENT:
THE WAVE OF THE PAST

A Personal Note

The great question which looms over the history of the British Isles in the period AD 400–800, the period traditionally called the Dark Ages, is: what happened in the British Isles that did not happen in Gaul, Iberia, Italy and other parts of the Roman Empire? Why did Britain apparently lose its history? Why, if he was so great a warrior and king, is the record silent about Arthur?

In the early 1980s, alongside Professor Mike Baillie, a dendrochronologist from Queen's University of Belfast, at first independently and then working together, I developed a theory which seemed, on the face of it, to provide at least a partial answer. Mike Baillie was working on the evidence of tree rings, and I was trawling through whatever hard copies of ancient documents I could find in the library of the University of Bristol, or borrow from, or consult in, other academic libraries. Based on the evidence then available to us, we formed the conjecture that an 'impact event' may have created the Dark Ages. We believed that this event occurred around AD 540, plus or minus ten years.

Baillie published an account of our reasoning in his book *Exodus to Arthur* (London: Batsford, 1993; see, in particular, pp. 125–126). I offer here a short account of the research which led me, initially independently, and then collaboratively, as described in Mike's book, to form that view. It was an exciting day when we first made contact with one another. I remember it well because I came back from a university meeting to be told that, responding to a letter I had written to him, he had telephoned when I was out of the office. My secretary told me: 'Your dendrochronologist says to give him a ring.'

The Wave of the Past

It is difficult to predict natural disasters such as the dreadful tsunami events of 26 December (Boxing Day) 2004. Those who can do it, whether they use satellites, remote sensing from space, deep ocean sensors or other methods, are rightly honoured. But in the days before scientific equipment allowed us to measure the mood of the surly Earth, when tsunamis and the like were attributed to the action of a capricious god (or gods), prediction was more difficult. Men looked at the sky, and into the scriptures, and thought they saw their future. One of the most successful heaven-watchers and readers was a monk called Gildas, and what he predicted, on the basis of his observations and his reading of the Bible, was the 'ruination of Britain', an event that came catastrophically to pass around the middle of the sixth century. In, or about, the fourth decade of that century, Gildas issued his prediction in the form of a sermon, what he called a little warning (*admonitiuncula*).[1] He warned the kings of western Britain that if they did not reform, they would be punished by God. They didn't, and they were.

Inundations

The legends of the period (there are no histories)[2] tell us that, in Wales, a whole *cantref* (district) belonging to a chieftain called *Gwyddno Garanhir* disappeared beneath the sea.[3] The *Chronica de Wallia*[4] lists three other named kingdoms submerged. The Menai Strait, part of the territory of another king called *Tyno Helig*, was scoured by great waves, and thereafter men had to use boats to pass across it.[5] *Maelgwn Gwynedd*, one of those kings warned by Gildas, was found, unmarked but dead, in the church of Rhos where he had tried to hide from the *fad felen* (which may have been a tidal wave).[6] In Cornwall, land submerged beneath the sea was recalled as the 'lost land of Lyonesse'.

There is no doubt that an inundation of some kind happened at some time in history. A change in sea level is evidenced by drowned or submerged forests around many of the coasts of western Britain. In England, they are seen at the mouth of the Char, in Tor Bay, Mount's Bay, the Hayle, and Camel estuaries, and further east at Minehead, Porlock and Sturt Flats. In Wales, they are seen at Carmarthen, Swansea and along the north coast.

On all these coasts, as far north as the Solway Firth, there are also large deposits of aeolian sand (sand that has attained a sufficient mass to be spread inland by the wind).[7] The extensive sand dunes of the Les Landes in south-western France may share a common origin. On the basis of studies carried out elsewhere in the world, such as on the coasts of Oregon in the USA, all such sand deposits should be regarded as the signs of an exhausted tsunami.[8]

There are additional geological signs that may betoken a great wave. Several beaches in Gower and Pembrokeshire display mixed sediments in a variable and sometimes bewildering order. There is no agreement about the stratigraphic relation of these deposits.[9] The coastal drifts of Cardigan Bay and Gower yield fragments of Mesozoic rocks and fossils of Liassic and Middle Jurassic age which may have come from the floor of the Irish Sea.[10] Other fine-ground erratic detritus from the Irish Sea has been noted on Welsh coasts. At Croyde in Devon, the 'blown sand', the raised beaches and erratics are all controversial. There is no full explanation of the erratics in the Axe Valley in south Devon, and in Cornwall there is no agreement on the age of the sand deposits around St Erth.[11] Further inland, in places such as the east Devon plateau and the Axe Valley, there are silty deposits of the kind associated with tsunamis when their progress over land is unimpeded.[12]

The debate among geologists about such matters has so far focused on glaciation. There appears to be little current doubt that the Devon erratics were transported to their present sites by known glaciers that brought material from Ireland and the north of Scotland. The suggestion that some of the stratigraphic puzzles that the erratics and other rocks and sands pose may have been caused by a notably large, sudden and catastrophic tsunami has not been examined.[13]

There are non-geological indications elsewhere that the inundation caused by the tsunami was indeed catastrophic. An account of alterations to the River Avon at Bristol in 1804 revealed around seventy trees which had all fallen in the same direction and at the same time. They were buried under levels of sand and gravel consistent with a wave deposit.[14] There is no current explanation of the force that felled them. To understand what may have happened at Bristol and elsewhere, we have to turn from science to history.

Procopius

Perhaps the best historical report of a tsunami event affecting Britain comes from the Byzantine historian Procopius. Writing not earlier than AD 530 and not later than AD 550, he gives a description of an island off north-west Europe called *Brittia* which appears to be western Britain.[15] It is worth repeating in detail.

> Now in this island of Brittia the men of ancient time built a long wall, cutting off a large part of it, and the climate and the soil and everything else is not alike on the two sides of it. For to the east of the wall there is salubrious air, changing with the seasons, being moderately warm in summer and cool in winter. And many people dwell there, living in the same fashion as other men, and the trees abound with fruits which ripen at the fitting season, and the corn lands flourish as any; furthermore, the land seems to display a genuine pride in abundance of springs of water. But on the west side everything is the reverse of this, so that it is actually impossible for a man to survive there even a half-hour, but countless snakes and every other kind of wild creature occupy this area as their own. And strangest of all, the inhabitants say that if any man crosses the wall and goes to the other side, he dies straight away, being quite unable to support the pestilential air of that region, and wild animals, likewise, which go there are instantly met and taken by death.[16]

Procopius continues with a story that he was at pains to say seemed to him close to mythology. Yet so many people told him the story he felt obliged to repeat it. It is about the souls of men being conveyed to Brittia. He says:

> Along the coast of the ocean which lies opposite Brittia there are numerous villages. These are inhabited by men who fish with nets or till the soil or carry on a sea-trade with this island, being in other respects subject to the Franks but never making them any tribute, that burden being remitted to them on account, they say, of a certain service...
>
> The men of this place say that the conduct of souls is laid upon them in turn ... As soon as darkness comes on, they retire to their houses and sleep ... And at a late hour of the

night they are conscious of a knocking on their doors and hear an indistinct voice calling them together for their task. And they with no hesitation rise from their beds and walk to the shore. There they see skiffs in readiness with no man in them at all ... and they are aware that the boats are burdened with a large number of passengers and are wet by the waves to the edge of the planks and the oarlocks, having not so much as one finger's breadth above the water ... After a single hour they put in at Brittia ... And yet when they make this passage in their own boats, not using sails but rowing, they with difficulty make this passage in a day and a night. When they have reached the island and have been relieved of their burden, their boats suddenly becoming light and riding high about the waves, for they sink no further in the water than the keel itself.

It is quite clear that when Procopius tells us of a dividing wall, he is not speaking of Hadrian's Wall. His division is east/west, not north/south. Walls of the kind he describes do exist close to the Hampshire coast. What is thought to be the beginning of the Wansdyke runs north/south from the coast near Bristol but that wall seems to begin at Bristol with an east/west wall. Such walls of course do not divide the whole island of Britain, but to an observer on the coast they might appear to do so. In Wales, Offa's Dyke, which does divide east from west, of course was not there when Procopius was writing, but there may have been some forerunner structure. We don't know. The question is: did these walls at one time make an east/west divide which, if a man were to cross, he might die?

The East/West Divide

Science has some answers. There is no doubt at all about an east/west divide in the settlement patterns of Britain which may reflect the destruction caused by the event. It is manifest in the pattern of Anglo-Saxon settlements revealed by archaeology and place-name studies. All Saxon names lie to the east, and there are no Saxon names in the west until at least the eighth or ninth century. In the far west, there are virtually no early names. Although Cornwall was settled in Roman times, and exported tin to Rome, there are no Cornish place names from that period. The earliest Cornish place names date from several centuries later.[17] In eastern Britain by contrast, there are commonly place names that date back at least to Roman times, and beyond. In the west, the human population that might have maintained knowledge and use of the names seems to have disappeared in the fifth or sixth century.

The same divide appears in studies of tree coverage. Western Britain has noticeably fewer trees than eastern Britain. Oliver Rackham used *Domesday Book* records to show that Cornwall (3 per cent) and Devon (4 per cent) had tree cover substantially less than the national average of 14 per cent.[18] There are no overt reasons in climate or soil for the difference. The archaeological record does not reveal the presence of larger population in the west who could have cleared the land more effectively than easterners did.

In any case, Rackham doubts the ability of early farmers to permanently destroy woods. Evidence from nineteenth-century New England in the USA, shows that the trees quickly regenerated where farmers abandoned the land, and recovered the landscape at the rate of approximately 3 acres of land per year.[19] The idea that Cornish and Devonian farmers were more successful in clearing trees than their more easterly fellow countrymen must clearly be an unjustified assertion.

The real reason for the lack of trees must be widespread species loss (as Procopius reports). To regenerate effectively, trees need the intervention of birds and animals to spread seeds. In the west of England that did not happen. Only old place names recall the former forests. The former name for St Michael's Mount, for example, was *carrek loes yn coes* – 'the grey rock in the forest'.[20]

Population Loss

The population loss in Britain was considerable. Roman Britain around AD 400 had a population estimated at 3 million. By AD 600, it had fallen to just over 1 million.[21] Historians cannot assign a cause for the decline, and there are no reliable data about the distribution of the population in either AD 400 or in AD 600. It appears, however, that the major population centres in AD 600 were in the east, in places such as London and York. Bath may have been already abandoned by AD 600, or, at least, was no longer important. Further west, the people appear to have gone completely. The Irish and Welsh saints who drifted into

Cornwall in the later sixth and seventh centuries found few human populations to welcome them, and were able easily, without having to overcome local resistance, to found settlements named after themselves.²² Archaeology and place-name studies show a degree of Irish colonisation which appears to have taken place from the mid-sixth century onwards.

Political and Cultural Change

There are also signs of the political and cultural damage that might be expected after a major disaster in the regions around southern Ireland, western England and the Irish Sea. In Munster, a king called Crimthann was deposed and none of his kin succeeded him. In south-east Ulster, the very powerful King Baetan MacCairill, who had exacted tribute from Skye to Munster, died, and his sons did not succeed him.²³ Geoffrey of Monmouth recorded a yarn about a conquering chieftain called Godmund Auffricaunus²⁴ who gained control over England, and then, for no given reason, disappears.²⁵ The French recorded an even more bizarre story in which the famous King Arthur was bested by a sea monster (*capalu*). This unusual animal also wore the crown of England, and then relinquished it.²⁶ It may be *capalu* was a mistranslation or misunderstanding of the name of the Irish king Muirchertach MacErc. He too died in mysterious circumstances, and about the same time (AD 540 plus or minus ten).

Taken together, the stories indicate a process that saw ruling powers replaced without military defeat by their political rivals in the period around AD 540. The kings deposed were all coastal rulers. Those who succeeded them (like the Ui Neills in Ireland) were more people from further inland. The tales indicate a collapse of the powers around the Irish Sea between AD 530 and AD 580.

That political collapse is matched by cultural changes indicating a wider social collapse. The Welsh language in this period, for example, stops being Late British, a heavily inflected language like Latin, and starts to become uninflected Early Welsh, the recognisable ancestor of modern Welsh. The fully developed Church described by Gildas, a body that had its own clergy (who cavorted, he complained, 'with foreign women'), had disappeared. By the time Saint Augustine of Canterbury arrived in 603, there was no discernible English Church to welcome or oppose him. There was only the pious queen of a Kentish king. The literate society for which Gildas was writing had disappeared too. No records were kept. It was left to another monk, Nennius, to try to re-create the records of the people of western Britain around three hundred years later. In Ireland, a country with a strong oral culture, written records began to be kept at Bangor around AD 550. Historians agree that date marks a sort of horizon. Before that date, we can see nothing distinctly, and in the west of England, virtually nothing at all. It seems that Procopius was right about the east/west divide, that there was an event that was disastrous for all the peoples around the Irish Sea.

The Nature of the Wave

The other part of the story told by Procopius indicates that a tsunami may have been involved in the disaster. He may have given us information that enables us to guess at its dimensions and place of origin. Procopius says that the men from the shore opposite *Brittia* (France, possibly Brittany) accomplished a journey in one hour that under normal trading circumstances they might expect to last a day and a night. Viking sailors later measured distance by *doegr*, the distance a boat could travel in one day. This has been calculated to be about 150 miles. If the sailors in the Procopius story had a similar measurement of their likely distance travelled, the normal journey of a day and a night might have been about 200 miles.

In the Procopius account, they accomplished that journey at very high speed, in scarcely more than one hour. That suggests that the wave they were borne by must have been moving at speeds of at least 150 mph. There is another indication of speed. The empty, but apparently heavily laden, boats described by the informants of Procopius were exhibiting a phenomenon that few sixth-century sailors could normally have witnessed. Boats at speed exhibit a phenomenon called 'squat', that is, they sit much lower in the water – as they would if they were heavily laden.[27] Boats of that period were not likely to be capable of the speeds necessary to achieve 'squatting' except in extreme sailing conditions.

Van Gestle, an eyewitness at the vast eruption at Krakatoa in August 1883, described how the rapid journey of the boats may have occurred. The first sign of the disaster at Krakatoa was that the boats in the bay before him all moved very swiftly and in the same direction.[28] In that case, they were eventually engulfed by the steam and boiling waters where the sea floor had opened.

Any tsunami is presaged by this draining of harbours and beaches, and the outward movement of poorly tethered boats. If, as at Krakatoa, the sea floor sank, the effect becomes magnified. The imminent arrival of a major tsunami, caused by the sudden sinking of the sea floor off the English coast, could have had the same effect on boats in the harbours of coastal France. As the waters rushed out, the boats would go with them. Alternatively, the *seiche* wave (the back wash) of a tsunami could also have carried the boats rapidly to Cornwall or Devon. But whatever the cause, the speed of the boats in making the journey to the English coast (perhaps 100–150 mph, we estimate) suggests that the original incoming tsunami was very fast.

The speed of the tsunami enables the probable point of origin to be calculated. Tsunami speed is a function of the depth of the sea where the event originates. The velocity is computed by the formula V = *the square root of g multiplied by D*, where V is the velocity, g the gravitational acceleration, and D the depth of water. Thus, a wave generated at the average of depth of the Pacific Ocean (18,480 feet – 5,633 m) could reach a speed of 524 miles per hour.[29] The continental shelf west of Britain and south of Ireland is about 630 feet (just under 200 m) deep, and an event there would produce tsunami travelling at about 100 mph. Further out, in the near Atlantic, speeds in excess of 200 mph could be generated. The evidence of the fishermen in Procopius's story suggests an event beyond the edge of the continental shelf.

More complex formulae govern the amplitude, or height, of the wave. A wave recorded in 1737 reached an estimated height of 210 feet (64 m), and the 1946 tsunami that destroyed the Scotch Cap lighthouse was at least 118 feet high (35.9 m). The so-called 'ultimate wave' of 1958 hit areas as high as 1,740 feet (530 m) in height, and reached 3,600 feet (914 m) inland. The trimline of denuded vegetation that marked its passage was 110 feet (33.5 m) high, and the speed was estimated to be between 97 and 130 mph.[30]

The shape and nature of the coast of western Britain may have enhanced the characteristics of the tsunami. The Severn Bore, generated in the Severn Estuary, for example, commonly generates a wave of 10 feet (3 m) or more under normal tidal forces. The forces that create the Bore would also act upon a tsunami. The configuration of the land and sea bottom in the west of England suggests that the wave may have been at least 70 feet (21 m) in height and may have been a great deal higher.[31]

Tidal reaction to the sea floor increases the speed of the Severn Bore. It would have enhanced the speed of the tsunami. It may have been travelling well over 100 miles per hour when it arrived at Avonmouth where the Severn Estuary starts to narrow. Upstream it may have increased its speed. Speed plus height adds to the considerable destructive force of tsunamis on impact.

The speed and height of the wave itself were not the only problems the people of the west faced. The storm waves familiar around the coasts of Britain rarely reach speeds in excess of 60 mph, or heights larger than 50 feet (15.25 m). Even so, the storm waves exert a pressure of about 4,000 pounds per square foot on impact.[32] The shock wave of displaced air that storm waves generate in front of them is even greater, exerting a pressure as great as 16,800 pounds per square foot. These forces are sufficient to destroy some of the strongest structures modern engineers can devise.

A tsunami in the sixth century would encounter only very rudimentary buildings. There were few Roman-style stone buildings in western Britain, and stone churches were only being built by one Church, centred in south-east Ulster. Most structures would have been either wooden, or wattle and daub. There were no buildings of any strength to resist the wave. As happened in Sumatra in 2004, whole communities would have been carried away. The evidence we have from Procopius, from archaeology, from place names and from legends is that this is exactly what happened.

The Cause of the Wave

That still leaves another big question: what caused the tsunami? One possibility is that there was a major tectonic shift South-West of the British Isles. The big Storegga land slip on the Norwegian coast about 7,300 years ago caused major tsunamis (some 40 feet (12 m) in height), and the evidence of it can still be seen on the seabed, and the waves it generated on some North Atlantic islands today.[33] There is currently no evidence of a similar very large slippage to the west of England at this time.

Yet there is no doubt that there has been a substantial change in sea levels. The Scilly Isles were apparently one island in the time of Sulpicius Severus (*fl*. AD 380). Two heretical bishops were exiled to Scilly which seems to have been one island then. Charles Thomas, who has investigated the Scillies, attributes the sea change to isostatic and eustatic adjustments. He, however, noted the view of Hawkins that the fall of the Scillies might be due to tectonic displacement. He also notes that Carter observed that the rising sea level in the Scillies was matched by a fall in sea level at Malin Head in the north of Ireland.[34] The level of the land seems to have risen too in Somerset. Islands around Glastonbury became landlocked, and still further east, in Gloucestershire, a Roman water mill appears now to be well above the present bed of the stream it used.[35] In Ireland, Lough Neagh increased in size[36] and some of the rivers feeding it may have changed course.[37] On this evidence there appears to have been a large tectonic adjustment south of Ireland and west of Britain.

While tectonic forces may have been the primary cause of the tsunami, other even more powerful forces may also have been involved. There is evidence that indicates that Gildas may have been right to suggest a heavenly origin for 'Britain's ruin'. The cosmologists Victor Clube and Bill Napier have identified what they call 'bombardment episodes' during which the Earth may be at enhanced risk of receiving material such as asteroids and meteorites from space. In particular they note two periods: around AD 450 and about AD 550. They further suggest that the arrival of a falling celestial body in the ocean could have a greater effect on human populations than a land-based impact. Tsunami-related damage is an intimate part of the process they imagine, but it is not the whole of the story.[38]

Clube and Napier calculated the effect of a body such as the asteroid *Hephaistos* striking the ocean. It would have an impact energy, they thought, of around 100 megatons. It would create a cavity in the ocean bed, and penetrate into the hot mantle of the Earth. It would create huge and very damaging tsunamis immediately.

The greatest damage, however, of an impact event of this kind would be long term. Clube and Napier speculate that plankton, and other biological material, would be drawn up into the plume that such an impact would create. Such plumes reach many kilometres into the sky. As the animals in the plume died, they would create a 'dust veil' (like the dust veils created by the ash of erupting volcanoes) that would inhibit the sun's rays from reaching the Earth. On land crops would fail, and in the sea the removal of the base of the food chain would lead to a mass extinction of species.

Effects of the Impact Event

Something very like their scenario appears in the annals of the sixth century. In Ireland, there were contemporaneous reports of red lakes (lakes and rivers of blood), which may indicate blooms of algae. Such blooms are not uncommon today, and are usually caused by a sudden access to nutrients. *Euglena*, for example, is bright red, and blooms when it has access to supplies of nitrogen and phosphorus, both of which, delivered by rainfall, are possible outcomes from an impact event.[39]

The dendrochronologist Mike Baillie, in a series of papers, articles and books, has demonstrated that there was indeed a 'dust veil' event around AD 540. It was hemispheric. Right across the northern part of the planet for a period of two or three years trees grew very little, and in Ireland around Lough Neagh oak trees took some twenty-five years to recover to normal growth patterns. There was a climatic change that cannot be explained by submarine tectonic changes alone. [40]

The usual explanation of 'dust veils' and other such climatic change events is a major volcanic eruption. The evidence for them is found in the international Greenland Ice Core Surveys. If there was a volcano involved in the event around AD 540, so far the guilty volcano has not been identified in the ice cores. The nearest one in time seems to be around AD 527 or 528.

An impact event of this magnitude, on the other hand, one that involved tsunamis and climate change, would have other consequences, and may have been recorded without being understood at the time. Noxious gases may have been liberated from the seabed 'boundary layers' (which might explain the strange unmarked death of Maelgwn and the sudden death of men and animals remarked by Procopius). Rain, and therefore water, supplies might have been contaminated. There is a report of Gwyddno's horses dying after drinking poisoned water from the river that flows into Bala lake.[41] A report of the death of the Irish saint Finnian in this period notes *'pestilentia in acqua'* (plague in the water).[42]

Ho 13

But if there were a comet, meteorite or other heavenly body, what was it and when did material from it fall to cause these effects on human and animal populations? Observers in China have kept a good record for over two thousand years of falling meteorites, and the appearance of comets associated with such falls. The celestial body responsible may be a comet (called Ho 13) that appeared in November AD 539. Its tail lengthened during the twenty-one days during which it was observed.[43] No meteorite was observed to fall. That, however, may not be significant. In 372 BC a comet was seen, and there were earthquakes and tidal waves at Achaea in Greece, but no meteorite was seen to fall.

It is impossible to say with accuracy where the object may have fallen, or what its flight path may have been. The currently available seabed studies do not reveal the high concentrations of metals such as palladium and iron-nickel that would indicate an impact site, although palladium minerals (mertieite and isomertiete with associated dendritic gold) have been noted at Torquay.[44] These minerals could have been deposited there by a tsunami.

No obvious crater appears, but prominent seabed features such as the 'Celtic Sea Deep' and the Mochras Fault off Wales may repay fresh study. Submarine landslides are commonly remarked in the Atlantic. Few have been dated. Any one of them could have been produced by an impact event, and thus in turn have produced an event such as the AD 540 tsunami.

The likeliest source of an earthquake-induced slide without an impact event would be the Azores–Gibraltar transform fault that produced the 1755 Lisbon earthquake (which did produce local effects in the Bristol area – ships in the harbour broke mooring lines and some local lakes turned black). The last major (8+) submarine earthquake on this fault was around 216 BC.[45] But there is nothing in the submarine record that suggests the climate-changing event demanded by dendrochronology.

The Evidence of Legends

We therefore have to turn again to legends. An impact event would have produced substantial shockwaves, perhaps experienced and understood by the people of the time as short-lived, very severe storm-force winds. Welsh tradition recalls a verse:

Ochenaid Gwyddno Garanhir
Pan droes y don dros ei dir

(the sigh of Gwyddno Garanhir when the wave covered his land)[46]

Welsh poetry often exaggerates, and is frequently ironic. There is no great difficulty in regarding Gwyddno's 'sigh' as a reference to a shock wave or short-lived storm-force wind. Muirchertach MacErc was also fatally involved with 'a sigh and a wind'. According to his death legend, a beautiful maiden called *Sin* offered herself to him as his paramour if he would agree never to speak her name. If he did say the name, she told him, he would be accursed. Muirchertach accepted her conditions. He turned his Christian queen and her children away from the court, and incurred the wrath of the clergy. Muirchertach did not care. He continued to enjoy the company of the lovely lady. But just after *Samhain* a great storm arose. 'This is the sigh of winter's night,' the king said. The girl reminded him that 'winter night' and 'storm' was her name. But Muirchertach repeated his remarks about the storm (*sin*) and she told him that he had invoked the curse. By naming her, he is doomed. She set the house on fire, and he was drowned trying to escape the flames in a vat of wine.[47] He may also have been struck by a roof beam.

It is clear that Muirchertach, like Gwyddno, dies just after a storm of an unusual, and perhaps magical, type. But Muirchertach's story gives us the time of year, just after *Samhain*, 1 November. That timing is consistent with the passing of the Ho 13 comet, and with the fallen trees found at Bristol. It suggests that the legendary traditions of Gwyddno and Muirchertach may refer to a real event that took place in the first week of November AD 539.

CONCLUSIONS

Legends cannot be pressed too far as history, and a great deal of the science that would tell us more about the event of 540 remains to be done. The AD 540 event will therefore continue to remain fairly obscure, but we can say that there was a traumatic event that drowned landscapes, led to widespread species loss, cultural, social, linguistic and political changes, and the death and/or forced migration of perhaps as many as two million people.[48] Trees and other plants took at least five years to recover, and in some places did not grow again at all. Human society in western England, and other affected regions, took centuries to recover. The impact on Britain – one of the most prosperous, powerful and sophisticated of Roman provinces in the third century – was so dreadful that historians coined a new phrase to describe the period after AD 540. They called it 'the Dark Ages', and Gildas the monk was its accurate prophet.

APPENDIX III

THE OLD CHURCH AT GLASTONBURY

The Old Church, or *vetusta ecclesia*, of Glastonbury is not directly connected with King Arthur. It is, however, very much part of his hinterland, the context in which he came to be viewed over the centuries. It is important in matters Arthurian for five reasons:

1. It may be on the site of one of the battles in his 'English campaign', the battle of Fort Guinnion.
2. It may be the place from which he expelled one of the figures involved in his Welsh campaign, *Henwen*.
3. If the bones in the grave excavated in 1190 in Glastonbury were his, someone thought this extraordinary holy site was a more appropriate resting place for them than the place where he was first buried. The Glastonbury grave is unlikely to have been his first resting place.
4. Glastonbury was regarded as a place of unusual sanctity for many centuries, and some famous saints were buried there. A Glastonbury burial may have been regarded as an honour as burial on the Mount of Olives is today in modern Israel. It may signal Arthur's perceived importance.
5. In the sixth century, Glastonbury was an Irish foundation, and that may be an indicator of Arthur's ethnicity.

The Oldest Church Anywhere?

In the earliest years of Christianity, there were no buildings anywhere dedicated solely to worship, the kind of structures that we today call 'churches'. There was also no formal organisation with priests and bishops, parishes, sees and dioceses. We might call that kind of 'Church' *ecclesia*, to distinguish it from 'church' meaning a 'building for worship'. Christians met to worship where they could in the first centuries of Christianity. Some met in private houses, and in Rome they met in the catacombs. There was almost no *ecclesia* and there were no churches. Glastonbury is therefore very unusual in claiming to have had a 'church' from the earliest times.

Although the church at Glastonbury was always regarded as being very ancient, the claim only became overt and documented in the twelfth century. For the clergy of the time, the date of the foundation mattered because it conveyed privileges and power in synods and councils of the Roman *ecclesia*. In England, the competition was with Westminster, which gradually moved its foundation back from King Sebert (AD 604), which trumped Glastonbury's King Ine, who issued a charter about a hundred years later (the first royal patron of Glastonbury was actually Centwine, AD 676–685). Glastonbury then discovered a King Lucius who granted a charter in AD 166, but Westminster claimed they too had a charter from this king. Glastonbury then asserted that its antiquity really dated from AD 63 'the thirty-first year from the Passion of the Lord and fifteenth since the Assumption of the Blessed Virgin'. The founder(s) was Joseph of Arimathea, or monks sent by Saint Philip the Apostle who was active in Gaul about then. If this story were true, the 'Old Church' at Glastonbury has a claim to be the first 'church' anywhere in the world.

The Investigation of William of Malmesbury
William of Malmesbury was a shrewd and assiduous investigator, and he had access to Glastonbury's own records. William knew this story of the very early foundation of the Old Church, or, at least, a version of it.

He described the Glastonbury church thus:

This church is certainly the oldest I am acquainted with in England, and from this circumstance derives its name. In it are preserved the mortal remains of many saints ... The very floor inlaid with polished stones and the sides of the altar, and even the altar itself, above and beneath, are laden with a multitude of relics. Moreover, in the pavement may be remarked on every side stones designedly interlaid in triangles and squares, and sealed with lead, under which if I believe some holy secret to be contained, I do no injustice to religion.

His own account of the story of the foundation of this manifestly holy place exists in several variations in his works (in the *Gesta Regum* and in *On the Antiquity of the Church at Glastonbury* particularly). We need to be careful because some texts of these works show signs of major later interpolations. The version in his *Gesta Regum* ('the Deeds of the Kings of England'), which most scholars who have studied William think is closest to his true words, says:

> There came therefore by the sending of Eleutherius (a Pope of the time) preachers to Britain, the effect of whose work will last forever though their names have perished through the long neglect of time. The work of these men was the Old Church of Saint Mary in Glastonbury, as antiquity has not failed to faithfully hand down through the ages of the past. There is also evidence of good credit found in certain places to this effect: The church of Glastonbury did none other men's hands make but actual disciples of Christ built it.
>
> Nor is this irreconcilable with truth for if the Apostle Philip preached to the Gauls, as Freculfus says in the fourth chapter of his second book, it may be believed that he cast the seeds of his doctrine across the sea as well. But lest I should seem to cheat the expectation of my readers by fanciful opinions, I will leave disputable matters and gird myself to the narration of solid facts.

The thing that strikes us most about this statement is its caution. William makes six statements:

1. Preachers (names unknown) brought Christianity in the Papacy of Eleutherius (AD 174–193).
2. These preachers may have built the church at Glastonbury at that time (*circa* AD 190).
3. There is a story on good authority that the church was built earlier than that by actual First Period Apostles (those appointed by Jesus himself [founded AD 63?]).

4. The most likely Apostle is Philip who preached in Gaul (authority – Freculfus, d. 852).
5. William does not mention any other Apostle, and does not mention Joseph of Arimathea.
6. William does not wish to speculate.

The last two points may indicate the reason for his caution. He may have discovered something that he thought it wise not to disclose, and he behaved as he always did when his research brought him into possible conflict with the orthodox Catholic and Benedictine world he inhabited. He reports the facts, and the authorities where he found the facts, and leaves it to his readers to think the dangerous thoughts, to make the heretical connections, and to initiate risky further inquiries. We see this in the lengths to which he went to conceal, or misdirect attention from, his love of pagan classical writers, or in the quiet note he makes to show that he had perceived that the Greek Orthodox version of the Nicene Creed is correct, and the Catholic one, to which he was obliged to adhere and affirm, was wrong (the word *filoque* was missing).

He also offers an apparently tentative complaint in his studies of the miracles of the Virgin Mary. William was devoted to the Virgin Mother, but he regrets that the Fathers of the Church did not provide more written contemporary accounts (there are none) of the Annunciation and the Bodily Assumption of the Virgin Mary. William accepted both – indeed he may have been in the forefront of those publicly espousing the doctrines which, in his day, had yet to be fully accepted across the Church – but his honesty as a researcher demanded of him that he report the lack of evidence.

This lack of evidence for doctrines that he held dear troubled him, and may be at the root of his diffidence concerning the founding of the Old Church at Glastonbury. William spent at least ten years travelling to Glastonbury, Worcester and other abbeys and religious houses. He examined charters, annals, and other documents wherever he went. He talked to senior monks and old monks about their personal knowledge, and he studied the inscriptions on all the distinguished graves. He correlated them, and used his critical intelligence to find a history within them. His historical judgments are often shrewd, and, for his time, accurate.

There can be very little doubt that he knew the practice of Celtic (Irish, Welsh) Christianity in relation to the dedication of churches. Virtually all Celtic churches bear the name of the founder, the saint who actually built it. Any church of a very early date in Britain was more likely to follow that custom, rather than the Roman habit of dedication to an admired hero/heroine of the church such as Peter, Paul, Andrew or James. A church bearing the name of Mary in the Roman manner would have been possibly the first such building above ground anywhere in the world. In Rome itself, there was no *ecclesia* and Christians were still worshipping in the catacombs in the first century, and the cult of Mary, the Virgin Mother, did not begin until the middle of the fourth century.

Mary Magdalene

It is clear that William saw something that troubled him. It seems possible that the documents he saw suggested a foundation date for the Old Church of AD 63. By that time, the Virgin Mary had died – she died fifteen years before the supposed foundation of the Glastonbury church, and so could not be its founder in the Celtic manner. There was therefore only one Mary who might have founded the church, and she was Mary Magdalene. The year of foundation was also reputed to be the year of her death. She may even have died at Glastonbury.

An important role for Mary Magdalene in the founding of the Old Church at Glastonbury – perhaps the first proper church of Christianity – posed a difficulty for William. The Eastern Church believed that, after the death and resurrection of Jesus, she retired to Ephesus, and died peacefully there after a quiet and virtuous life. Some parts of the Western Church, however, cherished a story that she had come as an Apostle to southern France, and had converted many people there before her death. She certainly was later venerated there. Saint-Maximin-la-Sainte-Baume built a basilica, and claimed it as her resting place. Her body may have been at Aix for a time, and the Cluniac Benedictines thought she had been transferred from Aix to Vézelay in Burgundy about AD 771. From around AD 1050, they certainly held her in veneration at Vézelay, and they built a great church dedicated to her there.

William was a Benedictine, and his abbot at Malmesbury, Peter, came from Cluny. Despite, or because of, the Cluniac connection, William could not safely have said anything within his order about a prominent role for Mary Magdalene in the founding of the Glastonbury church. His own abbey church of Malmesbury, after a period named after Saints Paul and Peter, had been rededicated to the other Mary, Saint Mary the Virgin Mother.

The Most Forgotten Woman in History

We need to ask why the name of Mary Magdalene as the founder may have enjoyed some currency in sixth-century Glastonbury. We can begin with Mary herself. Who was she and why would she be thought to have Glastonbury connections? We need to identify her and learn more about her.

There are several Marys to choose from in the Gospels. The most likely one is 'Mary of Bethany'. Bethany, in the time of Jesus, was a village near Jerusalem used as a kind of isolation unit for the sickly rich and a refuge for the poor and indigent. While Jesus was staying there in the house of friend, Simon the Pharisee (Simon the Leper), a woman anointed him. She used spikenard, a pleasant-smelling substance used in preparing food and as a medicine. It was very expensive, and she poured it abundantly either over his head or over his feet.

We can probably disregard the feet, but anointing the head was an action forever rich in significance and meaning. Pouring rare and valuable oil over the head of a living man is a rite of kingship and of kingmaking. It is still performed in the coronation of monarchs. In Roman Palestine, anointing a member of the House of David in this manner was making a statement of political and religious importance that could not, and would not, be ignored.

It was remarkable for several reasons. First, and it easy to miss it, it was an action done by a woman, not the High Priest in front of the Ark of the Covenant. That means this Mary was someone important, and it is not clear from what her importance derives. It was important too because this was the action that made 'Jesus of Nazareth' into 'Jesus the Christ' (Christ means 'the anointed one'). It was also the fulfilment of Biblical prophecy. It was, as Jesus himself noted, the first step that led to the Crucifixion. It was important politically, and could have been construed as raising the flag of revolt against the Roman occupation of Palestine. By this action, Jesus had been declared 'king of the Jews', the title he was to bear on the Cross.

At the time, the Disciples complained only about the manifest waste of a valuable resource. It should have been sold, they said, and the proceeds given to the poor who were everywhere around them in Bethany. Jesus told them they would always have the poor with them, but he would not always be there. He identified Mary's action as central to his mission. He said that wherever the Gospel (his story and his purpose) should be told, this woman's action should be remembered. Ironically, she has become the most forgotten woman in history, and we don't even know her name with certainty.

Tradition – never a good source – has identified her as Mary Magdalene. That doesn't help a lot. That may be more of a joke, or a title, than a name. The term *Mar* was used at that time and place to denote a 'rabbi' or 'religious leader', and in the first centuries it rapidly became attached to the name of Christian leaders as an alternative to the Latin word (*sanctus*) which gives us the title 'saint'. 'Magdalene' may indicate she came from Magdala, a village in Gallilee, but that is a flat place, and the root of the word *Magdala* implies a 'tower', possibly a pillar.

That is where the joke comes in. King Herod had executed his wife for suspected adultery with the commander of his guard while he was in Rome. He later regretted his action, and built a tower in her memory called the *Mariamne Magdalene* (the tower of Mary). We have no idea what it might have looked like, or might have been used for. It could simply have been a pillar, or ceremonial arch of the memorial type used by the Romans, or it might have been a useful military watchtower. It may have offered some sort of light in the darkness of the night. When Jesus was chided by disciples for the prominence he gave to Mary in his mission, he said, 'A city set on a hill cannot be hidden.' It was a joke. She may have been a tall woman, or he simply meant her importance to him and his mission; she was his tower, his 'memorial' pillar, his light unto the Gentiles. She was, in that sense, Mary Magdalene – like the Herodian tower.

There is no doubt that the woman that we call Mary Magdalene was an important figure in the life of Jesus. She was the first person he spoke to after the Resurrection. He greeted her as 'Mary' (which, as we have seen, may mean 'rabbi' or 'teacher'). She saluted him as '*Rabboni*' (one of only two occasions where the Bible uses this word). It means 'very superior rabbi'. He may have said the equivalent of, 'Hello, University teacher' and she responded by saying, 'Hello, Professor.' It was a light-hearted affectionate greeting between colleagues involved in a joint mission in which the woman acknowledged the higher status held by her male friend.

The relationship may have been deeper than that of friends. The Gnostic Gospels,[1] discovered at Nag Hamadi in southern Egypt in 1945, tell a story radically different from the one we are used to. In these new Gospels, particularly those of Philip, Thomas and Mary Magdalene, the relationship between Jesus and Mary is more one of lovers, or even of husband and wife. The Greek word *koinos* (companion, partner, spouse, co-worker) is used, a translation of Hebrew and Aramaic *rea* (companion, partner, spouse). We are told that Jesus kissed her on the lips many times, and that he loved her more than the other disciples. He wanted her to be the Apostle to the Apostles, in effect their chief in his absence. When Peter objected on gender grounds, he said he would make her into a man (*anthropos*, which is more like 'mankind' than 'male gender person'). What Jesus sought was a partnership between the *Logos* (the Word – him) and the *Sophia* (Wisdom – Mary), between male and female, a joint ministry, a manifestation of mankind that lay beyond gender or specific sex.

This partnership, or joint ministry, of men and women became the sign of the Magdalene. The other signs of her presence and her example became a tower, a pillar, a light and a caring and curing medical mission (her role at Bethany) to the people, offering them not only a spiritual consolation and a faith but a physical remedy for their illnesses and injuries.

There continued to be resistance to her, and the Apostles were divided. Peter and James (and later Paul) were opposed to her, and Philip and Levi supported her. That placed her in some difficulty as the *ecclesia* began to emerge as a movement or organisation. There was an apparent move to exclude her. By the time Eusebius (*c.* AD 260–340) wrote the first history of Christianity, he had Jesus speaking to Peter after the Resurrection, not Mary.

As the known partner of Jesus, she was possibly in some physical and political danger too. After the crucifixion, Zealots may have seen her as a focus for revolt against the Romans, and the Romans may have wished to remove her (and any children she may have had) for the same reason; she was the wife, or intimate companion, of the 'king of the Jews'. Mary may have been formally exiled, or simply fled from Palestine. She may have gone to the furthest corner of the earth. That corner, in AD 63, could well have been Glastonbury.

That all may be plausible while remaining doubtful. We can, however, be certain about one thing. She did not build a church at Glastonbury in the sense of a building devoted only to worship. Churches did not exist anywhere at that time. At best, she may have created a devotional space, a *monasterium*, in a villa or in a structure used for other purposes. Scarcely twenty years after the main Roman invasion of Britain, when their grip on the country may have been still uncertain, it may well have been merely a wattle hut in a Roman military frontier post.

The Heretical Reputation of Mary Magdalene the 'Sinner'

As time passed, in the Middle East another image of her emerged. A tradition preserved by the Gazan cleric historian Zacharias, Bishop of Mytilene on Lesbos (died *c.* AD 553), maintained that Mary Magdalene had been married to Jesus.[2] For many in the early centuries of Christianity, Mary Magdalene was either the wife of Jesus (a belief held by the Cathars in France who first appeared as a distinct people holding a discernible belief in southern France in the eleventh century),[3] or a repentant sinner (among Catholics) – an idea first mooted by Ephrem the Syrian (AD 300–373) who may have seen *Koinos* in the sense that Jews did – a descriptive word for something unclean because commonly or communally available (hence 'prostitute').[4] Alternatively he may have read *rea* (Hebrew and Aramaic 'companion' as Latin *rea* (originally an accused person but meaning now a 'wrongdoer' or 'sinner').

When William of Malmesbury was writing, Mary Magdalene thus carried a strong whiff of heresy. In the twelfth century, the widely culted 'composite Mary Magdalene' (sinner, reformed prostitute and repentant woman), whose name now attaches to so many churches, had yet to emerge. William may only have found information offering him two choices: Mary of Ephesus of the Eastern Church who lived and died in retirement, or a married Mary who acted as an Evangelist and Apostle. Any hint of a married Mary, with a child or children she had with Jesus, would have been frightening, and life- and faith-threatening. William therefore did what he often did. He shied away from the problem, but signalled to his friends who were readers in other monasteries that there was a matter here for thought or discussion that could not be stated. He provided a signpost for them, and the signpost was his mention of Philip the Apostle's mission to France and Britain. He told them where to look for the clue – in the books of Freculfus.

What excited William's interest there has not appeared (he may have had more ample texts than any currently available), but it seems possible he had before him an account of a successful joint ministry undertaken in southern and western France by Philip and Mary Magdalene.[5] There may have been some mention of a son called Joseph or Judah. At some point in that preaching journey, it was decided that the Gospel should be carried to Britain, and it may have fallen to Mary Magdalene to do it.

Quite where she might have landed and travelled is completely unknown to us, but at this time, hardly more than twenty years into the occupation of Britain by the Romans, she would have had to rely on the army and land wherever they might agree to accept her. Wareham – where the church (a medieval foundation) is dedicated to her – is a possible landing place, and she could have readily made her way from there to Ilchester, and along the emerging Roman Fosse Way to Glastonbury to build her first 'church'. She may have left her son there for his own protection. We can only make wild surmises about such matters, but whatever she did there (or, just as importantly, was believed to have done there) lies at the root of the unusual sanctity of Glastonbury and the peculiar status of the Old Church.

Saint Bridget

Christianity in Britain in the first centuries built few churches, and perhaps none at all. No dedicated or specially built church structure has been found by archaeologists. Religious services, activity and preaching seem to have taken place in houses and villas, and we can see archaeological evidence of that sort of

Christian activity in the mosaics in some of the Roman villas in southern England.

The first true 'church' at Glastonbury is likely to have been constructed by Saint Bridget of Ireland or her followers. We know, with about as much certainty as we know anything about the sixth century, that Saint Bridget of Ireland was associated with the earliest Christian phase at Glastonbury. She was an immensely important figure. There may have been Irish Christians in Ireland itself for all of the early Christian centuries, but the first phase of the widespread 'Christianisation' of Ireland itself seems to belong to the late fifth or early sixth century, and the person most responsible was not Patrick but Bridget. Bridget, from the first, asserted the joint ministry of men and women, and that characteristic is very much present in the first phase of Irish Christianisation. Bridget invited a monk called Cenleth to work with her when she found her monastery at Kildare (the church of the oak or oaks). Later, when the Irish Church was Romanised, her partnership was said to have been with Patrick.

Bridget's Church

What kind of church did Bridget build at Glastonbury? At Kildare, Bridget initially built her church of wattles, and set it in a sacred enclosure, also made of wattles. The location was alongside an oak tree which may have been originally a pagan sacred tree. The tree may have been set within a pagan grove of oak trees of the kind that Saint Martin of Tours went around felling in France. Apart from the oak tree as a symbol or focus, other pagan practices, such as sun worship, may have continued and been adopted or adapted for Christian use. Bridget and her followers have a very strong association with light. They maintained a perpetual flame, and may have used symbols based on the moon or the sun. Bridget's own name means 'bright or elevated', and a hymn to her draws on imagery close to paganism:

> Bright, ever-excellent woman,
> Golden sparkling flame,
> Lead us to the eternal kingdom,
> The dazzling resplendent sun.

At Kildare, Bridget administered not only the consolations of religion but also medicine and care of a high order. She may have worked with, taught or otherwise involved the Irish Saint Germanus of Man (said to be the nephew of Saint Patrick and a student of Saint Illtud who taught Gildas). His name was often invoked in medical matters as an aid in medieval times because of his skill as a doctor or surgeon.

The Kildare sacred enclosure appears to have been replicated at Glastonbury. Something very like a hospital for the wounded run by women, perhaps holy women, existed at Glastonbury around the sixth century. It may be the *castellum* (refuge is one meaning) *Puellarum* (of the maidens) mentioned by Geoffrey of Monmouth and other writers. Arthur, Yder and other wounded heroes were carried there for attention. Glastonbury too had a perpetual flame of a kind. A charter issued by King Ine provided for a perpetual candle to be maintained in the Old Church.

Architecture

The precise architectural nature of the Old Church built by the Irish is impossible to recover. Irish religious foundations were different from the continental monasteries and abbeys which were usually linked to great basilicas built in prominent positions in cities. The Romans never came to Ireland, and Ireland did not develop cities as the rest of Europe did. The Irish did not follow the pattern we see in Gaul in church building, and the Irish did not build vast basilicas when they founded churches or monasteries.

Irish monasteries were also different from those developed after the example of Pachomius (AD 292–348) in the deserts of Egypt. Irish abbots enjoyed regal powers, and the monasteries became substitute cities offering metalworking, market trading, military protection, and civil order and dwelling places for people who were not themselves monks. Some monks were married with children – the role of vice abbot at Armagh was actually a hereditary office passed from father to son within the same family. Monks seeking solitude sought the 'desert' – usually just up the road – and separated themselves from the hurly-burly life of the monastery.

If Bridget built a monastery at Glastonbury, it was probably for both sexes. Monks and nuns would be accommodated in single beehive huts, and only the hospital, the kitchens, the refectory and perhaps the stables would have been in a building of any size. If we judge from what has remained in Irish and Cornish examples, the building for worship, the church, would have been of modest size. It may very well have been made of wattle and daub, or wood.

Restoration, Repair and Respect

Something happened to whatever it was that Bridget built in the early sixth century. It is possible that she was expelled by Arthur (see the *Henwen* story in *Culhwch ac Olwen*) and the church was partially destroyed or damaged by his men. It may have been flattened by the encroaching sea in the AD 540 event. Whatever the reason, her church was in need of repair by the middle of the sixth century. Saint David of Wales proposed to replace it, but was persuaded to build his own church (or churches) a little to the west of it. The Old Church itself was restored by one Paulinus.

Always ready to find the most prestigious person, Glastonbury historians claim this was Paulinus, Archbishop of York, but there is no evidence that he ever took an interest in a place so far from his own diocese. The more likely candidate is the Welsh saint Paul Aurelian, who became more widely known as Saint Pol de Léon. This Welsh Paul was a pupil of Saint Illtud and Gildas, and was a known founder and restorer of churches. At Glastonbury, he is said to have provided the Old Church with a lead roof and strengthened its walls.

The structure appears to have remained mainly wood. The first Christian Saxon king of the area, King Ine, gave it a tax-free status of twelve hides, and made provision for it in a charter in which he called it the *ecclesia lignea* (the wooden church). He also called for a stone church to be built presumably alongside the old wooden one. It seems that the 'church of Mary the Apostle and Bridget' was too small, or too holy, to use. By Ine's time, it had become a sacred relic.

Saint Dunstan must have taken down the old wooden church, and perhaps also Ine's stone church because he raised the level of the whole abbey site at Glastonbury by at least 9 feet (around 3 m). F. Bligh Bond, the architect who uncovered the ruins of the abbey early in twentieth century, found wide footings just outside the main wall of the abbey church which he thought was Ine's church. When Ralegh Radford investigated the discovery of Arthur's body in the 1960s, he found burials at about 16 feet (4.9 m) below the surface. If we assume that 'normal burial' depth was around 6 feet (2 m), that depth confirms the extent of the backfilling by Dunstan. The Old Church appears to have been still at the same level as Dunstan's great new abbey. That can only mean that it was dismantled and re-erected.

On 25 May 1184 a great fire swept away the *vetusta ecclesia* (the Old Church)[6] and most of the other monastic buildings the site had acquired, leaving only a bell tower built by Henry de Blois, and a chamber and a chapel built by Abbot Robert. Only two years later, Reginald, Bishop of Bath, dedicated a new chapel of Saint Mary (now without question Mary *Theotakos*, Virgin and Mother). It took many more years before the abbey itself was restored and rebuilt.

Later History

In 1278, King Edward I decided to commemorate Arthur, the great hero, by building a shrine to him. Under the Abbot John of Taunton, work on the new abbey proceeded apace. In an elaborate ceremony, at which both the king and his queen were present, the relics of Arthur were duly placed before the High Altar. There Arthur remained until the abbey was sacked and its abbot hanged when King Henry VIII ordered the dissolution of the monasteries.

Holy Glastonbury declined to a half-forgotten ruin in a small market town, its hallowed stones used for more than four hundred years as a sort of convenient quarry by local builders. As the nineteenth century drew to a close, local clergymen became interested in its history. Their enthusiasm sometimes outran their good sense, but they succeeded in reviving (and partially reinventing) the old story of Mary Magdalene and Joseph of Arimathea and the Holy Grail. F. Bligh Bond FRIBA won a high reputation for his careful, knowledgeable and scholarly exposure and explanation of the ruins – until he revealed that he had been guided in his work by messages from medieval monks obtained through seances and automatic writing. Mystic interest in the site grew. It was based not on whatever fragments of the true record had survived but the vivid imaginations of everyone who had written about it. Glastonbury today is a centre for 'New Age' believers.

The Grail

What are we left with? Well, it is clear beyond any doubt that for five centuries or more, from about AD 500, everyone behaved as if Glastonbury was a site of unusual holiness. At the bottom of all the more recent mystical enthusiasms, there are some tantalising glimpses that may show that spiritual devotion of a deep kind is not entirely misplaced. The story of the Old Church is that Mary Magdalene, Joseph of Arimathea or preachers sent by Saint Philip the Apostle established some sort of Christian bridgehead in Britain. That, while not provable, is feasible. And then there is the Grail. Did Joseph bring two cruets (some rude people suggest on heraldic evidence that they were beer mugs) containing in one the blood and in the other the sweat of the crucified Saviour?

The answer to that should be a firm 'no'. Collecting relics of that kind was a fashion that only began in AD 304 when Saint Helena, the mother of the Emperor Constantine, persuaded herself that she had discovered remnants of the True Cross in Jerusalem. Whether she did or not, she ushered in an age of religious tourism, and souvenir and relic collecting. Before that, no one would have thought to collect and transport the blood and sweat from the Cross.

There is a more plausible version. Some old accounts say Joseph brought his son, or his nephew, to Glastonbury. The likely word at the root of the story is *nepos* which can be a grandson or granddaughter, a blood descendant. Over time *nepos* became limited to a 'nephew', and in Ireland acquired the meaning of 'heir'. It is best perhaps to think of it as 'blood descendant' without trying to stipulate a precise avenue of descent. Joseph of Arimathea may, or may not, have had a descendant called Joseph, but, as we noted earlier, there is also a story that says that Jesus and Mary Magdalene were married, and had a son who was called either Joseph or Judah.

If that story were true, or were believed to be true, then among those sent by Philip, and perhaps among those who accompanied Joseph of Arimathea was that Joseph. In the style and languages of the day he might very well have been seen, or reported, as 'a vessel of the true blood of the Saviour'. No grail or other dish or container was needed. All we need as a foundation for the legend is a young man of unique descent. Perhaps it was some evidence of, or reference to, that unsettling thought that spooked William of Malmesbury. Unless some fortunate piece of archaeology turns up in a mosaic villa pavement, or engraved on a newly discovered stone tablet, we shall never know. We are free to speculate and invent in the best traditions of the Old Church of Glastonbury.

Jerusalem – Using a Legend of the Old Church to Make a New Myth

For more than a hundred years, since 1895, the first week of September in London has been marked by the final concert in the series of orchestral entertainments called the 'Summer Proms'. Over the years, although there has always been a commitment to new pieces at the Proms, the concluding works of the final performance have been the same. They have formed – especially since they began to be shown on television – a sort of national celebration. There are two works that epitomise that feeling – the rousing 'Rule Britannia' (words by James Thomson and music by Thomas Arne, 1740) introduced into the repertoire by Henry Wood in 1905, and Hubert Parry's sonorous setting of William Blake's poem 'Jerusalem' introduced to the Queen's Hall Proms in 1916 and revived by Malcolm Sargent as part of the Royal Albert Hall Last Night performances in the 1950s.

'Rule Britannia' is frankly political, but the Parry/Blake piece 'Jerusalem' is very odd. Robert Bridges, after Britain experienced very heavy losses of soldiers in the fighting in the First World War, realised the need to catch and elevate the public mood. He brought the Blake poem back to public attention after a century of neglect, and he commissioned Parry to produce a musical setting of it. The music was intended to be sorrowful, recessional and inspiring, and, although Parry himself didn't initially care for it, it has proved to be so. The Suffragettes, the Mothers' Union, the Labour Party, the Conservative Party and the Last Night audiences have all welcomed it as speaking for, and to, them.

That is strange because Blake's words, in the form of a series of questions, are both mystical and religious:

> And did those feet in ancient time
> Walk upon England's mountains green?
> And was the Holy Lamb of God
> On England's pleasant pastures seen?

They should not really arouse the need to wave flags, and celebrate national identity even though they conclude with a resolve and dedication:

> I will not cease from mental fight
> Nor shall my sword sleep in my hand
> Till we have built Jerusalem
> In England's green and pleasant land.

What did he mean? And why did he choose this way of stating it? Blake saw himself as a social revolutionary; he went on supporting Napoleon long after the French general became Emperor, because he saw the French leader as a figure who was continuing what the French Revolution had begun. Blake thought that if all Christian believers could become prophets, society could be transformed. No child would go hungry and no man would live in fear. England could become the new Jerusalem, a light unto the Gentiles, the centre for world revolution.

The poem set by Parry occurs in a very long and very obscure work by Blake on Milton, another revolutionary. In that work, Blake turned to the legend of Joseph of Arimathea who, as the legend Blake knew had it, came to Britain bearing holy relics – the Grail – which might make, or inspire, radical change in society. For Blake that arrival, that brief shining moment, was 'Jerusalem'; for Jackie Kennedy, four days after the death of her husband, the American President, it was 'Camelot'; it was, for both of them, a time now lost when something new had been possible.

That shared perception places them both in the ambit of Arthur. The reaction of Last Night audiences also mimics the reaction people have had – at any rate since Dryden and Tennyson – to King Arthur. It is a kind of national, fervently felt nostalgia which is mystical, or even religious, in its effect. The feet of Jesus did not tread on England's pastures green, but nonetheless his ghostly step is heard by people as if it were true. There is absolutely no evidence whatever that Jesus, or Joseph of Arimathea, ever left Palestine. That faint stalking apparition started in the legends of the Old Church of Glastonbury.

Joseph and the Holy Descent of Arthur

In literature, the British legend of Joseph of Arimathea begins with
Robert de Boron, who between 1180 and 1199 wrote a French
poem which bears his name. According to that story, Joseph was
a soldier in the army of Pontius Pilate (a possible confusion with
the Jewish historian Josephus who really did serve with Roman
forces in Palestine in the time of Jesus). At the Crucifixion, Boron's
Joseph collected the blood of Christ in the chalice that had been
used at the Last Supper. After many adventures, Joseph brought the
chalice to *vaus d'avaron*, which William of Malmesbury concluded
was Glastonbury, or the Isle of Avalon. The story first appears in
the revised edition of William's *De Antiquate Glastoniae Ecclesiae*
('Concerning the age of the church of Glastonbury'), which was
written in the last years of the twelfth century, or the first years
of the thirteenth. It is, to that extent, tied in with the story of the
wooden church.

The Welsh Triad (TYP) 86 implies that *Peredur* (Perceval,
Parsifal) was a descendant of Joseph. Later Lancelot, Tristan and
even Arthur himself joined that descent. The fifteenth-century
Harley 200, folio 141 offers:

*Thelamis nepos Joseph ab Arimthea geuit Josue. Josue genuit
Ammadeb. Ammadeb genuit Castellys. Castellys genuit
manael. Manael genuit lambord ... lambord genuit filium qui
genuit ysernam (Igerne) de qau Rex Uter Pendragon genuit
nobilem et famosum Regem Arthurum quod patet quod Rex
Arthurus de Joseph descendit.*

(Thelamis the son [or nephew] of Joseph of Arimathea begat
Josue. Josue begat Ammadeb. Ammadeb begat Castellys.
Castellys begat Manuel. Manuel begat Lambord. Lambord
begat a son who begat Igerne with whom King Uther
Pendragon begat the noble and famous King Arthur.)

If that were true, and it manifestly isn't, Arthur was of the *sang
real*, the royal blood of Jesus and Mary Magdalene.

We don't need such pious associations or misconceived notions.
What we can see fairly plainly, even though we cannot prove
anything historically, is that Glastonbury was regarded as a place
of particular holiness, and those who believed that appear to

have thought that this reputation stretched all the way back to first-century Palestine. For those who believe in its legend, the Old Church and what it stood for is a matter of faith. For those who don't, it is a source of entertaining speculation that throws some sidelight on Arthur, the warrior and king. He was either its champion (Fort Guinnion) or he tried to suppress the power of the women clergy (*Henwen*) who served there. Perhaps he even threw down their wooden church.

The Sign of Saint Mary and Her Son

Nennius, or Harley 3859, tells us that King Arthur fought his eighth battle (of the English Campaign) under the sign of Saint Mary, and, through her power and that of her son Jesus, won victory. We have argued that that battle was fought at Glastonbury. That suggestion may not satisfy everyone interested in Arthur, and certainly other battle sites have been proposed. Our identification of Glastonbury as the site of the 'Fort Guinnion' battle is open to doubt. There is another element of doubt about that battle. It is extremely unlikely that anyone in England in the early sixth century had a particular devotion to the Virgin Mary. It is also certain that she did not have a sign associated with her of the kind twelfth-century heraldry later produced. That leads us to the question: if Arthur did fight with a sign on his shield, what was it and did it have any link with any Saint Mary and the Old Church?

Armies in the Age of Arthur are not known to have had many banners, or standards of the Roman legion type. They had shields which were usually about 3 feet (1 m) wide, made of wood and leather with a central metal boss. They were sometimes painted a single colour, and some elements of them may have had carved components (such as handles) in the form of stylised animals. None so far discovered by archaeology, other than manifestly ceremonial ones, had any symbols. The shield a warrior might carry in battle was plain and, colour aside, undecorated. A sign of any kind portrayed on a shield would have been unusual.

The Romans used military signs that included the sun and the eagle, but we are looking here for a Christian sign. The chi-rho and the cross are the only two known. There is no sign of early date known to have been associated directly with Mary Magdalene or the Virgin Mary. However, possibly, given Baetan's interest in collecting relics, and the likely presence at this time of Bridget or her cult at Glastonbury, we should look at Bridget and Ireland for some hint of what the sign might have been.

There is one potent sign that emerged around this time. It is sometimes called the 'Celtic Cross' although it is not specifically Celtic. It is better described as the 'Irish Wheel Cross', and began to be manifested in Ireland, certainly from the seventh century but possibly somewhat earlier. Its origins and meaning are obscure. If we postulate some sort of direct affiliation with Bridget and Mary Magdalene, it might represent the fusion of the Logos (Christ and the Cross) and the Sophia (Mary, Bridget and light – a circle representing a light source like the sun or the moon). By the eighth century this 'wheel-cross' or 'cross plus light' symbol had begun to be placed at the top of freestanding very tall 'high crosses' (like the 5.6 m one at Arboe in County Tyrone in, or close to, the territory of the *Airthir*).[7]

What the high crosses were used for is uncertain. They may have been 'preaching aids' because the carving on them often offers scenes drawn from the life of Jesus, or other Biblical themes. They could also have been memorials. Arthur was buried at Glastonbury between two such high crosses, the bases of which were seen by William of Malmesbury, and the foundations of which were uncovered by Ralegh Radford. We could choose to see them as representative 'towers' of the Herodian Magdalene type.[8] They may be signs of devotion to Mary Magdalene or Saint Bridget.

That notion could be merely fanciful and we should not read too much into it. There may, however, be a genuine link with 'the Cross imposed on the sun' symbol and the 'wheel cross'. We may conjecture that such a symbol, if it existed with the associations we have postulated, may have been used at the refuge offered by the holy women in Glastonbury. If Arthur ever fought using a Christian symbol, it might have been this one. It may even have signified Mary Magdalene to those who used it. Its symbolism may have included her son, if she had one. The reference in Nennius may be as much as anything an attempt to explain and adopt an inconvenient legend about a battle won through the merits of a saintly mother and her son whom the Roman *ecclesia* was not willing to recognise.

The Symbolic Arthur of the Old Church
On the current level of hard evidence from archaeology, or another scientific discipline, and the almost complete silence of the

documents referring to the period, there seems to be no way to advance this idea beyond mere speculation. The battle sign of Saint Mary may be no more than a pious invention by a ninth-century or later monk. In the end, all we can say is that 'the Old Church of Glastonbury' became, and remained, itself a very powerful symbol. Its precise meaning is lost to us now, but we can still see, although he may have tried to destroy it, that the Old Church captured Arthur, and made him a part of its own legend. He wound up buried either in it, or beside it, and whatever his views at the time may have been, the holy light, which the reputation of the Old Church casts, has now fallen on Arthur and made him, for our time, some sort of Christian hero.

APPENDIX IV

RELIGION IN THE AGE OF ARTHUR

We know, from Harley 3859, that King Arthur fought three battles with a religious dimension. At Fort Guinnion, he went into the fight 'with the image of Saint Mary on his shield'. Badon, Gildas says, was a Christian victory, and at Bravonium, Nennius says, he 'put the Pagans to flight' which suggests that, whatever else he was, Arthur was not a pagan, or fighting for Pagan interests on those occasions. That raises two questions: if Arthur was a Christian, or fought for a Christian overlord like Baetan MacCairill, what kind of Christian was he, and was there really a religious dimension to his wars? Did religion motivate his career as a warrior? Was he trying to suppress paganism and establish a Christian kingdom?

A Dream

To answer those questions, we must go back to the beginning of the fourth century, to the time of the Emperor Constantine. At a crucial stage of Constantine's campaign for the Imperial throne, the Battle of the Milvian Bridge, he had a dream. In his dream, he saw a vision showing him either the cross or the chi-rho (the Christian symbol formed of the first two letters of the word 'Christ' in Greek). He was told that, if he adopted this sign and this religion, he would be victorious.

The whole yarn is a bit dubious. Constantine changed his story on two occasions and suppressed a third version in which he said he saw a vision of the Sun God. When he erected a triumphal arch to mark the event, he hedged his bets a little, and attributed his victory to 'divine intervention' without being specific which God was involved. The precise nature of the vision before the Milvian Bridge in the end didn't matter very much; what mattered was that Constantine, in gratitude for that victory, and others that followed, which made him supreme Emperor ruling both the Western and Eastern Roman Empire, proclaimed Christianity to be the official Imperial religion.

The consequences of his decision were far-reaching. At the most trivial level, it led to the growth of a trade in religious relics. Small portions of the 'True Cross' his mother, Helena, found in Jerusalem were discovered to have miraculous powers to cure the sick, and to divine and decide issues where the results, sought by ordinary human and political argument, remained obscure. A trade in relics was created.

Imperial Christianity

At the most fundamental level, Constantine's conversion to the faith of Christ raised the question: who was a Christian? When Christians of all types had been persecuted, as they were in the reign of the Emperor Diocletian, such a question did not much matter. Christians of all kinds could feel themselves united in trying to survive in the darkness of paganism which everywhere surrounded them. When, after Constantine's decision, it became a question which of them should be the officially approved light unto the Gentiles, the candidates were many, and both the penalties for failure and the rewards of success were great.

The rewards offered by the new official Christianity were only partly doctrinal. They were also, in important respects, social, political and financial. The administrative and financial burdens of the Roman Empire until that time had fallen largely on the urban middle classes. The Senators and aristocrats in Rome, and in the larger provincial centres, had responsibilities only if they wished to exercise them. For the *decuriones* and town councillors, however, there was no escape. They were forbidden to go to their country estates, and could not opt out of the station in life to which their birth had called them. Even death provided no relief; their duties and obligations were inherited by their heirs, just like any other property. The advent of the official Church changed that. As the life of Saint Patrick of Ireland shows, it was possible for the son of a *decurion* to avoid his inheritance by joining the Church.

There was a double benefit for those who could make the transition. Not only did they escape the increasingly onerous responsibilities and financial penalties of the town councillor, but they gained access to unrivalled power, privilege and wealth. As William Frend puts it, 'Preferment in the Church was tending to become secularized and regarded as a "honour", the equivalent to the municipal "honour" held by the *curiales*.'[1] Bishops were using the Church's money as their own, there was a perpetual scramble to secure possession of the richer sees, and, in some favoured cities, rival factions of clergy fought street battles over the spoils of office.

With the money went political power. By the end of the fourth century – the time by which it can be said with some certainty that, in the influential circles of the Empire, the old Roman paganism was dead – it is possible to discern the force that replaced it: the rise of a class of men who can be best described as 'Prince-Bishops', men who wielded both spiritual and temporal power. The Western Empire no longer depended on the civil servants appointed in Rome to maintain its laws; Emperors had to rely on the only persons capable of ensuring their enforcement – the Catholic Bishops.[2] It was that fact, perhaps more than any other, which gave such immense force to the doctrinal disputes that raged throughout the early decades of the fifth century.

Augustine of Hippo and Catholic Christians

In AD 380 the Emperor Theodosius, seeking to further the idea of an official Church, one that might be, so to speak, 'the Roman Empire at prayer', declared that all those who followed the religious rules laid down by the Pope in Rome and the Bishop of Alexandria should henceforth be known as 'Catholic Christians'. Theodosius was not making a strongly doctrinal point. By pronouncing that there should be a 'Catholic Church', he meant little more than that he wished to see one broad version of Christianity.

Although his definition excluded the Arians and the Manichees, an official and broad church covering the whole Empire might well have been possible, but at Hippo in North Africa there was a group of Christians led by a young presbyter called Augustine who had different ideas. Less than thirty years later, they had successfully hijacked the term 'Catholic', and in a series of books, letters, sermons, political and sometimes riotous actions, laid the foundations for a vigorous, contentious and aggressive Church.

Augustine of Hippo was helped in that task by three major factors: the split between Rome and Constantinople gave him wider opportunities, the virtual collapse of the Western Empire allowed him and his allies to seize their political chances, and the emergence of strong, articulate and spirited doctrinal opponents forced him to define first what the Catholic Church was not, and then what it could become.

In North Africa, his first opponents were the Donatists. They were a tough, hard-fighting people who showed intolerance in victory and tenacity in defeat in equal measure, but by AD 410 the *Comes Africae* (the Count of Africa), the Imperial commander, had ended their resistance by military means. Augustine's task was not confined to his struggle with the Donatists, nor did it end with their defeat. Events in Italy brought him a newer and more difficult opponent, one who was his intellectual equal, a man from the British Isles called Pelagius.

Pelagius

His name doesn't allow us to identify him, but Saint Jerome tells us that 'he was born of Irish race, from the neighbourhood of the Britains'[3] (*habet progenium Scoticae gentis, de Britannorum vicinia*). He was of portly build, heavy and muscular like a wrestler. Jerome alleges that his bulk derived from his Irish diet – he was weighed down by eating Irish porridge (*Scotorum pultibus praegravatus*). He was 'like a great Wolfhound through whom the devil barks'. In Rome he was part of the circle of Melania the Elder who was a *confessor* (that is, a leader of worship), and he was protected by Stilicho the Vandal and his wife who were, at the time, the most powerful couple in the Western Empire. When Stilicho fell from power and was executed, and Alaric the Goth invaded Rome itself, Pelagius fled with the rest of the Roman aristocrats to North Africa where he met Augustine.

At first their relationship was one of guarded mutual respect, but strong differences soon emerged. Pelagius believed and taught that man could save himself by a single act of conversion; Augustine taught that man's salvation needed the constant, continuing and active involvement of an elite group – the Catholic priesthood. The row spread throughout the Mediterranean and synods took one side or the other. The finer points of doctrine need not detain us. What was at stake was the nature of the Church to be created.

Pelagius was something of a social revolutionary. Where Catholics under Augustine might forsake the world for a monastery, Pelagians sought to make the whole world a monastery. It was a monastery with gender equality. Pelagius not only supported Melania the Elder's role as *confessor* in Rome, but he also urged her granddaughter Melania the Younger and her husband Pinanius to sell what they had and give it to the poor, to live in a chaste marriage, and to found joint monasteries for men and women in Egypt and Palestine. His religious views were worked out in the same sort of detail as those of Augustine, his rival. They were coherent enough to be seen as a system – 'Pelagianism'.

'Pelagianism' provoked a particular wrath among Catholics, and special efforts were made to eradicate it. Not all those proscribed were really Pelagians. Versions of dissent from Augustine's Catholicism, some of them calling themselves Pelagian, flourished in Sicily, Southern Italy and Southern France where the monastery of Lérins, officially Catholic, taught 'semi-Pelagian' ideas. In Spain, the chief dissident group were the Priscillianists, named after the saintly Priscillian who had been executed at the behest of Catholics. In France, the ascetic Martin of Tours was perhaps fortunate not to share the fate of his friend Priscillian.

In general, Pelagians, or those to whom that title was applied, were, like Martin, rural, ascetic and frugal. In their religious practice, they had a prominent role for women, and they had a strong missionary urge. They tried hard to bring God's word to the heathens around them. For Catholics, unity under Rome was the issue. On the whole, Catholic leaders were more interested in putting right error among people who were nominally already Christians than in bringing new peoples to Christ.

British Christianity

Quite how this played out in Britain in the Age of Arthur is obscure. In the early stages of the contest between dissidents and Catholics, Britain was a place of exile, and perhaps, for some, refuge. Sulpicius Severus tells us that two Pricillianist bishops, Instantius and Tiberianus, were exiled to Scilly (then one island) in AD 380. A little later, Vitricius of Rouen procured himself an invitation from people in Britain, and (he told Saint Ambrose of Milan) 'filled the sensible with the love of peace, taught those who could be taught, subdued the ignorant, and attacked the opposition'.

The 'opposition' at this time could have been Arian, but more probably was Pelagian. Pelagianism had been brought to England by a bishop called Agricola who was the son of another Pelagian prelate called Severianus who was 'corrupting the churches of Britain by the secret inculcation (*insinuatio*) of his dogma'. A bishop called Fastidius was also active in the Pelagian cause.

Towards the end of the 420s, Pope Celestine sent Saint Germanus of Auxerre and Bishop Lupus of Troyes to help the British Christians surrounded by the enemies of grace (*inimici gratiae*). Germanus and Lupus met the heretical leaders (*sinistrae persuasionis auctores*) who came to the meeting in dazzling robes (*veste fulgentes*) and were attended by flatterers and hangers-on. With the aid of a local chieftain (a man wielding tribunical powers), and using a sneak attack signalled by the cry of 'Alleluia', they drove the evil ones (who included Picts and Scots) into a river where many perished. The heresy was completely destroyed (*deleta est*).

That account, if it were true, might be significant, but unfortunately our witness to these events is Prosper of Aquitaine who was a friend, supporter, and correspondent of Augustine of Hippo. Prosper's account of the 'Alleluia Victory' is a fiction based on North African rather than British experience. The richly dressed opponent met by Germanus in Britain is clearly based on a late fourth-century opponent of Augustine, Optatus of Timgad (in modern Algeria). Optatus was renowned for his love of regal ceremony and notorious for his hangers-on. He may have been among the Donatists who met Augustine in Carthage in 411 and who entered the city in a grand and spectacular religious procession (*cum tanto speciosi agminis pompa*).

Information about events like these from Augustine seems to lie at the heart of the Germanus mission to Britain, and that makes the whole account doubtful. It is extremely unlikely that the ascetic Celts (Picts and Scots) would have made any such display, and we can fairly certain there was no one in Britain wielding 'tribunic power' after the departure of the Romans. The result was at best exaggerated, and at worst a flat lie. Heresy, and dissent from the Catholic faith among the Britons, was not removed. We know that to be the case because even his most able propagandists had to admit that Germanus had to make a repeat visit some twenty years later to deal with a 'recrudescence of error'.

The plain fact is that the Catholics lost the Battle of Britain in the fifth century. There is no archaeological or documentary evidence that Britain developed bishops and dioceses on the Gaulish Catholic model. While some elements of the official Imperial religion may have remained as the faith of a few, perhaps even of prominent men and women, the archaeological and written record is silent about them. It would seem that, even in the south-east of Britain, the most urbanised and Romanised sector, Christianity suffered a decline, and Britons and Saxons alike again followed the path of paganism.

The Irish Christians

In the west and north of Britain, however, the Christian religion was thriving and expanding. A sturdy, self-confident, learned and missionary (mainly Irish) Church emerged which we can see, with increasing clarity, from the beginning of the seventh century. Before that date, and for some time afterwards, it would have seemed 'Pelagian' to Catholics of the time. Study in its monasteries encompassed not only the Bible, and the history of the fathers of the Church, but also some of the great literature of pagan Classical Greece and Rome. They knew the Earth was a sphere, and one of the greatest of them, Vergil (Fergal) of Strasbourgh, believed that there were people in the antipodes (the other side of the Earth). These clerics were totally confident in their views, and needed no Pope or Catholic synod to correct them. Columbanus, in the sixth century, thought nothing of correcting the Pope on religious matters in a series of trenchant letters. At the beginning of the seventh century, the monk Cummian complained about the confidence of the Irish in matters doctrinal: 'Rome is wrong, Jerusalem is wrong, Alexandria is wrong, Antioch is wrong, the whole world is wrong; only the Irish and the British know what is right' (*Roma errat, Hierosolyma errat, Alexandria errat, Antiocha errat, totus mundus errat; soli Scoti et Brittones rectum sapient*).

The Celtic clergy wanted to enrich men's minds as well as to save their souls. They wanted to save their bodies too. The Irish had a strong medical tradition. Patrick Sims Williams notes that many of the early medical terms used in Anglo-Saxon England in succeeding centuries derived from Irish sources and usages.[4] Women like Saint Bridget and Saint Issy played leading roles.

Irish monks, we are told, offered schooling and education in the marketplaces of Gaul to anyone who was interested. With an Irish teacher, the son of a peasant could, through education, walk with, and reprove, any king in the land. There was, above all, a strong and continuing commitment to spreading the Gospel which saw Irish monks take their missionary message right across Europe from the Atlantic coasts of their own small island to the great gates of Kiev.[5]

The roots the Irish planted struck deep, and the Catholic Church had to struggle for centuries to eradicate them. Theodore of Tarsus, the successor of Augustine of Canterbury, found it necessary (in contradiction of canon law) to re-baptise those who had been baptised by the Irish. Saint Boniface made similar efforts to bring pagan Germans converted by the Irish into the bounds of the Catholic Church. Saint Wilfrid, a hero to Bede, claimed to be the first to 'root out the poisonous weeds planted by the Irish'. Bede also tells us that Pope Honorius (Pope from AD 625–638) warned the Irish about raking over the ashes of the burned books of the Pelagians. Aldhelm complained in AD 731 to King Gerontius about the religious practices of the Celtic people of Devon, and in AD 909 Archbishop Plegmund added parishes to the see of Crediton 'for the purpose of rooting out their errors. For before that time, as much as in them lay, they resisted the truth and would not obey the Apostolic decrees'. As late as Henry II's day, heretics in the west were still being pursued by the rigors of the law for Pelagianism.

Christianity and King Arthur

King Arthur comes right at the beginning of the ministry of that Irish and Celtic Church. How much and how widely it had developed in his time must be purely speculative or merely conjectural. Gildas was part of it – with Saint David of Wales and other Celtic saints slightly later – but the *ecclesia* Gildas describes in his sermon sounds more like a Gaulish organisation based on Roman provinces than the family- or tribe-based Irish model. Writing at the start of the sixth century, Gildas could see a Christian Britain, but it was in poor shape. He said:

21.6 The flock of the Lord and his shepherds, who should have been an example to the whole people, lay about, most of them, in drunken stupor, as though sodden in wine. They were a prey to petty hatreds and contentious quarrels, the greedy talons of envy, judgment that made no distinction between good and evil ...

66.1 Britain has priests but they are fools. Very many ministers but they are shameless; clerics but they are treacherous grabbers.

Gildas complains that the priests 'drive religious sisters from their house and cavort with foreign women' and 'after that, they canvas posts in the Church more vigorously than in the kingdom of heaven; [when] they get them, they keep them like warlords, and bring to them no lustre of lawful behaviour'.

Gildas paints a picture of a widespread British Church with riches and powerful positions for those adept enough to gain ordination as a priest and apostolic blessing as a bishop. Yet archaeology so far has failed to uncover the basilicas and major buildings such a Church might have produced. Bede, writing his *Ecclesiastical History of the English People* about two hundred years later, also saw no sign of this Church, or perhaps, because of the venality and immorality that Gildas outlines, chose to ignore it. For Bede, a few isolated examples of piety aside, the Christian Church in England began with the arrival from Rome, on the invitation of the Christian wife of a pagan king of Kent, of Saint Augustine of Canterbury. Bede disapproved of the Irish, the Welsh and other British Christians. Augustine of Canterbury met them, and may have regarded them as his contemporary Saint Wilfrid did as 'false prophets'.

Bede of course may have been wrong to see Britain as a Christian wilderness before Augustine of Canterbury's mission. There is quite a lot of evidence of an organised Church of some kind in Britain. Tertullian (*fl.* AD 170) wrote that 'regions of Britain which have never been penetrated by the Roman arms have received the religion of Christ'. Origen, a generation later, said that 'the divine goodness of Our Lord and Saviour is equally diffused among the Britons, the Africans, and other nations of the world'. Eusebius, the first real historian of the Church, said that 'the Apostles passed beyond the ocean to the isles called the Britannic Isles'. Britain may have seemed like the end of the world, but British bishops were recorded as attending at the councils of Arles 314, Nicea in 325, Sardica in 347 and Ariminium (Rimini) in 359.

By the time we reach the Age of Arthur, the beginning of the sixth century, Christianity in Britain may have become a 'house church' again, a Church that had no need of vast buildings and scheming priests seeking preferment, but a faith practised quietly by an isolated social elite who paid pagan Saxon warlords to protect their worldly goods. Insofar as we can guess at the sees and dioceses of this Church, they appear to have been large and unorganised. The bishop at Dorchester-on-Thames, for example, looked after Wessex and Mercia. As they emerged as 'Saxon states' in the seventh century, he would have held spiritual sway from the Middle Severn to the Channel Coast, about one-third of the landmass of England.

A hundred years earlier, in the time of Arthur, most of the people in his vast territory may have been pagan, or were adhering to the Celtic Church. The Celtic Church did have its own bishops, but made them inferior in status to abbots when it came to leading a territory spiritually. The *termoin* (territorial rule) of the Celtic abbot in theory reached as far as the furthest missionary who looked back to the mother Church (the *familia*) from which he came. Wherever he was located, an Irish monk continued to regard himself as under the guidance of the abbot who was the head of the *familia* in Ireland. By the end of the sixth century, men like Columba and Columbanus had extended the *termoin* of the Irish abbots over much of England, and substantial areas of Europe.

They were not deterred by the dominating presence of Catholic Prince-Bishops. Missionaries, like Fursey in East Anglia, seemed to have occupied space for the Celtic Christ that nominally belonged in a see or diocese of the Catholic Church. Since that was accomplished apparently without bloodshed or armies or other violent reaction, we may assume that the people he found himself among were probably pagans, or that the forces of Catholic orthodoxy were weak at that time in that region. Eastern England was apparently religiously in the hands of the pagans in the Age of Arthur.

Arthur himself doesn't seem to have had doctrinal views. He didn't get involved in conflicts among Christians, or between Christians and pagans. He was motivated in his wars, as far as we can discern him, by the need to acquire land or defend it, not by a need to proselytise for Jesus, to promote heretical views, or to uproot them. He also showed no interest in converting the pagans he met in battle, and he doesn't seem to have subscribed to, or shared, the desire to collect relics of the saints attributed to his patron, Baetan MacCairill. Arthur interacted with the ascetic Christian saints of south Wales, but the relationship we see in the stories of their encounters is one of friendly co-habitation in the same landscape. Saints reproved Arthur for his behaviour, and he took their criticism in good part. When they outwitted him, he took his defeat with good grace. When they challenged his power, he expelled them.

In Ireland, just before the battles in south Wales began, he supported abbots who were possibly Catholic against Baetan, who was certainly Celtic in belief and may have been Pelagian. That action was more to do with opposition to Baetan than affection for Catholic orthodoxy. After some fighting, he offered a negotiated settlement. That shows he felt able to defy the wishes of the clergy he was nominally supporting. He was happy to accept a peace agreement. By and large, Catholic prelates, faced with Pelagian or quasi-Pelagian opposition, did not offer or allow truces. Their war on people they regarded as heretics was unrelenting, and was aimed at extermination.

We should not too readily assume that Arthur was pagan or deeply anti-religion. He simply – like Maelgwn Gwynedd and other rulers – wanted to affirm his desire to exercise both temporal and spiritual power. His opposition to Gildas and Bridget was part of his opposition to Baetan MacCairill and the *derbfine* (ruling elite), and the religious *familia* (Celtic Church structure) around the Ulster king.

As far as we can tell, the doctrinal contentions that had troubled the Roman Empire for nearly 200 years did not determine his actions. Arthur was entirely self-reliant. Triad 37 (TYP) tells us he exposed the three talismans guarding Britain because he thought the island should be protected by no power but his own. He did not want or need the power of Saint Mary or her son at Fort Guinnion. He didn't require the assistance of Mary Magdalene or Saint Bridget at Glastonbury. As we might say today, Arthur made no allowance for divided loyalties. No interfering priest or monk, not even one representing an Apostle, or the companion of Jesus himself, would stand between his people and him. His people were to be led by him and him alone, and he alone was to be the fount and origin of all benefit to them. That attitude is more or less what we might expect from a warlord.

When Arthur no longer had power (because he was seriously wounded or lacked executive competence as a result of his injuries), Saint David of Wales and Saint Paul Aurelian sought to restore 'holy Glastonbury'. Arthur did not interfere. He may not have had the military power to expel them again, or even to contest their presence. He may not have been aware enough to know that they were at Glastonbury, or what they were doing there. As matter of policy, he may have continued to be more or less indifferent to Christian leaders, provided his interests were not affected. If we accept the story of Columba's blessing of Arturbran, the good old pagan, Arthur was only brought within the ambit of Christianity when he could no longer think or act for himself. It was his interpreter who indicated his acceptance of baptism into the Christian faith. Arthur himself may have lacked all agency by then. And when men came to rebury him at Glastonbury, perhaps ignorant of Columba's action or doubting its 'Celtic Church validity', they remembered how he had lived his life, and entombed him as a 'pagan vainglorious king in the Isle of Avalon', not a Christian leader who had won significant victories with divine help for the cause of the Cross. Religion in the Age of Arthur was a very powerful force in Europe; in England, in the world of Arthur, in the motivation of the warrior and in the battles of the king, it appears to have been irrelevant.

APPENDIX V

OF LEGENDS AND CURIOSITIES

The Welsh Tradition and Ireland

The 'Welsh tradition' of King Arthur and his time is not wholly Welsh. There have been strong inputs from Brittany and Ireland. The *Welsh Annals* and other sources like the TYP are based partly on earlier Irish annals, Irish heroic poetry, and even Irish styles and techniques. Around 1100, *Gruffydd ap Cynan*, who was born in Ireland, invited some of the best musicians of that country to Wales. He had observed the abuses of the Welsh bards, and wished to reform them by setting up academies 'for the amendment of their manners and the correction of their arts and practices'.[1]

The result is that there is often a distinct Irish literary influence to be found in works like the *Mabinogion*. To this we may add the suspicion, widely held among distinguished scholars of early Wales and its culture, that Arthur and stories pertaining to him originated in the north, especially modern Scotland (Galloway and Edinburgh) and Northumbria. The Arthurian stories seem to some scholars to have been only re-localised in Wales; they did not originate there.

The basis of the Arthurian context, Arthur in his setting as it were, may, like the religious record, have come from Ireland, either from a northern Irish monastery like Bangor, or a centre further south like Clonmacnoise. The Brittany sources are harder to trace, but it is evident that most of the stories we know about Arthur had, at the very least, Brittany versions, if not Breton origins. At least some Bretons were 'Letavian Britons', the Britons from Devon and Cornwall. They may have taken Irish/Cornish/Welsh stories with them which were later repatriated. A 'green tinge' from Ireland may indicate an early source, and therefore may be a sign of authenticity.

Poetic Exaggeration and Modes of Expression

The Irish and Welsh traditional style of poetic exaggeration (as in *Culhwch ac Olwen* where a serious war is reduced to a boar hunt) influences how we see Arthur and his circle. For those who devised the exaggerated way of communication, they were simply a graceful literary device, a bit of fun. For example, the Welsh remembered three amazing travellers: *Hen Beddestyr*, whom no man could keep up with; *Hen Vas*, whose speed no four-footed animal could match; and *Sgilti Light-foot*, who preferred to run by stepping on mountain tops and tree tops rather than on roads or pathways. Then there was the chief leaper of Ireland, who could cover 300 acres in a single bound; *Sol* who had the unusual (and presumably rarely imitated) ability to stand all day on one foot; *Gwevyl* who, when he was sad, could let one eyelid drop to his navel and pull the other one over his head as a hood; and *Clust*, whose hearing was so acute that, even buried seven fathoms (12.8 m) deep in earth, he could hear an ant stirring from its bed in the morning 50 miles away.

Arthur's slaying of 960 men in one solo attack at the Battle of Badon may be an exaggeration of this kind. It may really have happened, but the numbers are a decoration, not a fact. We have to understand the mode of discourse to gain an insight into the story related. Read in the right way, the apparently far-fetched fables of the *Mabiogion*, for example, become practical guides and examples for a prince in training, a manual for the future King Henry II. He might learn, for example, not to pursue campaigns that left him victorious but militarily weak.

The Round Table

A series of *englynion* (verses) tell us the truth about Arthur's table. The poems have been given the title *A Dialogue between Arthur and His Second Wife Gwynhwyvar*. *Gwynhwyvar* (Guinevere) affects not to recognise a warrior at one of Arthur's feasts. She says:

> I have seen a man of moderate size
> At [Arthur's] long table in Devon
> Dealing out wine to his friends.

The substance of the poem between her and the warrior is about bravery, boasting and height. She encourages the man to challenge Kei the Tall. The point is in the incidental detail about the 'long table', which is exactly the kind of table we might expect in the sixth century from archaeology and other early documents. The great halls revealed by archaeology were only suitable for long tables. Arthur did not have a round table.

We can make a guess about how the Round Table story started. According to the somewhat untrustworthy testimony of Iolo Morgannwg, an eighteenth-century antiquarian and forger of documents, the Round Table story starts about 1080 when *Rhys ap Tewdwr* (*c.* 1065–1093)² brought knowledge of it to Wales, possibly in a document, and probably from Ireland. By fraud and deception, a document (which may or may not be the same one) called *The Roll of the Round Table* was taken to Cardiff where, by conquest, it fell into the hands of Robert Fitzhamon. By marriage, Fitzhamon's daughter Mabli then passed it to her husband, Robert, Earl of Gloucester. Robert himself was a sort of informal stepson of *Nest*, daughter of *Rhys ap Tewdwr* (she was said to have been the mistress for a time of his father King Henry I). Robert of Gloucester was the mentor of Henry II and may have passed it on to his nephew. Henry II and Robert were the chief patrons of those who wrote the romantic versions of King Arthur. Henry II may have made the document available to his writers, or told them about it. They seem to have conceived it as a register of the warriors at Arthur's court, so they may not have actually seen it.

The document did not survive, but its name, *The Roll of the Round Table*, is more likely to refer to its nature than its contents. Almost all books then were rolls of parchment – not more than 10 per cent of books were *codices* (books with leaves like modern books). There is therefore a 90 per cent chance that it was a goatskin parchment roll of the kind used to record the laws of kings. It may have contained an old battle, or *forsundud*, poem listing warriors, and Arthur may have been among them. Its name is likely to have been its library reference in an abbey, monastery or cathedral, rather than a register of names of knights or warriors. That is, it was the roll that was kept on the round table.

The Sword in the Stone

'Stones of Destiny' start in Ireland as part of the ritual enthroning a high-king at Tara. The Tara stone (*an lia fail*) was laid down flat like a flagstone, and may be the same stone, the *Stone of Scone*, that turned up later in Scotland, and which is still used as a 'stone of destiny' in the coronation of British monarchs. Ritual stones of this kind may have been later confused with memorial or grave stones which had an important role in Irish law relating to claims on land (*tellach*). A claim on land was made by entering over, or past, the memorial stones and graves.

A medieval author, dimly aware of the 'sovereignty' implied by stones of destiny and *tellach* (land holding) roles of grave stones, confronted with the Clifton *Sweordes Stone* (*sordes* or holy stone), may have used his imagination to conflate the two roles, and devise a sovereign-creating event – withdrawing the sword – to achieve a throne and a destiny. If it was in fact the success of the Battle of Badon which brought Arthur to the style and title of 'king', we should recall that Nennius says he alone won the battle. Figuratively, therefore, he was the only individual capable of 'drawing the sword of rule from the holy stone' on the very spot where the battle was fought. Such a figurative expression would be entirely appropriate in the poetic languages of his day.

The Other *Melwys*

In the Arthurian stories, *Melwys* (under various names) is cast as an abductor, a rapist or a rival-in-arms of Arthur. In Wales, another tradition survived in which he was a daring and successful lover. In this story, as related by the great Welsh medieval poet *Dafydd ap Gwilym*, he builds a concealed treehouse in the forest, and then climbs up to Guinevere's window to persuade her to join him there.

Dafydd was something of a lover himself. His poetry is concerned with the Triadic obstacles to the illicit loves he sought. The three enemies of love, he said, were a barking dog, a creaking door and an old woman. He saw himself as another Melwys.

This is a version of his poem *Och! Nad gwiw ocheaid gwas.*

> Oh damn, I need to find old Melwas's art –
> That subtle thief who, by his enchanting,

Lured his girl to the greenwood's heart –
Which I can't do for all my groans and panting.
To the world's end went that old deceiver
To concealing walls, a love-house in a tree.
Since I love her and know I cannot leave her,
Tonight I must climb there just as high as he.

Arthur in Old Age?

In the *Black Book of Carmarthen* (compiled about AD 1250) there
is a poem called *Pa Gur* after its first line, which is, in English,
'What man is the gate-keeper?' The question is a prelude to a
conversation between Arthur and a porter. Such conversations
between warriors entering a fort and the porter are common in
Welsh literature, and in other later places. A 'porter scene', for
example, is the only overt comedy in Shakespeare's *MacBeth*, and
serves to introduce Macduff as the focus of the forces that will
challenge and, in the end, overcome the murderous king.

Here the 'porter scene' introduces us to a non-heroic Arthur. Sir
Ifor Williams, noticing the lack of heroic action by King Arthur in
Welsh stories and the French romances, speculated that the king
had become old. In this book, it has been suggested he suffered
brain damage. Both conditions can lead to a querulous preference
for the 'good old days' which we see in this passage in *Pa Gur*
about the death of *Cei* and Arthur's son *Llacheu* – possibly in a
fatal encounter with a '*sea-cat*' or with King Murchada of Leinster.
This is what Arthur tells the porter:

I fear I shall find no fighters now
To match the men who marched and stood,
Braving my battle before the Lords of Gwynedd.
Here I proclaim Cei, Prince of Plunder,
Who stood tall and taunting, troubling our enemies.
His valour destroyed them, his vengeance was vexing.
In delight before battle, he could drink for a dozen.
Where war was to wage, he was worth regiments.
In the fair chance of fighting, no-one could fell him.
Only God's doom could determine disaster.
Mourn now for Cei, mourn too for my Llacheu.
In wars they worked wonders –
Spears of azure then ended their exploits.

Glastonbury and the War-dog

One of the kings condemned by Gildas was called *Cuneglas*. His name is composed of two elements: *cune* (Welsh or Irish for 'dog' with the additional meaning of 'guardian' or 'protector') and *glas*, which can be a blue-grey colour, but can also mean an oak or something holy. Gildas says to him *Cuneglase romana lingua lanio fulve*. The usual translation of the phrase is 'you Cuneglas – in Latin "red butcher"'. This is clearly not right. Gildas knew Latin and he knew Irish and Welsh, and there is no way Cuneglas can mean 'red butcher'.

The phrase needs to be looked at a possible example of Gildasian bitter humour. Gildas is more probably not saying the name but repeating its meaning, 'grey dog' or 'holy guardian'. 'Rome' in the time of Gildas did not always mean the city, and it never meant the Latin language. The 'soil of Rome' (*ruam* in Irish), for example, could mean either the veritable 'earth from the city in Italy', or merely some 'sanctified earth from a monastery'. If we read *romana* in that sense, the words of Gildas mean 'in the language of religion' or 'in religious terms'.

The 'red' reference may mean 'from Ulster' which in Ireland was associated with that colour, but may otherwise refer to the tawny coat of the typical Irish war dog. Gildas may be saying, 'You are called the guard dog of the holy grove, but really in religious terms you are an out-of-control wardog.' That at least fits the rest of his condemnation.

The idea of Cuneglas having a responsibility to guard religion may lead us to look again at Glastonbury as a name. We may translate the *bury* element as *caer* or fort. *Caer Glasten* in, say, Cornish means 'fort of the oaks' or perhaps 'Fort of the holy wood'. Insofar as *caer* may translate Latin *Castellum* (fort, refuge, or sanctuary), it may mean 'holy oak grove'.

'Holy woods' did exist, and still do. About 6 miles west of the great Irish abbey of Bangor there was a daughter house named *Sanctus Boscis* (the modern town of Holywood). A famous early mathematician at the University of Paris, John of Holywood, may have come from there. Gildas may simply be telling us that, in his time, Glastonbury was already important in religious terms, and its guardian or protector was not a suitable person for that role because he was an unrestrained ravager – a description of a trait that the TYP also applies to Arthur. That is about as close as Gildas comes to telling us that he knew Arthur, which he must have done. Was Cuneglas a nickname for Arthur? Unless we find another document from that period, there is no way to tell. The suggestion must remain little more than a curiosity.

A Glastonbury Mystery

William of Malmesbury tells us that if we want to know more about the mission of the Apostle Philip, we should look in Freculf. That is a signpost to a mystery. He follows it up with some remarks about the patterns on the tiled floor of the Old Church. He says they are pointed in lead, and may hide some secret of religious importance that he, personally, is unwilling to speculate further about. That is another signpost and another mystery. Both signposts indicate a story that William is unwilling to relate. What can it be?

According to the stories attached to Saint David of Wales and Saint Pol de Léon, the church of Mary at Glastonbury needed either replacement, or repair, in the mid-, or late, sixth century. Saint Pol gave it a new lead roof. That places skilled lead workers on the site. The lead pointing of the floor tiles could have been done at that time. But why do it at all? Why arrange a pattern of the kind William saw? Why, five centuries later, did William think it might have some important religious significance?

Then we have Abbot Richard Whiting, the last Abbot of Glastonbury. He seems, by all accounts, to have been a good abbot, and he initially did what a sensible man might do to preserve the abbey when, in 1534, King Henry VIII passed his Act of Supremacy, declaring himself 'Head of the Church in England'. Whiting signed the Act. In 1535, he could see the implications for Glastonbury of the Suppression of Religious Houses Act of that year. It applied only to the smaller houses, but by January 1539 Glastonbury was the only religious house left in Somerset. Abbot Richard knew that, sooner or later, the king, or his commissioners, would come for the treasures of Glastonbury.

When they came, the king's commissioners charged him with 'robbing Glastonbury church'. The commissioners found treasures valued at 200,000 crowns and a book supporting the cause of ex-Queen Katherine of Aragon. Supporting the former queen was in itself sufficient to place Abbot Richard in trouble, but the commissioners' charged him with the theft of something either they or the king wanted and believed was at Glastonbury. Their failure to find some other 'treasure of the church' beyond the extensive cash, ornaments and books they did find brought Abbot Richard and two companions to Glastonbury Tor. There they were hanged, drawn and quartered. The secret of Glastonbury died with him.

What was this missing 'treasure'? We can ask further questions: what did Abbot Richard hide (that is, 'steal' or 'rob') during the five-year build-up to the attack on his abbey and its treasures? Was the book supporting the ex-queen a deliberate misdirection? Were relics – whatever it was that made the Old Church holy, plus the bones of Arthur – the real target for the commissioners? Abbot Richard had plenty of warning, and more than enough time, to take action to conceal the 'treasures'. If you wanted to hide relics, where would you move them to?

The answer may have been to place them in plain sight, as priests and parishioners did in Bristol when they placed an altar upside down on the ground just outside the church and said it was a gravestone. When the winds of religion changed, they were able to restore it to its proper place in the church. Is there anywhere now in Glastonbury where, in the anxious time of Henry VIII, relics could have been concealed secretly, and without too much trouble, by men in a hurry?

There is food for thought here, and finding the answers, and indeed the treasures, requires a scheme capable of testing and implementation. Otherwise, we remain in the realms of faith, where almost anything is possible but nothing is provable. Finding out properly, initially at least, means doing something very like history. How can we do that at Glastonbury? Now that is a really big question.

Lost in Translation?

The strange tale told by Procopius (which may relate the story of the AD 540 event) is open to question because it is about an island called *Brittia*, and not overtly about Britain. It is unlikely that Procopius did not know and use *Brittania* or *Britanniae* to refer to Great Britain, and the geographical position given by Procopius is clearly that of Britain. Nonetheless, Procopius chose to use this term *Brittia* rather than *Britannia*. That may be because it was the term used by his informants, a name known to them, and applied by them in the sixth century (at least before AD 530) to a real land to which they made voyages. In any reality, it can only have meant some smaller part of the British Isles, perhaps western Britain. It may be therefore instructive to look more closely at *Brittia* to see what it might tell us.

There appears to be little doubt that the name *Brittia*, or a term similar to it, or derived from it, had become attached to the Glastonbury area by the twelfth century. It is mentioned by William of Malmesbury, and it seems to be entirely independent of the use of *Brittia* by Procopius. William does not refer to Procopius. There is a putative Early British form, *Ynys Witrin*, of uncertain antiquity. We do not know if that name was merely a translation of a still earlier Latin form, *Insula Vitrea*, or whether it comes from the *Brittia* name persisting in the area as a folk name with no linguistic heritage assigned to it. We can see clearly, however, that *Brittia* became *Vitrea* (the usual v for b pronunciation shift), and thus Glastonbury became the 'Isle of Glass' mentioned, and translated into French, in the twelfth-century romances.

We can go in the other direction in time and ask when, or why, or how, did a name like *Brittia* become attached to a part of western Britain, and indeed to the Glastonbury area. There is a vague possibility (and we should not put it any higher than that) that the term arises from the slight and shadowy information we have about Mary Magdalene in England. There is a term used in Arabic, Aramaic and Hebrew, which appears in forms such as *Barayeta*, *Boraitthoth*, *Baraita* and *Beraita*. Today, among Jews, as *Baraita*, it usually refers to 'secondary or less important teaching', not part of the *Mishnah*.[3]

In the Middle Eastern languages, words are formed from a core of consonants, and meaning and pronunciation is indicated by changing letter forms and punctuation marks to indicate the values of any vowels between them. The root form of this word is [BRT] with an A-sound vowel between them and after them which could be lengthened, shortened, or omitted to express related ideas (thus it could assume forms like *barata*, *brata*, *brita*, *berita*). The word used by Procopius and found later at Glastonbury by William of Malmesbury, *Brittia*, could readily be derived from this ancient root-form BRT. The BRT root-form means 'outside' or 'outsider', and thus could be extended to express notions such as 'outsider', 'exile' or, as among modern Jews, 'oral witness as opposed to written texts and therefore not quite so canonical'. In Christian terms, it could also mean a subsidiary witness, a gospel 'outside' the Bible, or a teaching that was not of the main stream.

This idea of 'outside-ness' and 'important but secondary' was of course was the view of Mary Magdalene taken by Peter, James and other Apostles who were Aramaic, Hebrew and/or Arabic speakers in the first century. *Insula Brittia* may mean 'the island of the outsider teaching', or 'the island of the exile'. It may thus represent, in a somewhat speculative way, a very early tradition of a secondary, alternative, orally transmitted teaching outside the mainstream of the developing Christian *ecclesia*. It may also reflect the 'exile' status of Mary Magdalene. Without further information, we cannot take it further, and it therefore must remain only a 'wild surmise'. While something very important may have been lost here in translation and/or transmission, we should only retain the notion of *Brittia* as *Beraita*, if at all, as a 'thought experiment' of the kind physicists use productively, a way of developing an idea in theory which may only be provable in the future as experimental data becomes available.

Arthur and *Stuf*

The *Anglo-Saxon Chronicle* says:

> AD 501 In this year Port came to Britain, and his two sons Bieda and Maegla with 2 ships to the place that is called Porthes Mutha and slew a young British man, a very princely man.

> AD 514 In this year came the West Saxons into Britain with 3 ships to the place that is called Cerdices ora, Stuf and Wihtgar. And fought against the Britons and put them to flight.

Stuf is not, as one might expect, a German or Saxon name. It appears to be derived from Latin *stuppa* which is tow, the coarse bit of flax or other similar grassy plants. In personal name terms, it is likely to have been descriptive, and for a meaning in modern English we might therefore turn to a word which describes hair quality and colour such as 'flaxen' or 'tow-headed'. *Stuf* may have been a blonde-haired warrior.

We know his name because Bishop Daniel of Winchester told it to Bede. It seems to have passed from Bede into *the Anglo-Saxon Chronicle*. Bede listed it, with *Wihtgar*, *Port*, *Bieda* and *Maegla*, as the names of the conquerors of early sixth-century Hampshire. In this book, we have suggested that *Bieda* is the Irish king *Baetan* Mac Cairill and *Maegla* is his son *Melwys*. *Port*, we think, may be the Welsh word *porth* and, in this context, means 'an army of assistance'. There is general agreement among scholars that *Port*, or *Porth*, is not a personal name.

Bieda is a personal name and occurs in Wiltshire place-names like Biddesham. Maegla (Melwys) is also a personal name. He may be the man whose name lies behind the modern river name *Malago* in Bristol. Only Stuf as a personal name remains unattested outside the *Anglo-Saxon Chronicle*.

That is not entirely surprising. The sixth century was an age of poor transmission of names, events and everything else. Spoken communication was in Welsh, Irish, Latin, Anglo-Saxon or the remnants of Old British, Brittonic. There may also have been languages spoken by the Picts and the mysterious Attacotti people, listed by Bede as inhabitants of the British Isles. The latter may be the Irish tribute-paying tribes (Primitive Irish *ateuiacototas* or Old Irish *aithechthuatha*) such as the *Airgialla*. No real trace of a Pictish or an Attacotti language has survived.

That may be because these two languages never achieved a written form. The written languages of transmission in this period appear to have been confined to Latin, Irish and Welsh (and there may be some doubt about Welsh at this date). Virtually all writers of such languages were monks, and the monks wrote down what they heard and their hearing may not have been well-adjusted to all of the tongues of the British Isles. The chance of garbled names is very high.

The monks also had to contend with languages which were in transition from inflected tongues to uninflected speech. Even in a language they knew quite well, monks had many chances of misunderstanding as names made the transition from inflected to uninflected. Bede (AD 673-735), for example, records the name of the Welsh Abbot *Dinoot* on its way from Latin *Donatus* to Welsh *Dinawd*. In such circumstances *Stuf* may not be merely descriptive ('tow-headed') but also, or instead, be a version of some other word or name which was near enough in pronunciation to be misheard, or which otherwise just sounded a bit like 'Stuf' to a monkish auditor.

One candidate word may be the Irish word *stiurthoir*. Normal processes in philology and orthography could just about remove the ending *oir* (final syllables were dropped because inflected case endings were disappearing) and the medial 'r' might have been absorbed in writing by the preceding 'u', thus giving us a form like *Stiuth*. A further voicing of the 'th' sound might produce an 'ff' sound. We can thus arrive at *Stuf* from *stiurthoir*, but by a somewhat dubious, unattested and uncertain route.

Stiurthoir means 'commander' or 'helmsman' and that may cause us to look again at the man Gildas calls *Cuneglas*. He is, in Latin, *'multorum sessor'* – the pilot, guide or commander of many men. *Cuneglas* is also described by Gildas as 'tawny' which might be another version of 'tow-headed'.

That can lead us to an interesting conjecture. If we exclude *Port* (the army) and *Wihtgar* (the people of the Isle of Wight), the entries for these two years in the *Anglo-Saxon Chronicle* give us the names of only three battle commanders: *Bieda*, *Maegla* and *Stuf*. The list of twelve battles in Nennius claims that Arthur was the sole *dux bellorum* (battle commander) of the forces engaged around this time and we have suggested that he fought in the interest of *Baetan MacCairill* and his son *Melwys*. Our suggestions about battle sites place him in southern Hampshire within a decade of the date assigned to the conquest of the area by the *Anglo-Saxon Chronicle*. That may lead us to suppose that, if *Stuf* was the name of a real commander who fought alongside *Bieda* (Baetan) and *Maegla* (Melwys) in southern Hampshire, the man we know as *Stuf* may well have been Arthur.

That identity may be confirmed in another source. *Stuf* may be another version (or a translation) of the personal name of a person referred to in *Berchan's Prophecy*. In the main part of this book, we have suggested that *Berchan's* Verse 24 refers to *Baetan*. The second line of that verse contrasts Baetan favourably with another man described only as *gairechtach glas-buidhi*. *Gairechtach* is roughly the equivalent of the Latin term *inclitus* used in its ironic sense of 'vainglorious'. We have found it applied in that sense to the Arthur of the Glastonbury grave. *Glas-buidi* combines two colours – *Glas* (grey) and *buidhi* (yellow) – and may be translated as 'pale yellow'. The line in Verse 24 may thus be a translation of *Stuf* ('flaxen', 'tow-headed') as *glas-buidhi* 'pale yellow'. If that were true, since Nennius tells us that the only military colleague of *Baetan* and *Melwys* in that place and at that time was Arthur, *Stuf* and the '*glas-buidhi* warrior' may both be references to Arthur. Arthur may be both the boastful blonde warrior we find in *Berchan* and the flaxen-haired fighter and leader in the *Anglo-Saxon Chronicle*.

Stuf (Arthur), the helmsman or commander, may also be the *Cuneglas*, the 'commander of many' condemned by Gildas. Arthur certainly fits the broad characterisation of *Cuneglas* that we see in Gildas; he is a warrior out of control (an unrestrained ravager and war-dog), charged with protecting a holy grove (the battle of Guinnion), but who is a sinker or suppressor of God's word (Arthur's opposition to *Henwen*). The 'Pale Yellow warrior' also exhibited a boastfulness later attributed to Arthur.

If Arthur were found to be *Cuneglas*, that would solve a major problem in this era of history. Saint Gildas was in a position to know everyone who really mattered in most of Britain and Ireland in the first half of the sixth century, yet he has nothing to say about any leader or commander called Arthur. We know that Arthur had emerged as a famous warrior by the middle or end of that century because prominent kings named their sons and grandsons after him. Three hundred years later, his name was still remembered and his reputation still invited the hostility of the monks of holy Glastonbury. Why did Gildas not mention Arthur by that name? Was it because he saw him only as the unworthy guardian of Glastonbury? Was that why he made a bitter pun of his name and addressed him as *Urthe* (bear) rather than *Airthir* (the Easterner)?

While it would be wonderful to be able to identify Arthur securely as *Cuneglas*, *Stuf* and the *glas-buidhi* warrior, we must admit that our whole argument is at best tenuous and at worst beyond credibility. It may be no more than an entertaining guess about an odd name in the *Anglo-Saxon Chronicle*, the sort of *Stuf* that dreams are made of.

There is also one major thing wrong with it. *Stiurthoir* looks like a borrowing into Irish from German, Icelandic or one of the other Scandinavian (Viking) languages. The root of the word implies 'guidance and leadership'. Old Mercian offers the verb *steran* with that sort of meaning and Early West Saxon offers *stieran*. The Irish noun seems to replicate the root of the West Saxon verb form. Unless it came into Irish in the sixth century from West Saxon (and we have absolutely no evidence to suggest that), *stiurthoir* is unlikely to have come into use in Irish much before AD 800, by which time Arthur, Bede and Bishop Daniel were all long dead. And that may knock the stuffing out of our argument. The fact is we know very little and we can prove nothing. *Stuf* and Arthur both remain fascinating mysteries.

APPENDIX VI

THE GLASTONBURY OAK COFFIN: EVIDENCE OF A HISTORICAL ARTHUR?

The oak coffin in the Glastonbury grave is, in many ways, the most interesting piece of information we can find in the accounts of the exhumation of Arthur by Gerald of Wales and Ralph of Coggeshall. We can trust it in a way we would not trust the lead cross and its inscription because the oak coffin of itself makes no overt claim about Arthur. It may nevertheless be one of the most persuasive pieces of evidence we have about him.

Coffins made of hollowed-out oaks have been used in the British Isles for more than a thousand years. Most oak coffins placed in the ground will of course have rotted, and there are not enough known examples of oak boat-style coffins to say much more. The Glastonbury oak coffin, however, seems to have survived because it was placed in a cist or lintel grave. That may have created anaerobic conditions, possibly aided by some gypsum either from the stone grave lining or originating from the oxidation of organic sulphur in the bodies, which preserved the coffin and its contents.

If the hollowed-out oak represents a boat, it may be a distinct sign of a Pagan burial (like Sutton Hoo) but it could also be a compelling sign of an Irish and Christian connection. *Bridei, son of Bili*, a Pictish king who was a friend of Adomnan (624–704), Abbot of Irish Iona, was remembered in a fragment of elegiac verse, possibly written in Adomnan's own hand. The verse says:

It is strange, it is strange,
That, after being in the kingship of the people,
A block of hollow withered oak
Should be about this son of the King of Dumbarton.

Bridei's last resting place appears to have been in, or otherwise involved, a hollowed-out oak coffin, and, given his close friendship with Adomnan, he was very probably a Christian. He died in AD 693, during the time Adomnan was Abbot of Iona. It appears on that evidence that hollowed-out oak coffins persisted in Irish contexts at least until that date. It is therefore feasible that the oak coffin in the Glastonbury grave is genuine and of the sixth century.

We can also say with some confidence that an oak coffin of this type is unlikely to have been forged in the twelfth century. Hollowing out an oak takes time and skill and finding a cist grave to put it in would have been almost impossible. No modern archaeologist would know where to find one without excavation. The monks of Glastonbury would not have been better placed to use a cist grave as part of their supposed deception. Forgers of that time, in any case, would not have known much about ancient oak-boat burials, Christian or Pagan, or indeed about cist graves.

What else does the oak coffin tell us? Although Irish slab-graves are known from the sixth century, in England there are few before the eighth century. Burial in a cist grave, either directly or in an oak coffin, in the sixth century in England would have been unusual, and, like the oak coffin itself, may be a sign of an Irish inhumation by people who shared the culture and practices of Iona and Dumbarton.

We can also say that an oak coffin could very well have survived at Glastonbury if it had been protected by being placed in the stone chamber or cist grave. That enclosure could have preserved the soft tissue of the two dead people as well as their skeletons. Arthur's wounds and Guinevere's hair may therefore have been, as reported by Gerald of Wales and Ralph of Coggeshall, readily observable by the monks of Glastonbury.

We can certainly say it was a high-status, probably Irish, burial. The male body buried may very well have been that of Arthur. The oak coffin may be at least an indication, if not a 'proof', of his historicity and that makes it superior to any other evidence in the Glastonbury grave. In the story of Arthur, King and Warrior, the oak coffin is very important.

NOTES

2 War in the Sixth Century

1. The *spatha* was about 0.75 to 1 m long. The *gladius* used by Roman infantrymen was about 0.5 m long. The *spatha* was used from the first century to the sixth century. It is thought to be the model for the swords used by the Vikings.

2. This is essentially the same word in all three tongues. The Welsh language was based on what is termed 'p-Celtic' (which gives words such as *Pen* for hill). Irish was based on 'q-Celtic' (which gives *Ken* for hill). In looking at names, we have to mind our Ps and Qs.

3. The Irish, however, displayed great interest in Romanised Britain. Romans coins and artefacts in Irish archaeology and some early loan words in the Irish language show a desire for contact beyond simple raiding.

4. *Chronica Gallica* AD 452. *Britanniae in dicionem Saxonum rediguntur* (The Britains (Britain) passed into the power of the Saxons). It was probably not a single event like a successful revolt in one location, but it was accomplished and visible by around AD 440–42.

5. *Ruari Ua Conchobair* (Rory O'Connor)

6. *Argent a saltire gules* (a red saltire on silver ground)

7. There is some doubt about when this title came into use. It appears in writing for the first time in the ninth century, but rulers in the

seventh century seem to have acquired it retrospectively. We can be certain it had no meaning in the sixth century.

8. Finn is said to have caused the 'Giant's Causeway' in North Antrim by flinging rocks at a Scottish giant who responded in kind.

9. There is no compelling evidence that the process was different from that followed by Richard de Clare and the Fitzgeralds.

10. Chapter 28 of *The Ruin of Britain* (*de excidio Britonum*).

11. Not necessarily homosexuality but just generalised sexual licence.

12. Eric Hamp and Patrick Sims Williams.

13. We cannot be certain but it seems likely their horsemen lacked stirrups and that governed how they fought. They did not fight like knights.

3 The English Campaign: Twelve Battles of King Arthur

1. Dumville, D. N., *History* 62(2) (1977), p. 187.

2. Hughes, K., *Early Christian Ireland: introduction to the sources* (London: Hodder and Stoughton, 1972), p. 224.

3. Halsall, G., *Worlds of Arthur* (OUP, 2013), pp. 168–171.

4. *Contra* Halsall *et al.*, writers of the period used Hiberno-Latin, Hisperica Famina, and other literary devices including numerology to decorate their texts and startle or amaze their readers. They did not change the basic material much. What mattered to early writers was the decoration, not the substance.

5. This assumes that the poorly explored fort, signal station or other form of fortification on St Catherine's Hill at Christchurch is Roman. A high proportion of bodies at a Saxon burial site at nearby Hengistbury Head were male and some were armed (about eleven out of thirty). No associated Saxon settlement has been found.

6. *Cabullus*, the Roman packhorse, produces by a similar process Late Latin *caballerius*, a horseman, and in French a *chevalier* and in English a *cavalier* (a knight) and *chevalier* (a horse soldier) and *chivalry* (the practice of knightly behaviour)

7. Birch, W. G., *JBAA*, Vol. XLIX (1893), p. 181.

8. The Earl of Caledon in County Tyrone in Ireland bears a title created in 1800. The family name is Alexander and the heir is called Viscount Alexander. There is no long history of the Caledon name in Tyrone before the creation of the title, and how the Alexander family, or the College of Heralds, hit on the name is not known. It may be a learned humorous reference to Caesar's campaign in a forested land

full of hostile natives and wild boars. Tyrone, even in 1800, merited that description.

9. It might safer to regard this catacomb image of a woman and child as only doubtful evidence of an early cult of the Virgin Mother Mary. A very similar image found at Herculaneum of a woman feeding a child held on her lap is thought to be simply a Pagan goddess.

10. There is a consensus that the text of Nennius dates from AD 830, give or take ten years.

11. Another Mary – Mary Magdalene – may be more likely. See Appendix III.

12. Cashel (the Rock of Cashel) in Ireland derives its name from Irish *caiseal* (stone ring-fort) but was never military. It was used as a ritual centre in the making of Irish kings. Although Irish language scholars discount it, it may be a borrowing of Latin *castellum*. Irish *caiseal*, a ritual centre, may lie behind the fort of the battle text.

13. There is a church in Cornwall dedicated to Saint Nonna who was said to be the mother of Saint David of Wales. The Turkish Saint Nonna was the mother of Gregory the Theologian.

14. Pliny mention a black dye which women used to paint their naked bodies before dancing to welcome returning warriors. He said it was called '*glastum*' in the British language of the time. That term may refer to some ritual meaning as well as to its colour. Oaks may have been involved in the making of the dye or in its sanctifying.

15. See Appendix III.

4 When Was Badon?

1. Kentish cemeteries of this period (fifth to sixth century) suggest an average age for males at death of twenty-five years. In later medieval times where more bodies have been studied, the average age at death for males was about thirty-one years. Much depends on how the age is calculated. If children are excluded, the average can rise by a few years. Few warriors can have expected to reach their thirtieth birthday.

5 Where Was Badon?

1. As we have seen in chapter 2, the Britons, the Welsh, the Bretons and the Cornish used p-Celtic and the Irish and the Goidels used q-Celtic. Latin Britannia thus became Welsh Prydein and Irish Cruithne. *Pen* and *ken* are essentially the same word.

2. See Appendix IV for a longer discussion.

3. 'B' becomes 'v or 'f' as Welsh develops as a language. Thus Badon moves to Vaddon. We have already seen in Bassas (chapter 3) one example of this change and will see other examples.

4. Brunel's famous Clifton Suspension Bridge which joins the three forts was completed in 1867 but eighteenth-century Bristol painters have recorded how it looked before that time. See Figs 5 and 6 in plates.

6 The Hill Forts of the Avon Gorge

1. Possibly the sign was thought to be doctrinally unsound in later years because it was associated with Pelagianism or a saint from whom the church had withdrawn recognition.

2. Apparently about 5 lb or 2.6 kg in weight.

3. The trebuchet, the latest artillery weapon, was introduced in a widespread way into Byzantine armies from Chinese examples by the mid-sixth century. It is unlikely to have featured at Badon.

7 What Happened at Badon?

1. C. 17 and c. 19 Gildas.

2. The plan worked well enough for Henry II's dynasty to use the Welsh form Plantagenet (Child of Anjou) as the family name.

3. The material of the bed may be significant. The Irish had a custom used to select a high-king. A recognised hero ate his fill of a roasted ox and went to bed. Whoever he dreamed of would be the new high-king. The ox hide may be intended to indicate a dream about sovereignty.

4. See poem in Appendix V.

5. There may have been long experience of manipulating the tides to create useful blockages and enhance water effects even at this early date. The Irish had tide mills dating back to the sixth century at Waterford, AD 630 at Cork and AD 787 at the monastery of Nendrum at Strangford Lough in Northern Ireland (where there were signs of a much earlier one). At Bristol there was an undated tide mill on the Malago River which may go back to Roman times. The River Malago is said to derive its name from the Brittonic *Melis* (a mill) and *agos* (a place). It may also be a version of the name of Melwys, a known hero of the time, which occurs in forms like *Malgo*, *Melga* and *Maelga*. That would make the etymology *Mael* (Irish, prince) linked with *agos* to mean 'prince's dwelling'. Tide mills were said to be used for Christian baptism, and may thus, in the manner of churches, have had someone's personal name attached

to them. A tide mill named after a prince is just about possible. In later centuries, the Bristol tide mill was called 'Treen Mills'. *Treen* means 'made entirely of wood' and usually applies now only to small objects. It derives from Old English *treowen* (trees). *Tre-owein* of course, if it were Cornish, would mean 'Owen's farm, homestead or settlement'. He may not be the Owein who commanded at Badon.

6. Gildas was using his experience to describe the effect of Roman legionary forces on raiding parties of Scots (Irish) and Picts about a hundred years before Badon.

7. Cameramen today filming tsunami events focus on both features as Gildas did; we are shown both the cloud-high wave-front and the streaming lines of the water following.

8. There may have been another battle on the same site as Badon twenty years later. In AD 675 (which may not be an accurate date) the *Anglo-Saxon Chronicle* tells us that Wulfhere, son of Penda, fought a battle at *Biedanheafod*. *Heafod* in Anglo Saxon is 'head'. In Irish that would be *ken* and in Welsh *pen*. Both are translated into Latin as *mons* (mount or hill) in physical geography. *Biedanheafod* as a name is another version of Mount Badon.

9. We cannot be sure that the obvious defence line, the Wansdyke, had been created, but the strategic pressure that created the Wansdyke may have suggested, to commanders at the time, a defence line that may have corresponded with it.

10. Based on the Burghal Hideage of King Alfred, which listed the numbers of men needed to mount an effective defence of a named location. It corresponded roughly to one man for every metre of wall.

8 The Glastonbury Grave

1. Henry II's grandson, Arthur of Brittany, was nominated as a child to be the successor of King Richard the Lionheart, but when Richard succumbed to wounds sustained in battle, King John captured and murdered the unfortunate Arthur. Thus, although Henry II's long-term scheme to use the prestige of King Arthur came to nothing in the end, Plantagenet interest in Arthur by then extended over four generations, and in as many countries.

2. See p. 98 *et seq.* P. O'hEaildhe in Rynne, E. (ed.), *Figures from the Past* (Dun Laoghaire: Glendale, 1987)

3. Radford appears to have realised that they were cross bases – see p. 51, Radford & Swanton, *Arthurian Sites in the West* (Exeter

University Press, 2002 edn). The cross base of the Rere Cross at Stainmore in England is rectangular at the base.

4. Baille, M. J. B., *Exodus to Arthur* (London: Batsford, 1993), p. 75 .

5. Barber and others attribute financial motives to the monks of Glastonbury in the 'fortunate finds' of ancient charters and relics of saints. This is to ignore or misunderstand profoundly the very powerful motivation that such discoveries had for people of faith. The benefits were spiritual rather than financial. Money may have helped in this world; for people who believed more in the next world, and that God and his saints were active and present in this one, objects conveying additional holiness in this world and benefits in the next world were to be sought after, and perhaps even manufactured for that reason. Monasteries where such relics were concentrated and aggregated were trying to build a sort of 'spiritual accelerator' (like the nuclear one today at CERN). Their aim, like that of CERN, was to access other dimensions.

6. The name Arator is otherwise unknown, but that conjecture would locate him securely in western Britain and he would thus become, delightfully, 'the only Ploughboy of the Western World'.

7. There are several kings of this name and in the fifth century they may have ruled a territory that stretched from Donegal to the headwaters of the River Boyne. One of them was an opponent of St Patrick.

8. Modern medical research by Professor Marta Karbonits of Queen Mary College London and Professor Patrick Morrison of Queen's University Belfast reveals that some County Tyrone/Armagh individuals, particularly those living by or near the Lough Neagh shore, have a gene that affects the pituitary gland which controls growth. In modern times it manifests as a benign tumour, but there is a long history of 'gigantism' stretching back over two thousand years. Some present-day examples of acromegaly in the area reach 2.3 m or more in height. The Irish Earl of Tyrone's men caused a sensation through their height when he visited the court of Elizabeth I. They were active warriors and must be seen as 'normally tall', not acromegalic, even though they too may have exceeded 2 m in height. If they were active warriors, they did not have pituitary problems.

9. One such Irish king may be the Owein who was Arthur's co-commander at Badon. There was an Owein, king of Clogher, around this time. The kings of Clogher ruled the Ui Crimthain, a relatively powerful tribe of central Ulster who were often

characterised in the lives of saints and elsewhere by an ox epithet. Archaeologists have discovered small iron oxheads at the site of their palace. One investigator, R. B. Warner, thought the 'ox people' of Clogher might be migrants from Romanised Britain. One of their rulers may also have had a Welsh dominion, and thus may have been the father of St Paul Aurelian, a pupil of St Illtud, whose father was one Perphirius (Peripherius? Odor, the border king? Rather than 'one who wore purple'?). Perphirius was *Penn Owen* (Latin *caput boum*) or 'chief of the Oxen'. The Oxen Ui Crimthain may, like their close neighbours, the Airthir, have been called to the hosting of the over-king. Welsh tradition recalls an *Owein Lawgoch*, Owein of the Red Hand which was later the heraldic symbol of Ulster. It seems possible that the exploits of this Irish Owein, of whom the Welsh poets knew very little, were assimilated by the great, but later, hero Owein map Urien. We may note in passing that Crimthain means 'cunning fox or wolf' – precisely the quality exhibited by Owein at Badon. Cunning, of course, we have identified via Gildas as one of the characteristics required to be a successful 'warlord' or 'tyrant'.

10. Paradise is from the Iranian *pairidaeza* –'enclosed park or surrounding wall' via Greek and Latin with the meaning 'garden'. Thus 'Avalonia' may mean here some sort of sacred, but not necessarily Christian, enclosure or precinct.

11. They were influenced by the work of the poet Ibn Hazm in Muslim Spain whose *The Ring of the Dove* is one of the first manifestations of what came to be called in the nineteenth century (not before) 'courtly love'. Hazm perhaps drew on the famous *Thousand and One Nights* saga which was then in the process of formation in the Islamic world.

9 A Life of Arthur

1. Unless we see the name as referring to whatever impetus took large numbers of people from England to Brittany in the sixth century at a currently undetermined date. Appendix II may offer one event which certainly caused a terrible commotion, but Arthur's mother was unlikely to have been involved in that.

2. Nendrum and Movilla are other possibilities. The inscription on the broken tile is similar to some at Nendrum.

3. We should note in passing that Bede uses the Latin word *imperium* to mean 'kingship' or 'realm of a king'.

4. See Appendix V.
5. If his sister really was called Morgan le Fay, and Arthur was indeed 'Airthir of Loughall' of the Oriel, she may be the Muirgen or Liban who lived near the southern shores of Lough Neagh. This Muirgen Liban started as a goddess and/or a pagan priestess. She became a Christian. Her name is interesting. Muirgen Liban becomes *Morgan li Fa* (possibly lengthened to ay or ey in speech) because the 'b' in Liban regularly became written and said as 'f' or 'v' in Wales and Ireland. The final 'n' often dropped out, or became a mistaken 'r' because of misreading of the Irish script. *Muirgen Liban* may thus become *Morgan Le Fay* or *Morgan le Fayr* or *Faery*. She appears under that name, or one very similar to it, in the romances, but we don't know that she was Arthur's sister.
6. This is the effect of q-Celtic, which demands a hard 'c' or a 'k' where p-Celtic has 'p'.
7. Benjamin Hudson, one of the latest people to write on Berchan, sees this section of the text as a description of the military exploits of *Causantin mac Fergus* who died in AD 820. He also favours wars against the Picts in Scotland but offers no detailed evidence of such wars. Hudson, B., *Prophecy of Berchan* (Westport, Conn: Greenwood, 1996), p. 83.
8. If his memorial said anything like 'Patrick', he was buried there by a Briton or a Welsh-speaker. An Irish memorial would have said 'Corthriche' or 'Korthriche'. The Latin form *Patricius* seems also to have been determined by a local p-Celtic speaker rather than the q-Celtic-speaking Irish of Iona. It is the same language point we have noted earlier in relation to *Pen* Badon or *Ken* Badon and *Mons Badonis*.
9. Patrick tells us in his confession that he was born at *Bann Avem Taberniae*. That translates as *bann* (mouth) *avon* (river) *taberniae* (*Sabrinae* [the Severn]). The exact location of 'Avonmouth' then may have been different from any place of that name that is important now, but, given that Patrick's father was a town councillor, it is likely to have been on a villa estate close to – that is within a comfortable day's journey of – a city (say about 12–15 miles). Bath or Gloucester are the most obvious candidates, but Caerleon-on-Usk or Abonae are also possible.
10. Another pagan custom.

10 The Man Who Was Badon

1. See earlier note about the River Malago in south Bristol which may record his name.

2. In the sixth century the people we now call 'Irish' were called 'Scots' and Scotland was named after them in much the same way and for much the same reasons as southern Britain became known as England after the Angles; they successfully invaded it and changed its language and culture.

3. *The Prophecy of Berchan*, as we have seen, is a difficult source to use. Hudson, one of the latest scholars to study the text, thought in 1996 that these words applied to a ninth-century Viking leader called Ivarr. Hudson translated *Alban* as Scotland rather than Britain (in AD 600 *Alban* was Britain; by AD 1000 it was limited to Scotland), he saw *gairechtach* as meaning 'boisterous' rather than 'showy' or 'boastful' (Latin *inclitus*), and 'the collection of relics' as an indirect way of saying that Ivarr looted monasteries.

4. His name *Fiachna* means 'raven' (and therefore by analogy with Welsh *bran* ['warrior']). *Lurgan* means 'the shin-shaped hill' and may be associated with the modern town of Lurgan in northern Ireland.

5. Thought by most scholars to be Portchester near modern Portsmouth.

6. See, for example, Higham, N. J. & Ryan, M. J., *The Anglo-Saxon World* (Yale, 2013), p. 72.

7. Bromwich, R., *Trioedd Ynys Pryden The Welsh Triads* (Cardiff: University of Wales Press, 1978), p. 82.

8. We can also recall the legend of 'Jews and Saracens' fighting at Clifton. The 'men of Edinburgh' (the city of *Iudeu*) could also become Jews (*Judeans*), and of course their opponents, the *Sassenachs* (Saxons), convert very readily into 'Saracens' of the kind King Richard I was fighting in the Middle East at the time the legend may have arisen. The Welsh word *Guieth* for a battle may lie behind the tale of the stone-throwing giant *Ghyst* current at the same time and place as the Jews and Saracens. There is a frequent confusion in Welsh texts using the word *gawr* which is sometimes a 'giant' and sometimes a 'warrior'.

9. Cut-up Roman silver has been found at Coleraine in Ireland and at Trapain Law in Scotland.

10. If we want to retain Bade in a combination name, we might look again at Bedminster just south and across the river from Clifton which appears to mean 'Baetan's church'. The earliest known

stone church there, however, is early medieval, although there may have been structures there before that date that have not come to light. Irish kings liked to have an alliance with an abbot of their own family. If the Clifton forts were indeed *Dun Baetan* (and *the city of Badde* of the romances), we would expect to see a monastery nearby. If it wasn't Westbury, a Saxon foundation, it may have been Bedminster. If Sibree was correct in his ideas about the origin of the name of the City of Bristol, it was an abbey founded by or dedicated to, or actually presided over by, Saint Bridget of Kildare.

11 The Welsh Campaign: The Rebellion of Arthur

1. Ireland later adopted the Scandinavian division *thrid* so we almost have the mathematical joy of the country of Ireland being divided into five great thirds.
2. Rachel Bromwich believed it was *gwas*, 'a lad', but 'a pig' makes more sense.
3. We can see another aspect of this rebellious war by Arthur against Baetan in the *Mabinogion* tale of *Culhwch ac Olwen*. He appears as the 'Chief Giant' (probably a mistake for Chief Warrior – the words are similar in Welsh) under the name of *Ysbaddaden*. The hero Culhwch, with Arthur's help, forces *Ysbaddaden* to give him his daughter Olwen in marriage, and then Goreu, son of Custennin, a Cornish leader, said elsewhere to be Arthur's cousin, kills him.
4. St Bridget of Ireland had a white cow with red ears.
5. The meaning of the bees in this context is obscure, but could be a sign of an early sixth-century origin to the story. Just about two generations before the events we have been describing, Childeric (AD 440–482), the father of Clovis, who united the Franks to form the land and nation of France, had 300 gold 'bees' (or 'winged insects') sewn on his funeral cloak. When in later centuries the cloak was discovered, Napoleon I of France believed that they signalled sovereignty, and adopted them as a symbol of the French Empire he founded. In the sixth century *Henwen*'s bees may be as much about sovereignty as they are about honey.
6. Arthur was renowned for destroying the three traditional talismans of Britain because he thought the island should be protected by no one but him.
7. Bedivere's name may derive from Baetan (*Baede*) and *gwyr*, a 'man' or a 'warrior' – thus 'Baetan's soldier'.

8. Unlocated, but the area between the two Roman walls in Scotland and Dyfed have been suggested. *Godden* means forest.

9. Thought to have been fought in Cumberland between rival British forces. The Angles or Saxons were not involved.

10. See a song recorded in 1930s by the BBC in Northern Ireland of Sarah Makem, mother of the famous folk singer Tommy Makem, singing a song with that title about betrayed love.

11. The younger sister may be the result of a false etymology which saw Guinevere's name as *Gwenhyw-mawr* (Gwen the great), and therefore could rise to another woman called *Gwenhyw-fach* (Gwen the little). It may be the case that Guinevere was 'slapped', but by a situation (slighted by a lack of respect) rather than by a person, and her 'sister' is a literary invention to cover an area of doubt.

12. Guinevere, or 'Holy Ghost', is a powerful name for an individual woman to bear. It is one part of the Trinity that the Irish taught and believed was the essence of God. It may have been not a name but a title. 'Little Gwen' may therefore be the title carried by the Vice-Abbess or Deputy Head of the Community. Guinevere may also be a name or title with religious significance by another route. It may have originated from '*Gwyn* (white or holy person) of *Fair* (Mary)'. As the place-name, Mary's Church (*Llanfair*), shows, 'm' became an 'f' sound, thus *Gwynyfair* may be a name signifying a holy woman devoted to, or following, St Mary Magdalene, or St Mary the Virgin Mother. In the context of a monastery, it may be the equivalent of *comarb* (successor), a name or title borne by the spiritual heirs of leaders like St Columba.

13. Other sources say AD 542. The difference, because of early dating systems, is not significant. It could be either 537, or 542, or some point in between.

12 King Arthur and the Rival Claimants to His Throne

1. We know what the sea-cat looked like. St Brendan encountered one at sea which his biographer described 'like a young ox or a three year old horse ... bigger than a brazen cauldron was each of his eyes, a boar's tusks had he. Furzy hair upon him and he had the maw of leopard with the strength of a lion and the voracity of a hound.' The zoologist Bernard Heuvelmans found over fifty sightings, some in recent years, of these creatures and thought that, as well as the spear-headed creature, there was another type which he called a 'mer-horse', which may be the one St Brendan met.

2. There is a link to, and perhaps a resemblance in head shape to, the African *meerkat* whose name derives from the Dutch word for 'sea or lake cat' – 'lake animal'. *Meerkats*, despite their name, live a thousand miles from the sea. The name is all about their appearance as they stand on their hind legs to look out for predators, presumably in a manner that recalled the appearance of a 'lake cat' or 'sea cat' known to the early settlers in South Africa. Or remembered accounts of the spear-headed animal of the Welsh and Irish stories.

3. Murchada is thought to have become, by well-understood scribal and spoken linguistic changes, the root of the modern names like Murphy Murrough and MacMurrow in various spellings.

4. The name may mean 'yellowish or swarthy' and later became associated with the surname Doran and O'Doran (exile). At least one Odor may be the 'tawny butcher' king denounced by Gildas. Another Oder (*Odran*) was the brother of St Madron, the favourite pupil of the prominent Irish Saint Ciaran of Saighir. Madron's name may lie behind the dedication of the church at Tintagel which would bring him into the orbit of Arthurian lore. Another monk called Odor was involved in the founding of Iona. That said, if we are looking for a warrior who may have attacked Arthur, we can ignore all the holy men. Saint Ciaran, however, is also involved with one of our warriors. He is Crimthann Odor, ruler of East Munster, who was effectively deposed and exiled by a *braithirse* or Synod of abbots and monks from a number of tribes (*tuatha*) convened by Ciaran. Saint Brendan of Birr, who attended the Synod, assured Crimthann Odor that 'the *tuatha* would have no king but the king of Cashel and the Synod acknowledged no king but the king of Heaven'. Another saint told him, 'There shall be no king of your progeny till Doom'. The curse of the saints in synod seems to have worked; no known children of *Crimthann Odor* appear in the lists of Irish kings. He may have sought an alternative kingdom by attacking Arthur.

5. R. B. Warner argues on the grounds of this archaeology that from the first century there had been Roman, or Romanised, settlers from Britain at Clogher. For discussion see Mallory, J. P., *The Origins of the Irish* (London: Thames and Hudson, 2015), pp. 195–6. If Warner is right, the likelihood of a 'Clogher presence' at Badon is increased. If the settler presence went beyond Clogher to neighbouring Loughgall, it may offer evidence of the link that brought Arthur to England.

6. We might suspect that *Caer Rian* (the fort of the woman or women) lies behind both the frogs and the spiders. *Caer* (fort, Welsh) regularly

is translated as *Dun* (fort, Cornish) and *Dun* is translated in turn as Latin *Mons*. If *Rian* is given a Latin ending it becomes *rianarum* (of the women) and could readily come into Latin as frogs (*ranarum*) and Norman French as *Ryenes* (spiders). The 'mount of Frogs and spiders' or fort of the women (*castellum rianarum*) seems to be the same place as the *castellum puellarum* and *chateau de pucelles* we have encountered earlier.

7. He lost a hand in battle and had prosthetic hand made in silver.

8. The sobriquet may hide a familiar character in Arthurian lore. The letter 'h' in Irish writing normally, and in most contexts, supressed the sound of the letter in front of it. Thus the modern city of Armagh does not end with a sound like Scottish *loch* but is said as 'Arma'. *Caech* in the same way for a non-Irish speaker could produce a written form such as Cei or Kay, the name of the warrior friend of Arthur who was known as 'Cei the Tall'. That may lead us to think that, like Arthur, he shared the Tyrone/Armagh DNA for 'normal great height', not the acromegalic gene for gigantism.

9. The bee sting led to a celebrated very early Irish law case. It was ruled that compensation was due from the man who owned the bees.

10. Quoted here in the English translation made about 1387 of John of Trevisa (1342-1402). John was a Cornishman and worked mainly at Berkeley Castle in Gloucestershire. He had considerable local knowledge and used it to inform his translation. Higden too was born in the West Country. Both knew local traditions.

11. The Byzantine historian Procopius tells us (in *The Vandal Wars*) that Gizeric the Vandal used fire ships to achieve the same effect in North Africa. In a very strange passage, he also reveals that Belisarius, the Byzantine general, offered to let the Vandals leave Africa and take up their abode in Britain. They were led at that time (*c.* AD 537) by one Gibamundus but he is thought to have died at Carthage. There is no record of any Vandal fleet arriving in Britain. Any fleet operating in the Irish Sea was likely to have been a Ulidian fleet, or one operating in some sort of alliance with other forces in Ireland.

12. In some sources Parsifal is Peredur son of Effrawc who may be the same man as Peredur son of Eliffer of the Great Warband. Eliffer is a strange name and it may be derived from *Leth-ri*, the joint king, also mentioned in Arthurian contexts.

13. This *Cunorix* appeared on an ogham stone (now lost) found at Uttoxeter which declared him to be the son or descendant of another warrior figure *Ceawlin*. Bede says the name was *Ceaulin*. On the missing stone it was written as *Colline*. Both versions may perhaps represent *Cu-Ullin*, a warrior named after the famous but fabulous 'Hound or Guardian of Ulster'.

14. Hwicce was probably pronounced with a soft c like the personal name Cicely. It sounded like Hw-issy.

15. Much of what we know about such events depends on the analysis of ice cores produced by drilling into glaciers. The material recovered exactly records the weather hundreds, and indeed thousands, of years ago.

16. See the Cosmic Winter, Victor Clube and Bill Napier, Blackwell, Oxford, 1990.

17. The arrival of the 'Letavian Britons' ('Britons requiring a sea voyage') in Armorica in either the late fifth century or the first half of the sixth century is currently otherwise unexplained and the sharp decline in the population of Britain from Roman times to the beginning of the seventh century also has no explanation.

18. A tradition still honoured by many books about King Arthur.

19. Perhaps this forced display of submission is the real reason for the appearance of Arthur as the leader of Gower before Columba. It may have been intended as another sign of submission. There is another story attached to Columba about *Maeluma* (Melwys). He took part in an old ceremony where he ate his fill of a roasted ox and then went to bed. Whoever he dreamed of was to be the next high-king of Ireland. Since he was the dreamer, it could not be him. The story may also be a sarcastic reference to the Oxen tribe of Clogher whose chieftain led troops with Arthur at Badon. All three elements may be submission propaganda.

20. 'These stories did not happen at all as they were told but it was to ingratiate themselves with the rude Ulster race that the smooth-tongued poets invented the lying fables.' An eleventh-century writer on Drumcett quoted by F. J. Byrne in his *Irish Kings and High-Kings*, p. 106.

13 The Quest Concluded

1. The two saints may of course have been restoring churches destroyed or damaged in the 540 event.

2. Higham, N. J. & Ryan, M. J., *The Anglo-Saxon World* (Yale, 2013), p. 143.

Afterword

1. I owe this version to Naomi Mitchison, the sister of J. B. S. Haldane.

Appendix II: The 540 Event

1. Gildas, *De Excidio Britonum* (trans. Michael Winterbottom) (London: Phillimore, 1978)
2. The sermon of Gildas is one of only three authentic British documents to survive from that period. The others are the Confession (*Confessio*) of St Patrick and a letter written by the saint to a British chieftain.
3. The word used for the sea is *don*, the singular form of the word for a wave. *Don* derives ultimately, through *tonn*, from Latin *Tumeo* (to swell). See *Trioedd Ynys Prydein* (TYP), 'the Welsh Triads', ed. and trans. Rachel Bromwich (Cardiff: University of Wales Press, 1978), p. 399.
4. *Ibid.*, p. xci.
5. *Ibid.*, p. 399, n. 1.
6. The words usually translated as 'yellow plague' (*fad felen*) may be a mistake for Breton *houlenn*, a wave. One *Maeldav Hynaf* made *Maelgwn* a chair of waxed wings in which he tried to show that he alone could defy the incoming tide in Cardigan Bay. Cardigan Bay is one of the supposed sites of the lost *cantref* of Gwyddno. St Gildas (c.17 *de Excidio*) may have witnessed the incoming wave or have spoken with men who did. See also p. 98 of this book.
7. Dewey (1935) believed that this sand was of sub-aqueous origin. Edmonds, E. A., McKeown, M. C. and M. Williams (eds), *British Regional Geology (BRG): South Western England* (London: HMSO, 1975), p. 81. Sand dunes are signs of a tsunami that has exhausted itself or has been successfully resisted by some geological feature. The great sandhills of western Oregon offer spectacular examples of exhausted Pacific tsunamis.
8. Personal communication from Professor Philip Drazin, University of Bristol.
9. *British Regional Geology (BRG), South Wales*, edited by T Neville George, HMSO, London, 1970., page 131.
10. BRG: South Wales, T Nevill George, HMSO, London, 1970, page 128.

11. *The Geology of Devon*, by E M Durrance and D J C Laming, University of Exeter Press, Exeter, 1982, page 272.

12. Durrance and Laming, University of Exeter Press, Exeter, 1982, pages 269 and 272.

13. John Rutter, the Quaker antiquarian, reported in 1829 that he had found what he thought was marine sand from an inundation of the sea below the cliff-top church at Uphill, near modern Weston-super-Mare. The area was a port in Roman times, and, although the present church is an eleventh-century foundation, there was a wooden church there at least as early as AD 700. Rutter thought the inundation had happened at some time in the previous 1,500 years. John Rutter, *Delineation of the North-West division of Somserset*, London, 1829, page 82. Rutter's observation, if confirmed by modern science, indicates a wave height in excess of 25 m.

14. See *A chronological outline of the History of Bristol and the Stranger's Guide*, by John Evans, Bristol, 1824, page 7, reporting an excavation in 1804. The roots lay towards Ashton and the branches towards Clifton (roughly North/South). Hazel nuts were present which suggest that the event took place in the autumn. John Loveless of the University of Bristol's hydrographic laboratory (personal communication) says that the deposits are consistent with debris left by a wave.

15. Almost certainly western Britain. The Welsh name for the area around Glastonbury was *Ynys Witrin* William of Malmesbury (*c.* 1125) and *Insula Vitrea* according to Gerald of Wales (also twelfth century). William was referring to a charter that purported to go back to AD 601. 'B' and 'v' are interchangeable in this period and a normal process of metathesis produces *Britea* or *Bitrea*.

16. Translation from Procopius, *History of the Wars*, Book VIII, xx (trans. H. B. Dewing) (Cambridge: Loeb's Classical Library, Harvard University Press, 1928), p. 267.

17. See Padel, O., *A Popular Dictionary of Cornish Place-names* (Penzance: Hodge, 1988), p. 26.

18. Rackham, O., *The History of the Countryside* (London: Dent, 1986), p. 78, table 5.1.

19. *Ibid.*, pp. 72–84.

20. Padel (*op. cit.*, p. 122) fears this may be a late invention, but other names such as Loswithiel imply wooded country but not of course in the middle of a bay as at St Michael's Mount.

21. Whittock, following J. C. Russell. Whittock, M., *The Origins of England* (London: Croom Helm, 1986), p. 118.

22. Padel, *op. cit.*, pp. 22 and 26. He says most Cornish names come from the ninth to twelfth centuries.

23. Baetan is difficult to date accurately but he flourished around AD 520–530 and was certainly dead by AD 560. He may have died in AD 540.

24. Apparently Godmund the African but more probably Godmundus from York (*Eboricanus*) or modern Goodmanham, formerly Godmunddingham in the Hundred of Weighton near York. Geoffrey of Monmouth, *The History of the Kings of England* (ed. and trans. Lewis Thorpe) (London: Penguin, 1966), pp. 263–265.

25. Geoffrey of Monmouth (*fl.* twelfth century) is not a reliable historian. William of Worcester (fl. fifteenth century), the father of English topography, is a sound source of anecdotes. He says Godmundus defeated a British king in AD 541. William of Worcester, *Itineraries* (ed. J. H. Harvey) (Oxford: Clarendon, 1969), p. 319.

26. *Trioedd Ynys Prydein* (TYP), 'the Welsh Triads', ed. and trans. Rachel Bromwich (Cardiff: University of Wales Press, 1978), p. 486.

27. The liner *Queen Elizabeth II* suffered from 'squat' and grounded. See *Daily Telegraph* 8 July 1993.

28. See Myles, D., *The Great Waves* (London: Hale, 1986), pp. 28–29. The tsunami at Krakatoa was over 120 feet high (36.5 m) and the volcanic explosive eruption was heard 3,000 miles away.

29. *Ibid.*, pp. 35–36.

30. *Ibid.*, pp. 147–148. The 1854 Lituya wave set a trimline of 395 feet, and that of 1936 one of 490 feet.

31. Apparently confirmed by Rutter's nineteenth-century observation.

32. Myles, *op. cit.*, pp. 61–62.

33. S. Bondevic et al., *EOS, Transactions of the American Geophysical Union*, Vol. 84, Number 31, 5 August 2003.

34. Thomas, C., *Exploration of a Drowned Landscape* (London: Batsford, 1985), p. 28; Clube, V. and B. Napier, *The Cosmic Winter* (Oxford: Blackwell, 1990), pp. 220–221.

35. Place-name evidence and personal communication from Mr Michael Burton, the landowner. Another landowner, the late Mr Charles Clarke, reported that archaeologists working on a Roman villa on his property at Gatcombe west of Bristol found a thin layer of grey-green silt which was possibly marine in origin.

36. Personal communication from Professor M. G. L. Baillie, Queen's University of Belfast.
37. Observation on-site and study of place-names by Don Carleton.
38. Clube and Napier, *op. cit.*, pp. 220 *et seq.*
39. Personal communication from Professor A. J. Walsby, University of Bristol.
40. See, for example, Baillie, M., *Exodus to Arthur* (London: Batsford, 1999), pp. 125–126, and Baillie, M., *A Slice Through Time* (London: Batsford, 1995).
41. Bromwich, *TYP*, p. 399.
42. In an annal in Angers Municipal Library found by David Dumville and cited by him in Lapidge, M. and D. Dumville (eds), *Gildas: New Approaches* (Woodbridge: Boydell, 1984), p. 211.
43. This comet is listed as Ho 13 or PIN 255 in the list of comets given by Donald K. Yeomans in *Comets* (New York: Wiley Science Editions, 1991), p. 363. Halley was the first Western scientist to note a real connection between the appearance of comets in the sky and events on earth. In 1688 and 1694 he suggested that the Biblical Flood was caused by an impact event. The indistinct murmur reported by Procopius could have been the sonic boom carpet it made on entry. The tertiary boom carpet is usually about 200 miles from the point of origin. That suggests that the entry flight path was about 100/150 miles east or west of western France.
44. Clark, A. H. and A. Criddle, *Minerals of Devon and Cornwall* (ed. P. G. Embrey and R. F. Symes) (London: British Museum, 1987), pp. 60 and 111.
45. Dr Simon Day, University of California and University College London, personal communication, July 2003.
46. Bromwich, *TYP*, p. 399.
47. Byrne, F. J., *Irish Kings and High Kings* (London: Batsford, 1973), pp. 100–101.
48. There are many records that indicate a mass migration from Devon and Cornwall to Brittany in the first half of the sixth century.

Appendix III: The Old Church at Glastonbury

1. 'Gnostic' is here more a term of abuse than a description. The name asserts the writers practised a vague form of spiritual exercise called Gnosticism, but that is by no means evident in the Gospels themselves, which sensationally revise how we might see Jesus, his circle and his teaching. See also Note 165.

2. British Library MS #17202.

3. The Cathars or Albigensians and their beliefs were brutally suppressed by a Crusade demanded by the Pope.

4. We can dismiss the idea that the Merovingian kings of France descended from this marriage. This appears to be a fiction created by Pierre Plantard and Patrice de Chérisy in the 1960s. It achieved international currency through two books in particular – *The Holy Blood and the Holy Grail* by Michael Baigent, Richard Leigh and Henry Lincoln (London: Cape, 1982) and the best-selling thriller *The Da Vinci Code* by Dan Brown which was based on Baigent, Leigh and Lincoln. It is, however, true that the Merovingians enjoyed a long-lasting reputation for sanctity. The last ruling king of the line, Childeric III, was deposed in AD 751 and sent to the monastery of Saint Omer. In later centuries, Saint Omer was the founding place of the Templars, and, as late as 1536, King Henry VIII of England sent there for a sanctified axeman to truncate his queen, Anne Boleyn.

5. A further note. The Gospel of Philip was discovered with other gospels in a cave in Southern Egypt in 1945 at Nag Hamadi. It tells us that Mary Magadalene was the Apostle to the Apostles, she was seen by Jesus as his successor and the leader of the Apostles, and she was opposed by Peter and James and supported by Philip and Levi. The value of the Nag Hamadi documents is that they have not been subjected to the long process of omission, destruction, amendment, obfuscation and invention that the Church has felt it necessary to impose on the history of Christianity in the interest of various orthodoxies and changes of doctrine, interest or fashions in piety. The Nag Hamadi texts are authentic early evidence of the era following the time of Jesus himself, the first two or three centuries of Christianity when many variants of Christian faith and practice flourished. It is therefore perfectly possible that Mary was, so to speak, the senior partner in the enterprise in Gaul with Philip, and decided herself to undertake the mission.

6. It is thought to have been a victim of Bridget and Mary's 'perpetual flame' – a candle kept always alight there.

7. The well-preserved and highly carved stone Arboe Cross is thought to date from about AD 900–1100, but may have replaced an earlier wooden one erected by Colman who founded a monastery at Arboe (the hill of the cow) in AD 590. A white or holy cow (with red ears) is associated with Saint Bridget.

8. Irish monastic round towers are also mysterious. They were supposed to be receptacles for valuables relics such as the bell of the monastery founder, places of refuge for monks under attack, or bell towers to sound the times for prayers and acts of devotion. They could not have been much use militarily. They would have been vulnerable to siege and fire attacks, and would have been of limited effectiveness in resisting determined attackers. That leaves one other explanation: that they were in some sense symbolic. The earliest date from the ninth century, and few were erected after the eleventh century. What they symbolised is probably lost beyond recovery, but whatever it was, it represented some very important aspect of belief, a belief that may also have been manifested in the High Crosses of the same period. It was a belief that had apparently no currency after about AD 1200.

Appendix IV: Religion in the Age of Arthur

1. Frend, W. H. C., *The Donatist Church* (Oxford: Clarendon Press, 1952), p. 245. *Curiales* were the merchants, businessmen and mid-level estate owners. Constantine effectively confiscated the endowments the cities of the Empire had built up, but demanded that the administration of cities should be paid by the *curiales* who already had considerable obligations in providing public events, celebrations and entertainment out of their own pockets.

2. See Brown, P., *Religion and Society in the age of Saint Augustine* (London: Faber and Faber, 1972), p. 321.

3. Not Britain, the 'Britains' – that is, Britain as it was for Roman military and administrative purposes.

4. Williams, P. S., *Religion and Literature in Western England 600-800AD* (Cambridge: CUP, 1990), p. 301.

5. Irish monks also enjoyed the gift of accurate prophesy which can still be verified today. Saint Magenn (aka Saint Mawnan and Mawgen) said, 'A time will come when girls will be pert and tart of tongue; when there will be grumbling and discontent among the lower classes; when there will be a lack of reverence to elders (old people and experienced political leaders); when the churches will be slackly attended; and when women will exercise wiles.'

Appendix V: Of Legends and Curiosities

1. Nash, D. W., *Taliesin or the Bards and Druids of Britain* (London: Smith, 1858), p. 27.

2. He was the remote ancestor of the fourteenth President of the USA, Franklin Pierce. Pierce may have been another 'Fitzgerald' by descent. The Norman warlord Gerald of Windsor, progenitor of the Irish Fitzgeralds, married Nest. President Kennedy was John Fitzgerald Kennedy. The descendants of warlords reached high places.

3. The first major written form or redaction of the Jewish oral tradition, sometimes called the oral *Torah*.

ACKNOWLEDGEMENTS

I should like to acknowledge with gratitude the friendship, patience, scholarly interest, advice and commentary of the following in shaping my ideas about Arthur and his context: Professor John Burrow, Dr Basil Cottle, Dr Martin Crossley Evans, Professor Philip Drazin, Dr John Loveless, Professor Richard Gregory, Professor Paddy McGrath, Dr Jonathan Musgrave, Professor Tony Walsby (all University of Bristol), Professor Jeremy Rayner (University of Leeds), and Professor Mike Baillie (Queen's University of Belfast); Hannah Lowry, Michael Richardson, and Nicholas Lee of the University of Bristol Library Special Collections; Mark Bolton, Ian Coates and Jamie Carstairs; Professor John Braidwood, who, when I was student in Belfast, taught me Anglo-Saxon and Middle English, and involved me in his study of the speech of the Ulster Scots; Professor Emyr Eyston Evans, who, although I was not one of his students, showed me how to read a landscape; my friend Deirdre Flanagan, who opened a door for me into the world of early Ireland and its language; Dr Mark Hempsell and Alan Bond of Reaction Engines Ltd for shared discussion of impact events; my friend Bryan MacCabe, printer and publisher, whose delight in this view of Arthur was a great joy; Shaun Barrington, Alex Bennett and Jonathan Jackson at Amberley Publishing, whose skills, enthusiasm, challenges, arguments and comments made this a better book than it otherwise would have been; and finally, and most importantly, my wife Janice, who has endured King Arthur for so many years with patience and love.

INDEX